HUMOR

A Series of Books in Psychology

Editors: Gardner Lindzey
Richard F. Thompson
Jonathan Freedman

HUMOR
Its Origin and
Development

Paul E. McGhee

TEXAS TECH UNIVERSITY

Illustrated by Edie Pistolesi

W. H. FREEMAN AND COMPANY
San Francisco

Sponsoring Editor: W. Hayward Rogers
Designer: Marie Carluccio
Production Coordinator: Linda Jupiter
Compositor: Typesetting Services of California
Printer and Binder: The Maple-Vail Book Manufacturing Group

Library of Congress Cataloging in Publication Data

McGhee, Paul E
    Humor, its origin and development.

    Includes index.
    1. Humor in children. 2. Wit and humor—
Psychology. I. Title.
BF723.H85M32   152.4   79-15401
ISBN 0-7167-1095-1
ISBN 0-7167-1096-X pbk.

Contents

Preface

This book is intended to acquaint the reader with the current knowledge and literature related to the development of children's humor. It is directed toward sophomore and junior college students, but it may also be used at the graduate level. It is suitable not only for seminars or other courses in which humor is the specific subject, but also for those undergraduate courses in child development in which students are assigned a particular aspect of development to study. Undergraduates find this topic fascinating and welcome the opportunity to learn more about it. As an accompaniment to a regular text on child development, then, this book offers the depth in a single area of development that textbooks cannot provide. Finally, it should be of interest to many readers outside the classroom who are simply curious about the nature and development of children's laughter and humor.

This book marks the achievement of a goal that I set out to reach more than ten years ago. As a graduate student, I sought a research topic in child development that would be both important and exciting to study, but about which very little was known. The first article that I came across concerned with children's humor convinced me that I had found a subject that could engage my attention for a lifetime. After examining reports of most of the studies of children's humor completed by psychologists, educators, sociologists, therapists, and others, I became increasingly impressed by the countless ways in which humor enters into the lives of both children and adults. Laughter and the development of humor seemed to be closely related to a child's intellectual, social, and emotional development, but there were obvious individual differences to be explained. Although children of the same age generally find the same kind of thing funny, a particular event might be hilarious to one child and produce no reaction at all in another. Most children seem to laugh and exhibit humor when in a playful frame of mind, but some are in this frame of mind more often than others.

I was surprised to find how little was known about children's humor (or about adult humor for that matter). Everyone attaches great importance to the possession of a good sense of humor; humor and laughter can often be used as an index of whether a person is depressed or in a good mood. We also assume a lack of laughter and humor in children to be a sign of distress. Once convinced of the importance of improving our understanding of the development of children's humor, the question was where to begin. Because no extensive studies had been made concerning any aspect of children's humor, it seemed reasonable to begin by studying the most basic or rudimentary forms of humor. Philosophers and other writers have debated the essence of humor for centuries, and there is accordingly considerable room for disagreement on which aspects of humor form its foundations. I concluded that humor seemed to be essentially a cognitive or intellectual experience, and that incongruity was a necessary (although not sufficient) prerequisite. Granted, there are important emotional influences upon humor. Social context also has an especially important bearing upon the funniness of an event. But these did not seem to be at the core of humor. This core seemed to consist of an incongruous or nonsensical relationship of which sense had to be made somehow. Sexual and aggressive elements play an important role in much (perhaps most) of our everyday humor, but sex and aggression are not funny in the absence of an incongruous context. It is because of this conviction that the basic building blocks of humor are cognitive in nature that my own research in the past ten years has been focused on the cognitive aspects of humor and on simple cases of incongruous relationships as the basis for humor. By achieving an understanding of the simplest cases of humor, we should be in a better position to understand the full complexity of humor found in the everyday world of cartoons, jokes, and humorous social interaction.

Consistent with this position, considerable attention has been given in this book to the origins of humor, with respect to both evolution and the development of an individual child. The theoretical views developed in Chapters 2 and 3 emphasize the

importance of specific cognitive acquisitions, particularly language skills, for the development of humor to begin. Chapter 5
discusses the general importance of other cognitive processes for
the enjoyment of humor.

Even though cognitive development and cognitive processes
are central to the origin and development of children's humor, it
is clear that we will only have begun to understand humor when
we finally do understand its cognitive properties. Humor also has
important social functions and psychodynamic properties that
would be missed by an exclusively cognitive analysis. Other investigators drawn to the study of humor development in the
1970s have focused their attention on these equally poorly understood facets of humor.

The present book summarizes all aspects of the recent re-
surgence of studies of children's humor. Chapter 1 gives the
reader a foundation for understanding these studies by reviewing
twentieth-century theories and conceptions of humor. Both general and developmental theories are discussed. My own views regarding the origin and development of humor are presented in
Chapters 2 and 3. Chapter 2 deals with the origin of incongruity
humor in infancy and describes four stages of humor development in early childhood. Chapter 3 addresses the question
whether animals other than human beings are capable of humor.
It is argued that, although other animals may exhibit behavior
similar to human smiling and laughter, no other species has
evolved a sense of humor. The capacity of apes to experience
humor is evident, though, in the fact that, when exposed to either
a verbal or a manual language system for a long period, they
exhibit humor similar to that of children. Playfulness and fantasy
are stressed as important prerequisites for humor both in young
children and in language-using apes.

Many of the studies completed on children's humor have
simply documented age differences in humor comprehension and
appreciation or in the ability to create or produce humor. Chapter
4 describes these studies and draws attention to the transition
period between ages six and eight during which the simple, perceptually oriented humor of the preschooler becomes the more
sophisticated and abstract humor of the school-aged child.
Specific changes in level of cognitive development are suggested
as an explanation for this transformation in the first or second

grade. Chapter 5 deals with other cognitive processes and factors related to the initiation or appreciation of humor: that is, the role of creativity, mood or frame of mind, and the importance of an optimal level of cognitive challenge.

Chapter 6 examines the social nature of most humor situations, focusing on the capacity of other persons to facilitate the appreciation of a joke, the contagious property of laughter, and the tendency to use laughter and joking as a means of gaining social approval. The relationship between personality and a child's sense of humor is also discussed. The origin of individual differences in laughter and humor is examined in Chapter 7. Consideration is given to the effect of early parental behavior and early characteristics of the child on subsequent initiation of and responsiveness to humor. It is concluded that, although humorists are not born, they may be predisposed toward humor by the early establishment of certain behavioral characteristics. An additional source of individual differences is the basis for Chapter 8, in which similarities and differences between the male and female sense of humor are described, both for children and adults. Although there are certain characteristic differences in humor between males and females, whether children or adults, these differences tend to disappear when liberated women are compared with men. This leads to the conclusion that sex-role expectations may play an important part in the overall development of a sense of humor that is distinctly male or female.

Finally, Chapter 9 treats the assumption that laughter and humor are somehow important in the maintenance of good mental health. Does humor serve as a coping mechanism for a child, assisting in dealing with anxiety or distress? Do laughter and humor in connection with sexual or aggressive ideas help the child inhibit the expression of sexual or aggressive impulses? In this chapter, findings pertinent to these questions are described, and attempts to use humor in therapy and as a diagnostic tool are discussed.

Together, these chapters point to the fact that humor has multiple origins. After tracing the archaic origins of the usage of the term humor, attention is given to its origin in (1) infant intellectual development and symbolic capacities, (2) evolution, (3) language learning, (4) playfulness and fantasy, (5) social interaction, (6) early childhood characteristics and experiences, (7) factors related to differences between the two sexes, and (8) coping with sources of stress and conflict. Only by comprehending all of these origins can we feel confident that we really understand how humor develops.

April 1979   Paul E. McGhee

HUMOR

Photographs by Edie Pistolesi

1 Explaining Humor: A Historical Overview

It is impossible to determine when human beings first began to puzzle over the nature and functions of humor. It is likely, though, that they have pondered over humor for as long as they have sought to understand their own nature. One longstanding approach to defining "human nature" has been to contrast human behavior and capacities with those of other animals. For example, human beings have always been thought to be unique because they possess language abilities, highly developed thought capacities, and a sense of humor. But these views have been undergoing radical changes in the past decade or so, especially as a result of recent efforts to teach some form of language to apes. It will be seen in Chapter 3 that the intellectual and language-learning capacities of chimpanzees and gorillas are far greater than has been believed. Most important, given the subject of this book, language-using apes seem to exhibit a sense of humor surprisingly similar to that of young preschool children. Thus, basic assumptions about capacities thought to be particularly human that have stood for centuries may soon need to be changed.

Explanations of humor by philosophers and other writers have been recorded at least as far back as the early Greeks. In many cases, in spite of differences in terminology, these early explanations emphasize qualities still thought to be of significance today. In fact, it is tempting, upon reading early philosophical writings about humor, to conclude that, just as there are really no new jokes (many comedians claim that there are no new jokes, arguing that each is simply a take-off on an old and familiar joke; the joke structure is the same, even though the specific content may vary), there are no completely new ideas when it comes to explaining humor. Has it all been said before? Actually, there are a few original breakthroughs in modern conceptions and theories of humor, even though most of the older ideas persist in a modified form. Unfortunately, an exhaustive review of early philosophical views of humor is beyond the scope of this book. Numerous reviews are already available elsewhere.[1] Rather, this chapter will focus only on twentieth-century psychological conceptions of humor. (The term "conceptions" is used here because in many cases the views offered are not developed as theories.)

To some extent, psychologists have fallen into the same "trap" that has ensnared philosophers for the past two thousand years: that is, they have (with few exceptions) developed explanations that are very effective in accounting for certain kinds or aspects of humor, while disregarding others. Like the three blind men who offered varying descriptions of an elephant, depending on which part of the animal's body they came into contact with, humor theorists interested in different aspects of humor have advanced a highly diverse set of explanations of humor. The main difference between current psychological views and earlier philosophical ones lies in the greater awareness of contemporary theorists that a given explanation is, in fact, limited to only one narrow aspect of humor. Philosophers through the centuries have been especially fond of arguing that their explanations accounted for all types or all aspects of humor. Psychologists today are quite aware of the complex and multifaceted nature of humor and realize that it is simply not possible at this time to develop a single broad theory that satisfactorily accounts for several key qualities of humor simultaneously. Thus, a theorist might focus on the stimulus events that serve as sources of humor (either those objectively represented in the real world, such as jokes and cartoons, or those in one's own head), whereas others may emphasize the intellectual process of evaluating those events, personality factors related to the kinds of humor appreciated, social influences, and so forth. The qualities that psychologists have considered important to achieving an overall understanding of humor are shown schematically on page 9.

---

[1]See KEITH-SPIEGEL, P. Early conceptions of humor: Varieties and issues. In J. H. Goldstein and P. E. McGhee (Eds.), *The psychology of humor: Theoretical perspectives and empirical issues.* New York: Academic Press, 1972.

Most humor theorists have been concerned with the appreciation of humor for which the source is external, rather than with the creation or production of humor. Some have focused exclusively upon the stimulus event that produces the perception of funniness, usually drawing attention to such qualities as sexual, aggressive, or superiority themes and incongruity. Others have attempted to determine whether a universal structure typifies all humor and whether there is an optimal level of complexity for humor appreciation. In the past decade, an increasing amount of their attention has been paid to how people make sense out of cartoons, jokes, and other sources of humor. These theorists are concerned with such questions as how information processing strategies in serious situations differ from those in playful or joking ones and whether there is a unique form of thinking in evaluating humor.

One of the most persistent views of humor is that it performs important dynamic functions for an individual, mainly as a result of the laughter that usually accompanies humor. It may release pent-up tensions or energy, permit the expression of ideas or feelings that would otherwise be difficult to express, facilitate coping with trying circumstances, and so forth. Currently, psychoanalytic writers are the strongest proponents of this view. Thus, tension-relief or energy-release views continue to be popular, but the terminology has generally been updated to refer to the underlying changes in physiological perceptions of tension. These arousal views are couched in contemporary theoretical terms, emphasizing that changes in arousal may be pleasurable in their own right (e.g., an increase in arousal followed by a sudden decrease, or moderate increases alone). Within these views, humor is just one example in a cluster of pleasurable events that produce such arousal fluctuations.

Other theorists have stressed the importance of a person's reaction to humor, regardless of the foregoing considerations. Were it not for the fact that people laugh and smile, or make statements indicating their feelings about a joke, cartoon, pratfall, and so forth, we would not be nearly as intrigued by humor as we are. Virtually everyone who tries to do some form of systematic research on humor relies on one of these forms of behavior as a measure of appreciation, although there have been attempts to relate these overt behaviors to underlying changes in arousal.

An additional major group of writers and theorists has considered the influence of other factors on humor, regardless of the kinds of mental processes associated with it or the behavioral reactions that it produces. Thus, basic motivation and personality characteristics may exert a strong influence on both the kinds of humor that are appreciated and the psychodynamic functions that humor serves for an individual. Similarly, the social context in which humor is experienced (or initiated) may influence both the level of appreciation and the functions served.

The brief review in this chapter of the various psychological views of humor should enable the reader to understand the research findings summarized in the rest of the book. Although developmental issues regarding humor have not received the amount of attention given to humor in general, it will be seen that investigators attempting to understand children's humor face many of the same kinds of problems that confront those who study humor in adults. The study of humor in children may be even more complicated than that in adults, however, because with increasing age there are changes in cognitive abilities, motivation, social interaction and skills, and a host of other factors that might have an important effect on humor. The principal concern of this book is to describe these developmental changes and the path of progressive change from the early laughter and smiling of the infant to the more sophisticated and adultlike humor of adolescence.

What Is Humor?

Archaic Origin

Current usage of the term "humor" has its origin in the Latin word of the same spelling, meaning fluid or moisture. According to ancient, medieval, and Renaissance physiology, there were four basic bodily humors or fluids: choler, or yellow bile; melancholy, or black bile; blood; and phlegm. The four humors were assumed to play a major role in determining a person's temperament, mood, or general disposition. A normal disposition was associated with a balanced or proper proportion between the humors. A disproportional amount of one of the humors was assumed to alter a person's temperament in characteristic ways:

1. Choler, or yellow bile, was thought to be produced by the gall bladder. An excess of choler led to a choleric mood or humor; that is, irascibility and proneness to upset or anger.
2. Melancholy, or black bile, referred to a thick, dark bile believed to be secreted by the kidneys or spleen. Heavy secretions of black bile presumably caused gloominess, dejection, or depression.
3. A person was considered to be in a sanguine mood when an excess of blood was present. This mood is characterized by confidence, hopefulness, and a cheerful spirit.
4. Phlegm referred to a cold, moist mucus believed to produce a phlegmatic temperament; that is sluggishness and apathy.

A person in whom the four humors were in correct balance came to be thought of as being in "good humor," whereas a person with any kind of imbalance was said to be "out of humor," or not himself. Through the centuries, the term humor gradually came to refer to one's mood or state of mind in a very general sense.

In addition to this general usage, the word humor began more than two thousand years ago to be used in reference to a specific mood or disposition, characterized by a sensitivity to, or appreciation of, ludicrous, absurd, incongruous, or comical events. As just noted, an imbalance in the amounts of the four humors present in the body was believed to be at the root of many forms of excessive behavior. As early as the time of Plato and Aristotle (fifth and fourth centuries B.C.), laughter was considered to be an effective means of correcting or controlling excessive, ridiculous, or otherwise unacceptable behavior. Accordingly, people believed to possess too much of one of the four humors became objects of laughter and ridicule and were referred to as "humorists." Once this connection was made, the term humorist was quickly extended to anyone who was highly skilled at producing amusing, incongruous, ridiculous, or ludicrous ideas and events.

Current Meanings

We continue to use the word humor in both the specific and the general senses described in the preceding section. It is especially important to acknowledge the influence of one's disposition or frame of mind on one's personal experience of humor. We may have difficulty defining humor, but we know it when we "see" it, and we know that we are more likely to see it in some moods than in others. Most dictionary definitions emphasize two distinct meanings of the more specific usage of the term. The basic one is the mental experience of discovering and appreciating ludicrous or absurdly incongruous ideas, events, or situations. When we speak of a person's having a sense of humor, we mean that that person is especially likely not only to perceive such events, but also to derive special enjoyment from them. Humor is also defined as those attributes of an event that make us laugh; namely, attributes that lead us to perceive the event as ludicrous or humorous. The problem is that this is a very circular definition. We must conclude, then, that humor (like beauty) is something that exists only in our minds and not in the real world. Humor is not a characteristic of certain events (such as cartoons, jokes, clowning behavior, etc), although certain stimulus events are more likely than others to produce the perception of humor. Humor is not an emotion, although it may alter our emotional state, and we are more likely to experience it in some emotional states than in others. Finally, humor is not a kind of behavior (such as laughter or smiling), although specific types of behavior are characteristically related to the perception of humor.

Related Terms If ideas or events that are judged to be incongruous, absurd, ridiculous, and so forth, are included in the definition of humor, then it is essential to clarify the meaning of these words. The following adjectives are commonly used to describe qualities of events associated with humor:

1. Absurd: An event or statement is considered absurd if it is illogical or inconsistent with what is either known or strongly believed to be true.

2. Incongruous: The notions of congruity and incongruity refer to the relationship between components of an object, event, idea, social expectation, and so forth. When the arrangement

of the constituent elements of an event is incompatible with the normal or expected pattern, the event is perceived as incongruous. The incongruity disappears only when the pattern is seen to be meaningful or compatible in a previously overlooked way. This discovery has long been considered to be important for humor, in that the nonsense that results from the perception of incongruity makes sense when we see the unexpected meaning or "get the point."

3. Ridiculous: This term is often used synonymously with "absurd," although it also refers to events that are laughable and not to be taken seriously. The intent of ridiculing a person or event is usually to belittle or disparage. Thus, laughter at the ridiculous often tends to be derisive, contemptuous, and hostile.

4. Ludicrous: This is a higher-order concept, referring to any event that produces laughter because of incongruity, absurdity, exaggeration, or ridiculousness.

5. Funny: This word is probably used more than any other to mean "humorous," especially as a result of perceiving something odd, incongruous, absurd, and so forth. It is interesting to note that this is the only term among those closely connected to humor that also refers to unusual or incongruous events that are puzzling, but not humorous. The use of the word "funny" in referring to something puzzling is puzzling in itself, because the word "funny" is derived from "fun," which does not have a comparable meaning. When we are having fun, we are playful, joking, merry, and generally lacking any serious intent. What's more, being in a playful frame of mind is central to the concept of fun, and we shall see that this frame of mind is an important prerequisite for humor.

6. Amusing: This term is sometimes used interchangeably with "funny," although it seems to describe a milder form of experience. This term will not be used to refer to humor in this book, however, because of its broader, common usage, which has nothing to do with humor. The occupying of one's attention in a pleasant and entertaining fashion is central to amusement. Although humor affords one means of achieving this, there are many others that do not involve humor at all. For example, television, theater, a light novel, or children at play may be entertaining and amusing in the absence of

humor. Furthermore, we go to amusement parks to play pinball, to go on rides, and generally have fun, not to find stand-up comedians, Laurel and Hardy films, or other sources of humor.

7. Mirthful: The term "mirth" is often used as if it were synonymous with humor. This is an inappropriate usage, and it will not be adopted in this book. We are mirthful when we are merry and in a generally lighthearted mood. The tendency to equate this with humor is probably because laughter usually accompanies mirth. Mirthful laughter may result from one's gay mood and a sense of fun and amusement, though, without anything being funny in a humorous sense.

Numerous other terms are commonly used to refer to some aspect of humor. Most of them are subcategories of the qualities just described. They will not be defined here, but a number of them are listed in order to impress on the reader both the overwhelming complexity of humor and the extent to which this is reflected in our language: clever, comic, corny, droll, dry, facetious, farce, inane, jocose, nonsense, parody, practical joke, sarcasm, satire, silly, slapstick, waggish, whimsical, and witty.

Kinds of Humor Although there has been widespread disagreement through the centuries about how many different kinds of humor exist, it has finally become clear that this is not really a meaningful question to debate. Some classifications of humor have been based on the structure of jokes and cartoons, whereas others have been based on content, complexity, style of expression, and a host of other qualities. The conclusion reached depends on the specific criteria used in conceptualizing humor. The number of discernible types is limited only by our own capacity to make distinctions between humorous events.

Pyschological Views of the Basic Characteristics of Humor

The model shown on the facing page will serve as a basis for organizing the material in this section, with discussion centered mainly on twentieth-century conceptions of humor.

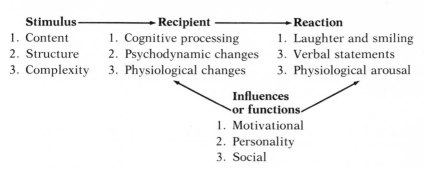

A general model of qualities accounted for in psychological theories of humor.

Stimulus Characteristics

One of the most popular approaches to explaining humor consists of an attempt to isolate the peculiar qualities of stimuli that lead to the perception of humor. This is not surprising, because much of the humor encountered in everyday living takes the form of specific jokes, cartoons, the behavior of others, and so forth. The quality most frequently emphasized through the centuries has been incongruity. Philosophers (e.g., Kant, Schopenhaur, and Bergson) have argued that incongruity is at the core of all humor experiences.[2] Many psychologists have agreed, although some, influenced by Freud and other psychoanalytic writers, believe that, even if incongruity is at the core of humor, other qualities are more important. For example, very few people really break up laughing at pure incongruities, but the addition of allusions to sex or aggression may produce this effect. Readers can draw their own conclusions about how funny the following jokes would be without the contribution of sex or aggression.

> One bachelor asked another, "How did you like your stay at the nudist camp?"
>
> "Well," he answered, "It was okay after a while. The first three days were the hardest."
>
> Mr. brown: "This is disgusting. I just found out that the janitor has made love to every woman in the building except one."
>
> His wife: "On, it must be that stuck-up Mrs. Johnson on the third floor."

[2]See Keith-Spiegel, Early conceptions of humor, for a discussion of them.

Accordingly, many theorists have simply taken the quality of incongruity (used here interchangeably with absurdity, ridiculousness, and the ludicrous) for granted, while turning their attention to other aspects of humor that they consider to be more important.

That incongruity is central to all humor is an assumption adopted throughout this book: that is, something unexpected, out of context, inappropriate, unreasonable, illogical, exaggerated, and so forth, must serve as the basic vehicle for the humor of an event, even though additional elements like sex and aggression maximize funniness. It should be made clear, though, that many writers who stress the central importance of incongruity for humor argue that incongruity may also produce reactions incompatible with humor (such as puzzlement or confusion, interest and curiosity, and anxiety or fear). In other words, incongruity is a necessary condition for humor, but not a sufficient one.

Other writers have focused on the thematic content of cartoons and jokes, arguing that sexual, aggressive, or superiority themes are essential for humor. The difficulty with these views is that we can easily point to humorous events in which these themes are completely lacking. It seems likely that they do make a major contribution to the funniness of cartoons and jokes, but they are certainly not prerequisites for humor. The fact that they do contribute so strongly to the level of appreciation experienced, however, suggests that we cannot claim to understand humor if we do not understand the process by which such themes contribute to funniness. The motivational dynamics of such humor will be discussed in a later section.

Finally, a number of writers, beginning with Freud, have stressed that some contribution to appreciation is made by the process of thinking. This has led to an emphasis on the importance of the complexity of the humor stimulus and to the conclusion that an optimal level of complexity maximizes appreciation. Such views will be discussed in detail in the next section.

Cognitive Characteristics

Freud argued nearly seventy-five years ago that part of the pleasure derived from humor merely results from exercising the

intellect in trying to understand a joke.] Subsequent research
has confirmed this view (see Chapters 2 and 5). Freud also emphasized that adults tire of society's demands for rigorous and
logical thinking and for rational and moral behavior. He felt that
we need periodic escapes from such demands, and that we enjoy
being able to revert to the playful feelings, actions, and thoughts
of childhood, where such demands are lacking. Humor affords
such an escape, and this is precisely why adults take such delight
in it.

A number of writers have used basic principles of Gestalt
psychology as a means of explaining the cognitive nature of
humor. Maier laid the foundation for a Gestalt theory of humor
half a century ago, adopting the traditional Gestalt view that the
meaning of an element or group of elements depends on the
whole configuration of which it is a part.[4] Changing only a single
part of the whole may change the meaning not only of that part,
but of the whole as well. In a joke, for example, the sudden
change in the expected meaning of certain words leads to a sudden restructuring and reinterpretation of the whole. This sudden
restructuring is the central cognitive factor in humor, according
to Maier, although similar processes are central to solving
nonhumorous problems. The factor unique to humor is the element of the ridiculous. Whereas the logic behind normal problem
solving tends to be consistent with one's past experience, the logic
behind humor is peculiar to the situation found to be humorous.

Bateson[5] and Fry[6] have advanced views closely related to
that of Maier. They suggest that a series of paradoxes is characteristic of humorous situations and that we only see the humor
when a punch line or other key information unexpectedly resolves
these paradoxes. Thus, Fry states: "During the unfolding of

---

[3]FREUD, S. *Jokes and their relation to the unconscious.* New York: Norton, 1960.
(Originally *Der Witz und seine Beziehung zum Unbewussten.* Leipzig and Vienna:
Deuticke, 1905.)

[4]MAIER, N. R. F. A Gestalt theory of humour. *British Journal of Psychology,* 1932,
23, 69–74.

[5]BATESON, G. The role of humor in human communication. In H. von Foerster
(Ed.), *Cybernetics.* New York: Macy Foundation, 1953.

[6]FRY, W. F., JR. *Sweet madness: A study of humor.* Palo Alto, California: Pacific,
1963.

humor, one is suddenly confronted by an explicit-implicit reversal when the punch line is delivered . . . but the reversal also has the unique effect of forcing upon the humor participants an internal redefining of reality." Like Maier, Bateson stressed the fact that figure and ground are reversed when we get the point of a joke. The structure of the joke draws our attention to certain elements while deemphasizing others, forming a background or setting for the apparent focal points of the joke. When the punch line is delivered, the background material is suddenly and unexpectedly brought to the center of attention. Both Fry and Bateson emphasize that a playful state or the presence of a play signal is essential to perceiving such restructuring as humorous. The following joke cited by Bateson demonstrates how this restructuring is assumed to occur.

> A man who works in an atomic plant carries a wheelbarrow full of excelsior past a gate guard every day for some period of time. The worker repeatedly states that there's nothing in the wheelbarrow except excelsior, but the guard finally threatens to put him on the suspect list unless he tells what he is stealing. The worker then admits that he has been stealing wheelbarrows.

The well-known writer Arthur Koestler argued that humor, scientific insight, art, and other forms of creativity are all based on a characteristic mental process that he calls "bisociation," defined as "the perceiving of a situation or idea . . . in two self-consistent but habitually incompatible frames of reference."[7] In the case of humor, bisociation "causes an abrupt transfer of the train of thought from one matrix to another governed by a different logic or 'rule of the game.' But certain emotions, owing to their greater inertia and persistence, cannot follow such nimble jumps of thought; discarded by reason, they are worked off along channels of least resistance in the form of laughter."[8] Koestler feels that emotions related to anxiety or aggression play a key role in all humorous situations. This "aggressive defensive" element produces the emotional arousal released through laughter. Laughter is necessary because one's emotions are left in an aroused state after one's intellect has understood the point of the humor.

---

[7]KOESTLER, A. *The act of creation.* New York: Dell, 1964.
[8]Ibid., p. 95.

More recently, Suls has proposed a two-stage model of humor, arguing that two key processes characterize the cognitive activities required to comprehend and appreciate cartoons and verbal jokes:

> In the first stage, the perceiver finds his expectations about the text disconfirmed by the ending of the joke or, in the case of a cartoon, his expectations about the picture disconfirmed by the caption. In other words, the recipient encounters an incongruity—the punch line. In the second stage, the perceiver engages in a form of problem solving to find a cognitive rule which makes the punch line follow from the main part of the joke and reconciles the incongruous parts. A cognitive rule is defined as a logical proposition, a definition, or a fact of experience. The retrieval of such information makes it possible to reconcile the incongruous parts of the joke.[9]

Suls offers the following joke in support of his position:

> One prostitute said to another, "Can you lend me ten dollars until I get back on my back?"

The incongruity here is created by the unexpected ending, for we expect the last word to be "feet." The ending makes sense and the humor is appreciated when we realize that a prostitute earns a living by working on her back. Shultz advanced a similar position at about the same time, arguing that jokes and cartoons contain two distinct structural dimensions: incongruity and resolution. We must both identify the incongruity and resolve it in order to appreciate the humor.[10]

Rothbart has questioned the view of Suls and Shultz that incongruities must be resolved in order for humor to be appreciated, arguing that some jokes do not allow for complete resolution.[11] The punch line may afford partial resolution, but in so

---

[9]SULS, J. M. A two-stage model for the appreciation of jokes and cartoons: An information-processing analysis. In J. H. Goldstein and P. E. McGhee (Eds.), *The psychology of humor: Theoretical perspectives and empirical issues.* New York: Academic Press, 1972, p. 82.

[10]SHULTZ, T. R. The role of incongruity and resolution in children's appreciation of cartoon humor. *Journal of Experimental Child Psychology,* 1972, 13, 456–477. SHULTZ, T. R. A cognitive-developmental analysis of humour. In A. J. Chapman and H. C. Foot (Eds.), *Humour and laughter: Theory, research, and applications.* London: Wiley, 1976.

[11]ROTHBART, M. K. Psychological approaches to the study of humour. In A. J. Chapman and H. C. Foot (Eds.), *It's a funny thing, humour.* Oxford, England: Pergamon, 1977.

doing it creates new incongruities. For example, consider the following joke from Rothbart:

"What is grey, has four legs, and a trunk?"
"A mouse on vacation."

Although "elephant" would be a reasonable answer, we know it is not correct because it is not a joking answer. But even though the answer given does supply resolution information, as described by Suls and Shultz, there remains the incongruity of a mouse packing its bags and going on vacation. So, in one sense we have resolution, and in another we do not. It is not clear just how much this leftover incongruity contributes to the overall funniness of the joke (the reader should remember that this is a children's joke and is not likely to be funny to adults).

The broadest cognitive theory of humor advanced so far is Nerhardt's.[12] In his view, "humor is seen as a consequence of the discrepancy between two mental representations, one of which is an expectation and the other is some other idea or percept." The unique part of this view stems from the fact that the funniness of an event is assumed to depend on the degree of divergence of an event from expectations, with funniness increasing as divergence increases. Nerhardt found supporting evidence for this view even in the unlikely circumstance of lifting weights. If a container of a certain weight is lifted repeatedly, lifting either a lighter container or a heavier one tends to produce laughter.

Physiological Characteristics

A number of views have been advanced suggesting that the most important qualities of humor are to be found at the physiological level. A prominent nineteenth-century conception of the nervous system seems to have set the stage for these views. This conception is exemplified by Charles Darwin's "principle of the direct action of the nervous system." This principle states that "when the sensorium is strongly excited, nerve force is generated

---

[12]NERHARDT, G. Incongruity and funniness: Towards a new descriptive model. In A. J. Chapman and H. C. Foot (Eds.), *Humour and laughter: Theory, research, and applications*. London: Wiley, 1976. NERHARDT, G. Operationalization of incongruity in humour research: A critique and suggestions. In A. J. Chapman and H. C. Foot (Eds.), *It's a funny thing, humour*. Oxford, England: Pergamon, 1977.

in excess, and is transmitted in certain definite directions, depending on the connection of the nerve cells and partly on habit."[13] Spencer linked humor to this view of the nervous system by arguing that laughter served as a form of "safety valve" for excess energy built up in the nervous system.[14] There have been many supporters of this view since it was initially advanced 120 years ago. Most notable among them is Freud, who thought laughter was a means of releasing excessive amounts of "psychic energy."[15] The late eminent behavior theorist Daniel Berlyne was highly critical of this view, noting that

> This kind of hypothesis is not viewed very favorably nowadays, mainly because the underlying notion of a quantity of pent-up "nerve force," "energy," "excitation," or "tension" that demands release receives little support from our present knowledge of how the nervous system works. Nevertheless, laughter seems clearly to be capable of a cathartic effect.[16]

It is precisely because of this cathartic effect that a strong belief in such a physiological function of humor has persisted. People feel as if excess energy has been drained away following laughter. There is no evidence, though, that this feeling corresponds to a physiological release of energy within the nervous system.

Modern physiological theories of humor are concerned with the nature of measurable arousal changes that accompany humor. Berlyne, for example, linked arousal changes operating in humor to two types of arousal fluctuation assumed to be related to pleasure in a general sense: (1) the reduction of high arousal and (2) moderate increases in arousal followed by a sudden drop.[17] An especially important aspect of Berlyne's position is his view that a curvilinear relationship exists between arousal level and amount of pleasure: that is, moderate levels of arousal are more enjoyable than either very high or very low levels. The

---

[13]Darwin, C. *The expression of the emotions in man and animals.* London: Murray, 1872.

[14]Spencer, H. Physiology of laughter. *Macmillan's Magazine,* 1860, 1, 395.

[15]Freud, *Jokes and the unconscious.*

[16]Berlyne, D. E. Humor and its kin. In J. H. Goldstein and P. E. McGhee (Eds.), *The psychology of humor: Theoretical perspectives and empirical issues.* New York: Academic Press, 1972, p. 52.

[17]Ibid. Berlyne, D. E. *Conflict, arousal, and curiosity.* New York: McGraw-Hill, 1960.

arousal Berlyne is talking about might come from any of a number of sources, including sexual, aggressive, or anxiety-arousing themes in a joke, as well as such "intellectually arousing" qualities as incongruity and complexity. Regardless of why we are aroused, we tend to find extremely high and extremely low levels of arousal unpleasant.

A number of investigators have interpreted Berlyne's position to mean that funniness ratings or laughter should be greatest at moderate levels of arousal. There are data both in favor of and against this interpretation.[18] One of the difficulties in testing Berlyne's position is that there is considerable uncertainty regarding just how arousal should be measured in the context of a particular joke or cartoon. (For example, should arousal be measured before, during, or after the punch line? Should absolute level of arousal be considered, or only relative changes in arousal?) Furthermore, different investigators have used widely varying procedures to test this relationship, so that it is not clear to what extent the variation in findings is due to a difference in measurement procedures and to what extent it reveals the true state of affairs in humor. Intuitively, the theory seems quite convincing, but it is likely to be some years before we will be able to fully accept or reject it.

Rothbart extended Berlyne's position, arguing that "arousal increases of any size will be accompanied by pleasurable affect when they are associated with the subject's judgment that the situation is a 'safe' or nonthreatening one."[19] This view primarily applies to young children, however, and so it will be discussed later in this chapter.

---

[18]CHAPMAN, A. J. Social aspects of humorous laughter. In A. J. Chapman and H. C. Foot (Eds.), *Humour and laughter: Theory, research, and applications.* London: Wiley, 1976. GODKEWITSCH, M. Physiological and verbal indices of arousal in rated humour. Ibid. GOLDSTEIN, J. H., HARMAN, J., McGHEE, P. E., and KARASIK, R. Test of an information-processing model of humor: Physiological response changes during problem- and riddle-solving. *Journal of General Psychology,* 1975, 92, 59–68. LANGEVIN, R. and DAY, H. I. Physiological correlates of humor. In J. H. Goldstein and P. E. McGhee (Eds)., *The psychology of humor: Theoretical perspectives and empirical issues.* New York: Academic Press, 1972. SHELLBERG, L. G. Arousal and humor preference: A theoretical formulation and empirical test. Paper presented at meeting of the Western Psychological Association, Vancouver, Canada, 1969.

[19]ROTHBART, Psychological approaches, p. 88. See also ROTHBART, M. K. Laughter in young children. *Psychological Bulletin,* 1973, 80, 247–256.

Tomkins suggested that laughter and other positive affects result from sudden drops in stimulation and the accompanying changes in neural firing. He considered laughter to be an intense form of smiling: "As such it is activated in the same way as the smile except that the general density of stimulation which is suddenly reduced begins at a higher level in the case of laughter compared with the smile."[20] Actually, the combination of the original intensity level and the suddenness of the drop in neural firing determines whether smiling or laughing occurs. Although the terminology used by Tomkins differs from that of Berlyne, the similarity between their views is certainly more striking than the differences.

It seems virtually certain that the results obtained from future research will be supportive of the views of Berlyne and Tomkins. However, it is worth questioning what this really tells us about the nature of humor. In effect, according to these views, there are physiological correlates of the mental experience we know as humor. We become increasingly aroused as we listen to the development of a joke, with perhaps the greatest increase in arousal coming either when our expectation of the punch line is greatest or when it is being delivered. Once we get the point of the joke, arousal decreases and we smile or laugh. Both the level of arousal reached and the steepness of the drop are likely to be increased by the addition of sexual or aggressive themes, or by the inclusion of any other material that is in some way emotionally arousing to the recipient of the joke. But these arousal changes are certainly not unique to humor, for simply asking a person a question that requires thought before answering produces a similar pattern: an increase in arousal is followed by a decrease once the answer is found.

Berlyne recognized this problem and questioned how humor differs from other psychological phenomena (such as exploration, problem solving, and artistic forms of appreciation) accompanied by similar arousal fluctuations. He acknowledges that older cognitive or psychodynamic theories sometimes point in the right direction, but that they are simply too narrow in scope to supply a

---

[20]TOMKINS, S. *Affect, imagery, consciousness.* Vol. I. New York: Springer, 1962, p. 370.

satisfactory solution. He suggests that two arousal-related dimensions and one cognitive factor may be critical in differentiating between humor and nonhumor reactions having similar physiological characteristics. First, there may be a difference in the time scale of arousal changes. For most jokes, there is a prolonged expectation of the punch line, during which arousal increases slowly. This prolonged expectation is probably enjoyable in its own right, "but the humorous configuration itself appears suddenly and is over quickly."[21] However, many humorous events do not produce prolonged expectation. In a cartoon without a caption, for example, we sometimes immediately recognize the visual incongruity forming the basis for humor. The same statements could be made about general exploration out of a sense of curiosity.

Berlyne further speculates that humor might differ from other psychological events experienced as pleasurable in that humor is always characterized by either a sudden drop in arousal or an increase followed by a decrease. Some pleasurable events involve only moderate increases in arousal and are never followed by a sudden drop. He feels, however, that this probably never occurs with humor. Again, although this is certainly a reasonable position, we are left with the fact that many nonhumorous events also are accompanied only by increases followed by decreases in arousal, and not by increases alone. So this also fails to get at the essential qualities that differentiate humor from other psychological events.

The two most promising suggestions by Berlyne regarding the unique qualities of humor are that the important differentiating factors may be of a cognitive nature. He suggests that, whereas humor thrives on extreme divergences from what is expected, aesthetic appreciation and exploration of a general nature thrive better on milder deviations from what is known. Moreover, he adds that most humorous situations contain cues indicating that the events are not to be taken seriously. This is a view that I have stressed in my own earlier writing, and its significance will be elaborated upon in Chapters 2 and 3.

At this point, then, the strongest conclusion to be drawn about the relationship between arousal and humor is that the

---

[21]BERLYNE, Humor and its kin.

kinds of arousal fluctuations described by Berlyne and Tomkins seem to be inherently pleasurable, so that human beings and other animals might be expected to seek out conditions that produce them. Humor is only one of the sources of this pleasure available to us, however; so, although arousal explanations do improve our overall understanding of humor, they do not seem to supply the essential means for differentiating humor from other related psychological experiences. Arousal-based pleasure may be central to experiencing humor, but we seek out humor and enjoy it in other ways as well. Thus, there may be basic cognitive, social, or psychodynamic sources of pleasure in humor. To a great extent, they simply amount to a different level of analysis of phenomena related to humor. The crucial question is whether one level of analysis and explanation is better equipped than the others to account for the central differentiating qualities of humor.

Psychodynamic Characteristics

Several twentieth-century writers have extended Spencer's nineteenth-century "surplus nervous energy" theory to refer to psychological or subjectively experienced tension.[22] They typically assume that laughter (as the natural response to humor) somehow releases this tension, regardless of its source, leaving the laugher feeling noticeably more relaxed. Presumably, it is this quality of humor that leads us to seek it out, or to react in a more exaggerated manner, when in a state of heightened tension or arousal. We have all experienced "nervous laughter"; that is, feeling so tense or uneasy that we are likely to laugh at anything, including things our intellect tells us are not really very funny. It seems likely, then, that the release of tension is a basic function or property of humor from a psychodynamic point of view. Unfortunately, it is difficult to test this view, because it is not clear how physiological changes should correspond to psychological feelings of tension reduction through humor. But such experimental testing may not be important. If people who are tense and anxious report feeling less so after a humorous experience, this is important in its own right.

---

[22]See KEITH-SPIEGEL, Early conceptions of humor, for a review of them.

How laughter came to serve this function has long been a source of puzzlement to those interested in humor, but the way in which the tension is reduced is relatively easy to explain. We have known for some time that a brief tensing of a muscle system leads to feelings of relaxation with respect to that muscle system. A number of forms of therapy now utilize muscle extension-relaxation techniques as a means of either directly reducing tension or creating a state in which a person can more easily talk about sources of distress. Vigorous laughter seems ideally suited for this purpose, because many different muscle systems are activated during laughter. Thus, it is precisely this sequence of spasmodic muscle tensing followed by relaxation that produces the sense of relaxation or relief as a result of laughter. Other sources of muscle tension relaxation can also produce this effect, but laughter seems to be especially well suited both physiologically and socially for performing this function.

The best-known tension relief theory of humor is that initially advanced by Freud, and subsequently elaborated upon by several other psychoanalytic writers. In what continues to be the most impressive single volume devoted to a psychological analysis of humor, Freud wrote more than seventy years ago that in most cases the main source of pleasure in humor (he drew a distinction between wit, humor, and the comic) stems from the fact that people have strong sexual and aggressive impulses or wishes at the unconscious level that are seeking expression.[23] Because society does not allow us to directly express these impulses, an indirect and socially acceptable means of doing so is needed. Humor does this in a manner that is not only socially acceptable, but sought out and valued. The sexual or hostile nature of the emotion expressed in reaction to a joke is usually not even noticed, because the sexual or aggressive content is typically disguised (at least to some extent, although this may not be the case with children), and the context suggests that the event is a trivial one (after all, it's only a joke!). In fact, Freud emphasized that the success of a joke in supplying vicarious gratification of repressed desires or impulses depends on the quality of the structural properties of the joke (incongruity and other aspects of the "joke

---

[23]FREUD, *Jokes and the unconscious.*

work"). A joke whose sexual or aggressive nature is poorly disguised should be less funny than a well-disguised joke, although
this seems to be more important for aggressive than sexual
humor in our culture. Also, this should have a greater influence
on appreciation by a person who is especially anxious about expression of sexual or aggressive feelings. According to Freud,
then, humor serves a crucial social function, in that it helps
people regulate or control the expression of sexual and aggressive
feelings—an essential capacity for members of a civilized society.

Humor has also been assumed by a number of psychoanalytic and nonpsychoanalytic writers to function as a "coping
mechanism" in a very general sense. All of us are confronted with
conflicts or problems that must be dealt with. By occasionally
stepping back from the seriousness of the situation and approaching it with a sense of humor (sometimes called "looking on the
light side"), we are presumably better able to deal with the
source of the problem. If laughter does serve the tension-relief
and impulse-control functions discussed, a person must be in a
better position to cope with conflict after humor than before it.
Some have argued that it is actually the "liberating" quality of
humor that accounts for this coping function.[24]

Along these same lines, there has been considerable controversy over whether a strong "humor orientation" is a sign of a
healthy or an unhealthy personality. Does frequent joke-telling or
clowning, or intense laughter at the jokes of others, indicate that
a person is well adjusted or poorly adjusted? Either position
seems to have some validity. When we are unburdened of anxiety,
tension, conflict, and other "heavies," our outlook on life is a
bright one, and a generally positive mood prevails. This kind of
mood is essential for a playful frame of mind, and (as will be
noted throughout this book) it is only in this frame of mind that
there can be genuine perceptions of humor. We might understand
the point of a given joke when not in this frame of mind, but we
would be less likely to appreciate the humor depicted; it would
simply not be very funny. Even if joking and exaggerated responsiveness to humor is assumed to result from ongoing attempts to

---

[24]GROTJAHN, M. *Beyond laughter.* McGraw-Hill: New York, 1957. MINDESS, H.
Laughter and liberation. Los Angeles: Nash, 1971.

cope with underlying sources of distress, their occurrence might be taken as evidence that the person is coping quite well.

On the other hand, it might be argued that sources of distress are more extreme for some people than for others and that initiating or responding to humor in the extreme must be taken as an index of serious problems. Regardless of how good a job humor does in helping a person to cope, the fact remains that the chronic clown or jokester must have serious problems if it is necessary to rely so heavily on the coping functions of humor. Such a person might be considered to be "on the edge" of being unable to cope, although managing satisfactorily at the moment. As the early social psychologist McDougall noted, "The perfectly happy man does not laugh, for he has no need for laughter."[25]

One of the most popular views of humor through the centuries has stressed that the most important characteristic of humor is that it allows us to feel superior to others who are depicted as incompetent, stupid, foolish, ugly, and so forth. In fact, some have argued that the original cause of laughter in early man was related to this sense of superiority over a defeated enemy.[26] The list of philosophers and writers emphasizing the centrality of feelings of superiority to the appreciation of humor is a lengthy one, including Plato, Aristotle, Hobbes, Hazlitt, Bain, Bergson, Ludovici, Leacock, and others.[27] Contemporary psychological theorists point out that these early views are much too general, in that degree of enjoyment derived from seeing someone else ridiculed, put down, embarrassed, or made to feel incompetent or stupid depends wholly on just who the person is. Wolff, Smith, and Murray first pointed out in 1934 that the enjoyment due to feeling superior that is derived from humor is likely to occur only in connection with persons, ideas, or events toward which we have no positive feelings or affiliation.[28]

More recently, LaFave extended superiority theory to draw attention to the nature of the joke recipient's "attitude" toward

---

[25]McDougall, W. *An outline of psychology.* London: Methuen, 1923.

[26]Rapp, A. *The origins of wit and humor.* New York: Dutton, 1951.

[27]See Keith-Spiegel, Early conceptions of humor.

[28]Wolff, H. A., Smith, C. E., and Murray, H. A. The psychology of humor. I. A study of responses to race-disparagement jokes. *Journal of Abnormal and Social Psychology*, 1934, 28, 341–365.

the person, idea, or "class" of event disparaged in the joke.[29] Most jokes that give rise to vicarious feelings of superiority contain one (or more) person or idea that is victorious and another that is the butt of the joke. According to LaFave, the more positive one's attitude toward the victor and the more negative one's attitude toward the butt, the greater the appreciation of humor. Thus, males should find it funnier when men or boys in a joke win out over women and girls, and vice versa. Similarly, blacks should derive greater enjoyment from seeing another black victimize a white in a joke, whereas whites should show the reverse trend in appreciation. In the same fashion, the disparagement of highly valued ideas should meet with little humor, whereas the disparagement of unacceptable ideas should be thoroughly enjoyed. LaFave has completed a number of studies that support this view. In a closely related view, Zillman and Cantor proposed that

> the intensity of the response to humorous presentations critically depends upon the respondent's affective disposition toward the protagonists involved . . . humor appreciation is facilitated when the respondent feels antipathy or resentment toward disparaged protagonists and impaired when he feels sympathy or liking for those protagonists.[30]

The importance of the identity of the aggressor and victim for funniness can be seen in the cartoons on the preceding page.

Overt Behavioral Characteristics: Laughter and Smiling

Individual differences in personality lead some people to laugh more than others at cartoons, jokes, and other humorous events, but we usually assume laughter to be a reliable index that

---

[29]LaFave, L. Humor judgments as a function of reference group and identification classes. In J. H. Goldstein and P. E. McGhee (Eds.), *The psychology of humor: Theoretical perspectives and empirical issues.* New York: Academic Press, 1972. LaFave, L., Haddad, J., and Maesen, W. A. Superiority, enhanced self-esteem, and perceived incongruity humour theory. In A. J. Chapman and H. C. Foot (Eds.), *Humour and laughter: Theory, research and applications.* London: Wiley, 1976. LaFave, L. Ethnic humour: From paradoxes towards principles. In A. J. Chapman and H. C. Foot (Eds.), *It's a funny thing, humour.* Oxford, England: Pergamon, 1977.

[30]Zillman, D., and Cantor, J. R. A dispositional theory of humour and mirth. In A. J. Chapman and H. C. Foot (Eds.), *Humour and laughter: Theory, research, and applications.* London: Wiley, 1976, p. 93.

someone has found something funny. We further assume that the more intense and extended the laughter, the greater the level of appreciation experienced. For the most part, humor researchers have also adopted this assumption. Apreciation is measured by rating the intensity of a person's laughter (usually a three- to five-point rating scale is used, ranging from no reaction at all, through smiling and light laughter, to hearty laughter) to a specific cartoon or joke. However, most investigators also ask their subjects to indicate how funny the event is by giving it a funniness rating themselves.

Using laughter as an index of humor appreciation seems safe enough, but there are actually many hazards with this approach, because we have long known that humor is only one among several possible causes of laughter. Giles and Oxford, for example, described various conditions under which seven distinctive forms of laughter might occur, noting that the list is certainly not exhaustive: (1) humorous, (2) social, (3) ignorance, (4) anxiety, (5) derision, (6) apologetic, and (7) tickling.[31] Each form of laughter is characterized by different underlying motivation and occurs in a relatively unique set of circumstances. For example, the laughter that is induced by tickling and certain occurrences of apologetic and social laughter have nothing to do with humor. All of the others, however, commonly cloud over genuine humorous laughter, making it difficult to separate the appreciation of humor from other forms of social behavior.

Theorists have paid very little attention to the reactive aspects of humor. Most of what has been written has concerned the social functions of humorous laughter (which will be discussed in the following section). Those investigating humor have been especially concerned about how we can be confident that our measure of laughter is a valid index of level of appreciation. The many possible sources of laughter that have nothing to do with humor make this a forbidding task. For example, if we are shown a group of jokes or cartoons in an "experiment," we know that the socially appropriate response is laughter. In order to oblige the experimenter, we are likely to laugh even at punch lines that we do not

---

[31]GILES H., and OXFORD, G. S. Towards a multidimensional theory of laughter causation and its social implications. *Bulletin of the British Psychological Society*, 1970, 23, 97–105.

understand. Thus, the experimenter must try to sort out how much of the laughter is due to genuine appreciation and how much is due to artificial causes (assuming that "polite" laughter is artificial). Unfortunately, most of the studies for which the findings are discussed throughout this book did not adequately deal with this problem.

One way of avoiding the problem is to simply ask people to evaluate the cartoons or jokes presented to them by giving an "intellectual" rating of how funny they are. Because the rating is not a public behavior, it should be a more genuine index of appreciation. On the other hand, it may be that asking people to "sit back" and examine their own reactions to a cartoon or joke actually interferes with the enjoyment that would normally result from it. A commonly held assumption about humor is that one of the best ways to destroy funniness is to try to analyze why it is funny. Such intellectualizing seems to reduce our spontaneous emotional response to humor, but it is not clear that it necessarily lowers our appreciation in general. For example, upon reflection we may see things we were not aware of initially, and this may boost our appreciation. The question is, Which is the more valid indicator? a rating of the amount of smiling or laughing? or a personal judgment about funniness? Both are important in that they give us two different looks at the overall experience of humor. Some people seem more inclined to reflect about what causes our laughter. To them, the intellectual awareness is central to appreciation. Others prefer not to think about the reasons for their reactions. For them, the spontaneous expression of laughter may be a more valid index of appreciation (although we must not forget about the other influences on laughter noted above). Both types of people intuitively grasp the point of the intended humor, but the latter is more likely to let it go at that, whereas the former is inclined to think about the joke in greater detail.

Social Characteristics

Henri Bergson realized that "to understand laughter, we must put it back into its natural environment, which is society, and above all must we determine the unity of its function, which is a social one."[32] Psychologists have generally acknowledged this property of laughter, and numerous studies have been undertaken to examine the social aspects or functions of laughter and humor (see Chapter 6). Few theories have been developed to deal with the social qualities of humor, however, and, of those that have been advanced, some say more about laughter than about humor.

> Social laughter can be thought of as a behavioural response serving to integrate the individual within a particular social group. In other words, the individual does not experience the situation as a paradigm of humorous laughter (although he does comprehend the situation), yet nevertheless emits laughing responses either directly because other members of this group are laughing, or because expectancies exist with respect to his laughter emission by a group member or members.[33]

It is always difficult to distinguish between humorous and social forms of laughter when the humorous event occurs in a social context, but an attempt will be made to confine the discussion that follows to social aspects or functions of humor and humorous laughter.

The well-known natural scientist Konrad Lorenz was struck by the social significance of humor, arguing that

> laughter (as the overt expression of humor) produces simultaneously a strong fellow feeling among participants and joint aggressiveness against outsiders. Heartily laughing together at the same thing forms an immediate bond, much as enthusiasm for the same ideal does. Finding the same thing funny is not only a prerequisite to a real friendship, but very often the first step to its formation. Laughter forms a bond and simultaneously draws a line. If you cannot laugh with the others, you feel an outsider, even if the laughter is in no way directed against yourself or indeed against anything at all.[34]

The anthropologist Radcliffe-Brown argued that in most cultures people sometimes find themselves thrust into close interper-

---

[32]BERGSON, H. *Laughter: An essay on the meaning of the comic.* New York: Macmillan, 1911.

[33]GILES and OXFORD, Multidimensional theory of laughter causation, p. 97.

[34]LORENZ, K. *On aggression.* New York: Bantam, 1963, p. 284.

sonal situations with people with whom they have little in common, and whom they would not normally befriend. An in-law relationship is the best example of this type of situation, in which conflict and antagonism is very likely to occur at some point. Radcliffe-Brown argued that it is under just this kind of circumstance that a "joking relationship" is likely to develop. The joking relationship is defined as

> a relation between two persons in which one is by custom permitted, and in some instances required, to tease or make fun of the other, who in turn is required to take no offence . . . . The joking relationship is a peculiar combination of friendliness and antagonism.[35]

This kind of social relationship seems to be very common in Asia, Africa, and Oceania, as well as in North America. In many cases, these joking insults take on the form of ritual. Their value is considered to lie in their ability to provide a harmless release for antagonistic feelings that develop. This view is similar to the psychoanalytic one that humor affords an indirect means of regulating the expression of sexual and aggressive impulses.

Middleton and Moland concluded that sociologists approach their investigations of humor with three distinct focuses, viewing it (1) as an index of intergroup conflict, (2) as a means of controlling intragroup behavior and maintaining a sense of solidarity and and intimacy within the group, and (3) as a joking relationship.[36] Martineau extended the first two of these approaches in developing the most extensive formal model of the social functions of humor yet advanced. Because of the uniqueness and breadth of this model, it will be described in some detail here. According to Martineau, the functions served by humor initiated in an *intragroup* situation depend on how it is judged by the members of that group.

1. When the humor is judged as esteeming the ingroup, it functions to solidify the group.

---

[35]RADCLIFFE-BROWN, A. R. On joking relationships. *Africa*, 1940, 13, 195–210.

[36]MIDDLETON, R., and MOLAND, J. Humor in Negro and white subcultures: A study of jokes among university students. *American Sociological Review*, 1959, 24, 61–69.

2. When the humor is judged as disparaging the ingroup, it may function
   a. to control ingroup behavior;
   b. to solidify the ingroup;
   c. to introduce or foster conflict already present in the group;
   d. to foster demoralization and social disintegration of the group.

3. When humor is judged as esteeming an outgroup, it functions to solidify the group.

4. When the humor is judged as disparaging an outgroup, it may function
   a. to increase morale and solidify the ingroup;
   b. To introduce and foster a hostile disposition toward that outgroup.[37]

Very opposing functions may be served by humor initiated within a group setting, then, depending on other group characteristics specified by Martineau. He gave examples to support the existence of each of these functions.

When humor is initiated in an *intergroup* situation, it influences both the ingroup members and the interaction between the two groups. The effect on ingroup members of humor initiated by an outgroup member depends on how that humor is perceived by ingroup members.

1. When the humor is judged as esteeming the ingroup, it functions to increase morale and solidify the ingroup.

2. When the humor is judged as disparaging the ingroup, it may function
   a. to increase morale and solidify the ingroup;
   b. to control the behavior of the ingroup;
   c. to foster demoralization and disintegration of the ingroup.

3. When the humor is judged as esteeming the outgroup, it may function
   a. to introduce or foster a hostile disposition toward the outgroup initiating the humor;
   b. To solidify the ingroup.

---

[37]MARTINEAU, W. H. A model of the social functions of humor. In J. H. Goldstein and P. E. McGhee (Eds.), *The psychology of humor: Theoretical perspectives and empirical issues.* New York: Academic Press, 1972, pp. 116–119.

4. When the humor is judged as disparaging the outgroup, it may function
   a. to increase morale and solidify the ingroup;
   b. to introduce and foster a hostile disposition toward the outgroup.[38]

Finally, the effect of humor initiated in an *intergroup* situation upon the interaction between the groups depends on how each group perceives the humor.

1. When the humor is judged as esteeming one of the groups, it may function
   a. to foster concensus and social integration;
   b. to foster disintegration of the relationship.
2. When the humor is judged as disparaging one of the groups, it may function
   a. to foster integration of the relationship.
   b. to redefine the relationship.[39]

The reader should refer to Martineau's work for examples supportive of this model.

Kane, Suls, and Tedeschi noted that, although Martineau's model does an excellent job of describing the functions that humor might serve either within a group or between groups, "it fails to take into account or explain why humour should be used where praise or criticism would seemingly serve just as well." They conceptualize humor as a tool of social influence. The power of this tool lies in the ambiguous nature of humor; that is, humorous communications can be interpreted in more than one way, always allowing for social recovery if the humor is responded to unfavorably:

> The source's use of humour serves as a rather safe way of self-disclosing taboo interests or values and to probe the values, intentions and/or motives of others, is a decommitment tactic allowing the source to dissociate himself from responsibility for performing a prior action, is a face-saving device that helps preserve a person's identity after an embarrassing incident, is an unmasking tactic that reveals the hypocrisy and pretentions of persons, groups, institutions, and nations, provides a basis for forming positive and long-standing relationships with others, and allows for safe practice of

---

[38]Ibid., pp. 119–121.
[39]Ibid., pp. 122–123.

ingratiation of powerful others. In each instance, laughter can be used to initiate a cognitive transformation of a situation into a non-serious one or it may indicate acceptance of the meanings conveyed by a source of humor.[40]

Theories of Humor Development

Few theories of humor have been concerned with specific questions related to its development in childhood. Those that have been proposed fall into two distinct categories. The first and oldest group of developmental theories consists of psychoanalytically oriented views, most of which extend parts of Freudian theory. The second group consists of views advanced within the past decade and is more strictly concerned with the cognitive aspects of children's humor. Most of these views are directed toward an explanation of incongruity-based humor.

Psychoanalytic Theories

Freud did not pay much attention to children's humor in his book *Jokes and their relation to the unconscious.* He did note, however, that children pass through three separate stages in the development of joking. The first stage, called "play," refers to the incongruous or absurd combinations of objects, words, or ideas that children begin to exhibit before age two. As they begin to feel either a desire or social pressure to make these incongruities and absurdities more meaningful, they enter a stage called "jesting." This is the point at which they first begin to use the various joke techniques described by Freud. In the final stage, these techniques begin to be used as a means of obtaining vicarious gratification of sexual or aggressive impulses, through the development of the "joke facade." The joke facade serves to disguise the true sexual or aggressive nature of the joke, thereby permitting momentary gratification of these impulses.[41] It is the lack of such

---

[40]KANE, T. R., SULS, J., and TEDESCHI, J. T. Humour as a tool of social interaction. In A. J. Chapman and H. C. Foot (Eds.), *It's a funny thing, humour.* Oxford, England: Pergamon, 1977, p. 16.

[41]FREUD, *Jokes and the unconscious.*

a facade that makes young children's humor seem so cruel or openly expressive of "taboo" ideas or behavior.

Freud believed that one of the most important functions of humor was its use as a coping mechanism. A source of distress or anxiety is presumably easier to deal with if the person adopts a humorous or playful attitude toward it. Several psychoanalytic writers have extended the notion that a child enjoys mastering physical, cognitive, and other aspects of its interaction with the environment to include the view that mastering its problems and anxieties also plays a key role in the child's humor. Levine recently summarized these views by suggesting

> the conceptualization of two components in the development of the humour process. The first component is the innate pleasure in mastery. The second is the learned "whistling in the dark" or "laughing it off" phenomenon, in which we use humour to restore those familiar feelings of mastery when we are made anxious or are threatened.
>
> As a process of adaptation, humour provides the individual with the opportunity to re-experience the gratifications of cognitive and interpersonal mastery. The child learns that humour, like play, is a source of pleasure at each stage of development by momentarily re-experiencing the mastery of functions and relations of earlier stages ... Whether in reality or fantasy, and whether under stress or relaxation, humour reasserts one's mastery over the environment. In fact, humour flourishes best when fertilized by newly mastered anxieties ... [42]

Kris was one of the earliest psychoanalytic writers after Freud to emphasize the importance of mastery in children's humor. He argued that, in order to experience the comic,

> a preliminary condition is complete control over the function in question. An absurd movement on the part of another person will seem funny to a child *only* when it has itself mastered the movement. At a later stage of development, it will laugh at a mistake in thinking, only when its own powers of thought are firmly established.[43]

---

[42]LEVINE, J. Humour as a form of therapy: Introduction to symposium. In A. J. Chapman and H. C. Foot (Eds.), *It's a funny thing, humour.* Oxford, England: Pergamon, 1977, p. 129.

[43]KRIS, E. Ego development and the comic. *International Journal of Psychoanalysis,* 1938, 19, 77–90 (p. 83).

Martha Wolfenstein wrote the first book concerned exclusively with a psychological analysis of children's humor twenty-five years ago. She shared the view that humor can help children overcome the distress and anxiety that automatically results from being a child in an adult's world. But she also gave considerable attention to the more general concept of a child's achievement of intellectual mastery in understanding the environment. She noted that, even though a child seems to have achieved a high level of understanding of a given activity, idea, or event, distorting it or depicting it in an incongruous manner does not automatically mean that the child will perceive it as humorous. Whether or not humor is perceived depends on who has created the strange event and under what circumstances: "While they can easily break away from the demands of reason on their own initiative and enjoy fantasy or nonsense, it is not always clear to them when others, especially their elders, make this shift."[44] As will be seen in Chapter 2, if the available cues in the situation suggest that the child should interpret the incongruity in a realistic way, not in a playful way, the humor of the situation is likely to be lost.

Grotjahn suggested that early physical activity may be especially important in the initial development of a sense of humor. He felt that children first discover comic situations when they begin to feel superior to other children in this respect. Once they achieve a sense of mastery and enjoyment relative to their own bodily movements, they are likely to see the mistakes or reduced coordination of other children as being funny.[45]

Helmers advanced a mastery view of children's humor that takes a somewhat different stance on the motivation behind humor from the child's own perspective. He maintained that children's creation of nonsense and absurdity in jokes is really aimed at reconfirming their belief that the world is organized and orderly.

> Words form one of the basic order carriers of a child's world. Every joke, every departure from the norm, means an attempt to shake up this order himself or to hear it pushed around by another.

---

[44]WOLFENSTEIN, M. *Children's humor.* Glencoe, Illinois: Free Press, 1954, p. 196.
[45]GROTJAHN, *Beyond laughter.*

> But, in the final analysis, the order emerges unscathed. The child's relief that the order has proved unshakable is felt as happiness and breaks through as laughter.[46]

Helmers felt that about two-thirds of all laughter before age 12 can be characterized in this way. Aggressive humor is also typically a fantasy-reordering of the world. If the child were not aware of the fantasy nature of aggressive humor, it would not be funny. Whether a child is laughing because he knocked daddy down or because a cartoon character has been run over by a steam roller, it is funny (at least in the mentally healthy child) only because there is no doubt that each will get up again, totally unscathed. If this did not occur, the child might be either confused or frightened, but it certainly would not be funny.

In addition to conceptualizing humor as a result of achieving prior cognitive mastery over an event, and as a means of achieving mastery over sources of anxiety or distress, a third major contribution of psychoanalytic writers to our understanding of children's humor concerns the development of the joke facade, which was briefly described earlier.

> We learn to circumvent prohibitions of conduct by being humorous. Thus, young children will violate social prohibitions by exposing themselves, making fun of other children's immaturities, or telling jokes about other children's indiscretions. The aggression in the humour of young children is direct and open. Poking fun, teasing, taunting, and even physical attacks are all forms of aggression in children's humour. But, as they grow, and increased internalization of social controls occurs, the humour of children becomes less direct, and the children dissociate themselves increasingly from the aggressive impulses in the humour. The jokes become more impersonal and aggression is more indirect.
>
> Thus, as Freud pointed out, the development of humour is characterized by the increasing use of indirect expressions of aggression shifting from motoric to verbal attack. The latter he has called "tendentious" humour. The indirect expression of aggression in humour is achieved by what Freud called the "joke work" or "joke facade." The construction of a joke which children must learn

---

[46]HELMERS, H. *Sprache und Humor des Kindes*. Stuttgart, Germany: Ernst Klett Verlag, 1965. (Quote taken from Alice Shabecoff, *New York Times Magazine*, September 15, 1968, p. 119.)

involves techniques like absurdity, incongruity, puns, and plays on words which in themselves give pleasure by providing a cognitive challenge to resolve. But Freud's great insight was to recognize that this joke facade, although in itself gratifying, serves as a distraction from the underlying aggressive or sexual theme.[47]

Wolfenstein noted that at about six years of age children begin to feel the need for a joke facade to disguise the sexual, aggressive, or otherwise taboo nature of their jokes. Whereas a three- or four-year-old might take great delight in calling someone "pee-pee" or "ka-ka," a six-year-old probably will not. It should be less funny to the older child both because it is too simple to be intellectually challenging and because of the absence of a more indirect means of expressing the taboo words or ideas. This necessity for a cognitive "vehicle" to carry the humor has recently led theorists concerned with the development of a sense of humor to focus on incongruity as a basis for humor and on the cognitive processes by which incongruities are interpreted as being humorous.

Incongruity Theories

The view that has recently stimulated the greatest amount of both research and controversy is that of Thomas Shultz. In his view, humor can be separated into two parts, the discovery and the resolution of incongruity. He has suggested that, until a child is seven or eight years of age, the resolution of incongruity does not contribute to the appreciation of humor. Rather, the young child is said to appreciate "pure incongruity."[48] Even if information is available that resolves the incongruity (i.e., makes it meaningful in some way), the restricted cognitive capacities of a young child presumably interfere with appreciation of it. Even though the information is acknowledged by the child, it is simply not brought to bear on the incongruous relationship. The incongruity

---

[47]LEVINE, Humour as a form of therapy, p. 132.
[48]SHULTZ, Cognitive-developmental analysis of humour.

is funny because it makes no sense, not because it makes sense in an unexpected way. For example, consider the following riddle supplied by Shultz:

> Why did the farmer name his hog Ink? (Question)
> Because he kept running out of the pen. (Original answer)
> Because he kept getting away. (Resolution-removed answer)[49]

Children less than seven or eight years of age should find the second answer just as funny as the first one, because they are responding only to the incongruous idea of naming a pig "Ink." They have no awareness of the way in which the original answer makes this a reasonable (at least in one respect) name for a pig. For an older child, this connection with one of the properties of a fountain pen provides the resolution of the incongruity needed to see it as being funny. Consider the following additional examples:

> Why did the cookie cry? (Question)
> Because its mother had been a wafer so long. (Original answer)
> Because its mother was a wafer. (Resolution-removed answer)

> How far can a dog run into the forest? (Question)
> Only halfway. After that, he will be running out. (Original answer)
> Only halfway. (Resolution-removed answer)[50]

Shultz has obtained data indicating that older children find the first answer funnier, whereas younger children find the two answers equally funny. These findings will be discussed in Chapter 4.

Pien and Rothbart have recently questioned Shultz's view that younger children appreciate humor on the basis of incongruity alone.[51] They argue that Shultz developed this view because of the kinds of cartoons and jokes that he used: that is, they were too complex for preschoolers to understand. The lack of greater appreciation for original jokes than for resolution-removed jokes is not surprising, because four- to six-year-olds are

---

[49]SHULTZ, T. R. Development of the appreciation of riddles. *Child Development,* 1974, 45, 100–105.

[50]Ibid.

[51]PIEN, D., and ROTHBART, M. K. Incongruity and resolution in children's humor: A reexamination. *Child Development,* 1976, 47, 966–971.

not able to understand the linguistic ambiguity responsible for the humor. Appreciation of the resolution information in a joke requires awareness of this ambiguity, and Shultz himself has found that children do not become aware of different forms of linguistic ambiguity until about age seven.[52]

Pien and Rothbart found that even four- and five-year-olds are capable of appreciating the resolution of a cartoon or a joke if the cartoon or joke is simplified. Sequential cartoons containing visual incongruities provide such simplicity. For example, in one of the cartoons that they showed to young children, a boy is sitting in a chair reading a book that is upside-down. In the second frame, an adult tells him, "You're holding the book upside down." The children were then given two alternate forms of the final frame and were asked to indicate which was funnier. In the original version, the boy is shown reading the book while "standing" on his head in the chair, with the book remaining in its original position. In the second version, the boy is shown standing on his head in the chair, but not reading the book (which is sitting on the arm of the chair). In the original version, then, the humor results from the unexpected resolution of the incongruous act of reading an upside-down book by turning one's body upside down instead of changing the position of the book. In the second version, sitting upside down does not resolve the initial incongruity, because the child is no longer reading the book. Four- and five-year-olds not only said they preferred the original to the second version, but also smiled more and laughed harder in reaction to it.

It would seem, then, that the age of transition from Shultz's first stage to the second stage must be lowered at least to age four. There does not seem to be any doubt among those studying humor that it is meaningful to distinguish between the perception of an incongruity and its resolution. But, at this point, it is not clear how much each contributes to funniness, or whether the contribution of each changes as the child gets older. In my own view, it is questionable whether children ever pass through a "stage" in which they are capable of appreciating only the fact

---

[52]SHULTZ, T. R., and PILON, R. Development of the ability to detect linguistic ambiguity. *Child Development*, 1973, 44, 728–733.

that an incongruity exists. Many forms of humor can truly be called nonsense humor, in the sense that there is no resolution intended. Both children and adults are capable of perceiving humor in events that are absurd or impossibly incongruous (such as an elephant flying or a stone talking, in the case of young children), but this does not mean that they are not capable of appreciating other forms of humor in which the resolution of incongruities is intended. It is a basic contention of this book, in agreement with the psychoanalytic position, that prior cognitive mastery or a firmly established expectation of "how things should be" is a basic prerequisite for humor. It is this prior mastery of the situation that enables a child to recognize when an incongruous event has been substituted for the expected congruous one. Rather than trying to determine the point at which children begin to appreciate resolution information in humor, *we should trace the path of developmental change in the types of resolutions employed by children.* In order to do this, however, we must first identify the kinds of incongruities thought to be humorous by very young children (see Chapter 2). The earliest form of resolution (in the two-year-old) may consist of a simple mental substitution of the normal or expected elements of a situation for the funny incongruous ones. Thus, if a two- or three-year-old finds it funny to call another child or an object by the wrong name, the resolution may lie in the child's awareness of what the real name is.

The level of cognitive mastery achieved by a child was singled out first by Zigler, Levine, and Gould[53] and later in my own work[54] as having a special bearing on children's appreciation of humor. In our view, once a child has reached a sufficient level of cognitive development (and has had the necessary prior experience) to recognize humor in incongruous depictions of objects and events, the level of appreciation experienced depends on how much effort is exerted in making sense out of the incongruity.

---

[53]Zigler, E., Levine, J., and Gould, L. Cognitive processes in the development of children's appreciation of humor. *Child Development,* 1966, 37, 507–518. Zigler, E., Levine, J., and Gould, L. Cognitive challenge as a factor in children's humor appreciation. *Journal of Personality and Social Psychology,* 1967, 6, 332–336.

[54]McGhee, P. E. Cognitive mastery and children's humor. *Psychological Bulletin,* 1974, 81, 721–730. McGhee, P. E. Children's appreciation of humor: A test of the cognitive congruency principle. *Child Development,* 1976, 47, 420–426.

Presumably, there is an optimal moderate amount of cognitive challenge that maximizes funniness (other things being equal). Jokes that are too easy to figure out are not very funny because we get the point immediately. Adults find most children's jokes very unfunny (we sometimes call them "cute") for precisely this reason. We think of them as simplistic and boring when other adults try to tell them as legitimate jokes (many adults have this reaction to puns). On the other hand, very complicated and intellectually demanding jokes tend not to be very funny for the opposite reason. They require so much effortful thought that the "fun" is taken out of what is supposed to be funny. When figuring out the point of a joke becomes work, we are taken out of the mood to enjoy the humor even if we do finally understand it. Both of these processes are assumed to operate in children and adults of all ages, as we shall see in Chapter 5. Humor appreciation is greatest, then, when we do not immediately see the point, and yet are not required to think laboriously about it. In my opinion, the addition of sexual or aggressive elements in a joke probably has the effect of increasing the enjoyment of jokes that are otherwise boring because of their simplicity. The jokes that produce the greatest belly laughs on late night talk shows seem to support this view.

Rothbart extended Berlyne's arousal theory of humor in developing an "arousal safety" model of infants' and young children's laughter. She proposed that

> Laughter occurs when a person has experienced heightened arousal but at the same time (or soon after arousal) evaluates the stimulus as safe or inconsequential. Emotional reponses other than laughter to arousing stimuli are likely to occur if arousal increases to a very high level or if the stimulus is identified by the person as dangerous.[55]

This view has some similarity to older "tension reduction" views, in that laughter is assumed to result from the tension release that follows heightened arousal. It differs from most other incongruity theories both in its emphasis on the importance of arousal changes and in its suggestion that contextual factors influence the form of emotional reaction likely to occur. I agree that contextual

---

[55]ROTHBART, Laughter in young children, p. 249.

cues influence how children interpret incongruous events and feel that humor is likely only if such events are believed to occur in a fantasy sense.[56] Rothbart agrees with Tomkins's view (discussed earlier) that lower levels of arousal result only in smiling, whereas higher levels lead to laughter.

Stroufe and his associates advanced a view similar to that of Rothbart.[57] They suggested (in the Berlyne tradition) that an increase in tension followed by a decrease is required for smiling or laughter to occur. The greater and more rapid the build-up of tension, the greater the probability of laughter occurring instead of smiling. They also emphasize the importance of contextual factors as determinants of whether underlying tension or arousal fluctuations produce positive or negative forms of affect. It should be noted that neither of these views deals with the "ticklish" problem of trying to determine the nature of humor, its connection to smiling and laughter, and the manner in which these change as a function of the child's development. Pien and Rothbart have recently taken a stand on this problem, however, arguing that infants as young as four months of age can experience humor because they have the capacity for play and are able to detect incongruities.[58]

Shultz has also recently suggested that infants are able to appreciate several primitive forms of humor as early as the first year, some months before they can begin to represent their world in terms of symbols.[59] Appreciation of one such form is "characterized principally in terms of pleasure in cognitive mastery" (see Chapters 2 and 5). The difficulty with this view is that it does not specify how the humorous form of pleasure in such mastery dif-

---

[56]McGhee, P. E. On the cognitive origins of incongruity humor: Fantasy assimilation versus reality assimilation. In J. H. Goldstein and P. E. McGhee (Eds.), *The psychology of humor: Theoretical perspectives and empirical issues.* New York: Academic Press, 1972.

[57]Sroufe, L. A., and Waters, E. The ontogenesis of smiling and laughter: A perspective on the organization of development in infancy. *Psychological Review,* 1976, 83, 173–189. Sroufe, L. A., and Wunsch, J. P. The development of laughter in the first year of life. *Child Development,* 1972, 43, 1326–1344.

[58]Pien, D., and Rothbart, M. K. Incongruity humour, play, and self-regulation of arousal in young children. In P. E. McGhee and A. J. Chapman (Eds.), *Children's humour.* London: Wiley, forthcoming.

[59]Shultz, Cognitive-developmental analysis of humour.

fers from the nonhumorous pleasure derived from the mere exercising on the intellect in a mildly taxing way. He further suggests that humor is experienced in connection with certain games in the first year, such as peek-a-boo, the tickling game, and chasing games. Shultz feels that the smiling and laughter that accompany these activities indicate early appreciation of humor because of the biphasic sequence of arousal increase followed by a decrease, which is assumed to correspond to the identification and resolution of incongruities among older children and adults. As already noted, however, this pattern of arousal fluctuation is related to nonhumorous reactions in adults. So, this does not appear to be a sufficient basis for labeling laughter in these conditions as humorous laughter.

A General Theory of Humor?

To what extent, then, can we say that we understand humor? As described in this chapter, there is a diverse range of views designed to explain various stimulus, cognitive, response, physiological, psychodynamic, and social characteristics of humor. Intuitively, one is inclined to believe that most of the views discussed have some degree of validity. In most cases, they have the ring of truth because of their consistency with our own private experience. Yet, each position seems very narrow, leaving unexplained much more than is explained. Especially regarding children's humor, most of the knowledge that has been gained is not explained by any of the theories presented. In spite of the numerous conceptions of humor advanced through the centuries, then, it seems that we are only beginning to develop satisfactory theoretical conceptions of how a sense of humor develops.

Considerable disagreement exists among those who study humor regarding how broad theoretical explanations of humor should be. Should we be striving to explain all aspects of humor in a single global theory? Or should we develop a large number of more limited theories, each designed to account for a specific aspect or characteristic of humor? A survey of humor researchers attending the International Conference on Humour and Laughter in Cardiff, Wales, in 1976 indicated an even split of views on this question.[60] Approximately one-third of those responding felt that we have been much too piecemeal and narrow in the past and that we should develop very global explanations of humor. Another third felt that we simply do not yet know enough about humor to develop all-inclusive explanations. In their view (and mine), it is preposterous at this point to try to explain cognitive, social, motivational, and physiological aspects of humor within a single explanatory system. By developing satisfactory accounts of more limited aspects of humor and its development, we would then be in a better position to combine theories to form higher-order explanations. Finally, an additional third believed that we should be moving in both directions at the same time: that is, we should continue to develop more restricted theories but consolidate existing theories whenever possible.

A Definition of Humor

The developmental theory advanced in Chapter 2 is of the more restricted variety and stems from my own belief that the perception of an incongruous relationship (absurd, unexpected, inappropriate, and otherwise out-of-context events are included in this term) forms the basic foundation for all humor experiences. Incongruity is considered here to be a necessary, but insufficient, prerequisite for humor. It was noted earlier in this chapter that incongruity may give rise to interest (curiosity) or anxiety, as well as humor. It is suggested here that the way in which the incongruous event is interpreted determines which of these reactions is likely to occur. Thus, considerable attention will be given in Chapter 2 to factors that determine the way in which incongruities are mentally processed; that is, the mental operations we go through to derive meaning from the initially incongruous situation.

Humor is defined here as a form of intellectual play. Two forms of such play will be distinguished: one is relatively serious in nature and is characterized by a desire to expand existing

---

[60]McGHEE, P. E. The humour questionnaire: An analysis of humour researchers' views of appropriate directions for future research. Paper presented at the International Conference on Humour and Laughter, Cardiff, Wales, July, 1976.

knowledge, and the other lacks serious intent and is characterized by a playful consideration in fantasy of events or relationships known to be impossible or improbable. It is this playful, rather than the serious, interpretation of fantasy incongruities that constitutes the essence of the young child's humor. The specific operation of this fantasy-assimilation process and the kinds of incongruities found to be humorous change with the child's progressive development. The cognitive experience of humor has characteristic underlying physiological (arousal) changes and overt behavioral reactions (smiling and laughter) associated with it, but these are byproducts of humor. Social, motivational, and other psychodynamic factors closely linked to humor are added to these basic fantasy-play processes but are considered to serve only as modifiers and sources of enrichment (albeit very important ones) of the basic humor experience—which can occur in their absence.

2 The Origin and Early Development of Children's Humor

Chapter 1 clearly demonstrates the complexity of the mental experience we call humor. The reader should bear in mind throughout this book that, in any given humor situation, we might consider many different characteristics in our attempt to understand and explain humor. We might talk separately about the stimulus situation itself (e.g., the joke, cartoon, social behavior, etc.), rather than focusing on what goes on in the person who finds it to be funny. This would lead us to focus on incongruities, sexual and aggressive themes, complexity, and other important stimulus qualities. A second approach would be to focus on what goes on in the mind of the appreciator of humor. With this approach, we would feel that we understand the nature of humor when we understand the thought processes of both understanding the "point" of the humor and appreciating it in a humorous sense. Thus, we would have to separately study factors related to the comprehension and appreciation of humor. We would also have to consider those factors that lead us to see a situation as a joking circumstance in the first place, instead of a circumstance to be taken seriously. A third approach to understanding humor would oblige us to examine the role of social influences on different aspects of the overall humor experience. It is immediately apparent to anyone who takes the time to ponder over the nature of humor that most occurrences of humor have a strong social component. Although we may appreciate humor when alone, it is much more enjoyable in the presence of others (at least we laugh more with others than when alone).

Each of these approaches to studying children's humor will be discussed at different points in this book. My own bias, however, is strongly toward the second of these approaches. Although philosophers and other writers have been discussing the nature of humor for centuries, virtually no attention has been given to how the capacity for humor develops in the very young child. Are human infants born with the ability to experience humor, or does it develop at some point later in infancy or childhood? If we do not have the capacity for humor at birth, what is it about the child's development that leads to humor later on? In my view, there can be only one answer to this question: humor requires a certain level of cognitive, or intellectual, development. Surely it is precisely the intellectual superiority of human beings over other animals that makes them alone capable of humor. Before discussing what has been learned about children's humor from research findings, then, consideration will be given to issues related to the origin of humor in infancy.

To a great extent, any position taken on the origin and nature of a child's earliest experience of humor must come down to a matter of definitions. Is there only one kind of humor, or many kinds? Is smiling or laughter a criterion for humor? or should some other criterion be used to define it? The position taken in this book is that there are as many different kinds of humor as our conceptual capacities permit us to distinguish. Thus, the argument about how many kinds exist is a fruitless one. But not all types of humor are equally central to humor in a general sense. It is assumed throughout this book that incongruity comes closest to being the foundation stone of humor. In the simplest sense, incongruous relationships are the essence of what is seen as humorous. Whether in the realm of objects, behavior, social norms, or language, some form of nonfitting, unexpected, inappropriate, surprising, or incongruous relationship is always present in humor. Humor invariably requires a comparison of what is expected and what is encountered instead. This comparison automatically occurs, regardless of the individual's age; although we shall see that the child's developmental level determines just how the comparison is made and what conclusions are drawn as a result.

Incongruity, then, is considered to be a necessary prerequisite for all occurrences of humor. It should be noted from the outset, however, that the perception of incongruity by a child might lead to any of at least three different reactions: (1) interest or curiosity, (2) anxiety or fear, (3) humor or amusement. Clearly, then, although incongruity is a necessary condition for humor, it cannot be a sufficient condition. There are no sufficient conditions for humor. A primary concern of this book is to clarify the many different conditions that both determine whether an incongruity is perceived as humorous, rather than interesting or frightening, and influence just how funny it is considered to be. For the former, attention will be given primarily to the importance of "play signals"; that is, cues in the environment or in the behavior of others that communicate to the person pondering over the incongruity that "this is not a situation to be taken seriously." Again, such signals are necessary, but not sufficient, conditions for humor. In the absence of a play signal, an attempt will be made to make sense out of the incongruity in a realistic or adaptive fashion—a condition incompatible with humor.

The present chapter, then, offers a theoretical perspective on the origin and early development of a limited type of humor. In my view, we must start with simple cases of incongruity if we are to ultimately develop a satisfactory explanation of the development of children's humor in a more general sense. It is precisely because the simplest and most basic forms of humor derive from incongruity in the absence of elements of sex, aggression, superiority, and so forth, that I have chosen to advance a model of humor development focusing exclusively on incongruity in relation to humor. The reader should rest assured that I am not proposing that all humor (whether that appreciated by children or by adults) can be reduced to incongruity alone. In the real world of cartoons, jokes, and social situations, the basic elements of incongruity involved may in fact play a minor role in determining how funny an event is. Clearly, it is the addition of sexual, aggressive, and other "emotionally salient" themes that produce belly laughs. However, if we attempt to understand humor with all of these factors contributing simultaneously, we immediately become overwhelmed by its complexity. Only after we have achieved an initial understanding of simpler forms of humor can we effectively study more complicated ones. The present chapter is designed to provide that first step.

Finally, imagination, make-believe, and fantasy (these are considered to be equivalent) are emphasized as playing a central role in children's humor. In comparing what is expected with what is encountered, the perceived incongruity must be believed to exist only at a fantasy level in order to be perceived as humorous. However, the importance of fantasy is considered to decrease as the child approaches adolescence.

The Meaning of Smiling and Laughter in Infancy

It is tempting to argue that infants first begin to experience humor when they begin to show vigorous laughter, or when they begin to smile at external events. The difficulty with this reasoning is that, if we cannot equate smiling or laughter with humor among adults, we certainly cannot do so with infants. It was noted in the preceding chapter that smiling and laughter have many different meanings, only one of which applies to humor. For example, children commonly smile and laugh during play activities. The high amount of affect shown in such play is a stronger index of general enjoyment than of the funniness of events occurring during play. But, even with full awareness of this characteristic of children's play, it is difficult to observe the toddler's hearty laughter without concluding that something must be terribly funny to the child. Accordingly, we will examine in more detail the explanations advanced for infant smiling and laughter that do not rely on humor-related causes. The reader is reminded that the central concern here is to determine how infants and young children respond to perceived incongruities; that is, events that are inconsistent with the child's previous understanding or experience with them. At what point in development, and under what conditions, does the infant begin to find such inconsistencies to be funny?

Smiling typically occurs three to four months before laughter in infants, making its initial appearance during sleep within the first week after birth. This early smile is not a "gas" smile, as commonly assumed, but results from spontaneous activity of the central nervous system during sleep.[1] The first wakeful smile follows within about two weeks and tends to occur just after feeding, when the infant is drowsy and satiated. The first fully alert smile occurs toward the end of the first month and is most effec-

---

[1]For an extended discussion of this subject, see SROUFE, L. A., and WATERS, E. The ontogenesis of smiling and laughter: A perspective on the organization of development in infancy. *Psychological Review*, 1976, 83, 173–189.

tively brought about by a combination of the mother's voice and some form of tactile stimulation (tickling or rubbing the stomach being the most common). In the second month, the smile develops into a broader grin and tends to occur in connection with a much broader range of events. The infant is now becoming increasingly interested in sights and sounds and less exclusively concerned with some form of physical pleasure. Thus, moving objects or lights are most interesting (especially if they also make a sound) and most likely to produce smiling.

By the third or fourth month, the meaningfulness of events begins to play an important role in infants' smiling. For example, an unmoving human face is one of the most consistent sources of smiling in the three- to four-month-old child (more effective than a moving face). The distinguished Swiss observer of child behavior Jean Piaget emphasized more than three decades ago that this smile might best be conceptualized as a smile of recognition (or mastery):[2] that is, through repeated examination of faces (especially the mother's) during the first three months, an infant finally develops a sufficient memory of the basic features of the face to recognize a face as being familiar. This memory (or "schema," as Piaget calls it) is initially of only the general features of a face, however. Parents who think that their child has finally learned to recognize them are disheartened to find that one face is as likely to make the infant smile as another. It is only by the fifth or sixth month that the stored memory for faces improves to the point that the mother's face (or those of other persons in close, regular contact with the child) can be discriminated at a glance from other faces. This discrimination usually produces selective smiling at the mother and is typically taken as an indication of the child's growing attachment to the mother.

The development of the smile of recognition between the ages of three and six months is more complicated than it seems. Studies in the past decade have shown that infants do not restrict their smiling to highly familiar faces or objects. If the child is so familiar with the object that it is immediately recognizable, little interest is aroused, and smiling does not occur. Rather, it is objects that are recognizable only after some initial effort that are

---

[2]PIAGET, J. *Play, dreams, and imitation in childhood.* New York: Norton, 1962. PIAGET, J. *The origins of intelligence in children.* New York: International Universities Press, 1952.

most interesting and most likely to be smiled at. In fact, it has been suggested that smiling is most likely when an optimal amount of effort is required to recognize events.[3] If the new object is sufficiently different from objects that the child has encountered before, the process of trying to understand (that is, recognize through memories or schemas) that object seems to be so mentally demanding or fatiguing that smiling does not occur even after the object is finally recognized as being similar to other familiar objects. The fact that this pattern of findings occurs as early as it does suggests that gaining the greatest amount of pleasure from thinking that requires the exertion of moderate amounts of effort may be built into children (in a biological sense). This pleasure is manifest in the form of a smile.

Several lines of evidence support the existence of such a relationship between amount of mental effort exerted and smiling. First, when a totally unfamiliar object is presented to an infant, there is no smiling initially. Rather, the infant looks at it, manipulates it, and generally explores it in an effort to recognize it and make some sense out of it. In other words, the infant relates (although with no conscious awareness) this new event to previous ones experienced. As the object is repeatedly presented to the infant, smiling gradually begins to appear. The child is building a schema for the object with each successive presentation and eventually achieves a sufficient memory to permit recognition. As the object is continuously presented, however, smiling reaches a peak and subsequently begins to subside.[4] Boredom sets in because eventually the object is recognizable with virtually no effort at all.

A second line of evidence stems from demonstrations that infants are most likely to smile at stimulus events that are moderately different from those with which they have become familiar.[5] This is typically accomplished by first presenting the same pattern (e.g., an upside-down "y") repeatedly until the infant no longer shows any interest in it; that is, spends very little time

[3]Ibid. KAGAN, J. *Change and continuity in infancy.* New York: Wiley, 1971.

[4]Ibid. SHULTZ, T. R., and ZIGLER, E. Emotional concomitants of visual mastery in infants: the effects of stimulus movement on smiling and vocalizing. *Journal of Experimental Child Psychology,* 1970, 10, 390–402.

[5]McCALL, R. B., and McGHEE, P. E. The discrepancy hypothesis of attention and affect in infants. In I. C. Uzgiris and F. Weizmann (Eds.), *The structuring of experience.* New York: Plenum, 1977.

looking at it. When this occurs, habituation is said to have taken place, meaning that a stable memory, or schema, has been developed for the pattern. The important test is made after habituation to the original pattern has occurred. At that point, one of several graded levels of discrepancy from the original pattern is presented: that is, a series of patterns is used, with one end of the series being very similar to the upside-down "y" and the other end being very dissimilar to it. Under these conditions, infants are most likely to smile at patterns that are in the middle of the range of discrepancy. Again, the amount of effort required to relate the discrepant event to the memory of the original pattern seems to be the important factor in determining whether smiling occurs.

In a later chapter, we shall see that a comparable process seems to contribute to children's appreciation of humor: that is, if we hold constant or eliminate such factors as sexual and aggressive content, those jokes or cartoons that are moderately challenging to our intellect are the funniest.[6] Puns are not very funny to adults because they are too simple. Puns are funny to children, however, presumably because they are more challenging to a child's mind. In a sense, then, we can think of jokes and cartoons as a kind of problem-solving task. We enjoy engaging in this task in order to get the point of the intended humor as long as the task does not get too difficult. In a nonhumorous situation—for example, in performing tasks with embedded figures or anagrams—children have similarly been found to smile after getting the solution.[7] More important, smiling tends to be maximized following the solution of more difficult problems. We must conclude, then, that children enjoy exercising their intellectual powers. When new or incongruous events are encountered, they make the effort to understand them and derive great pleasure from being successful at it. This source of pleasure may contribute to the enjoyment derived from humor, but it certainly cannot be equated with humor. So we are again forced to conclude that this source of smiling in infants has no implications for whether infants are capable of humor.

---

[6]McGhee, P. E. Children's appreciation of humor: A test of the cognitive congruency principle. *Child Development*, 1976, 47, 420–426.

[7]Kagan, *Change and continuity in infancy.* Harter, S. Pleasure derived by children from cognitive challenge and mastery. *Child Development*, 1974, 45, 661–669.

In addition to this parallel between humorous and non-humorous forms of problem solving at the cognitive level, a second parallel exists at the physiological level. It was noted in Chapter 1 that sudden drops in measures of physiological arousal (some have described this as tension reduction) are related to the appreciation of humor. Arousal increases as we listen to the development of a joke and sharply decreases when we "get the point" of the punch line. Recent studies have shown that a similar process occurs when infants are confronted with new or discrepant stimuli.[8] We have already noted that smiling occurs as a result of this sudden tension reduction.[9] With repeated presentations of the same stimulus, smiling presumably becomes less frequent because there is no build-up of tension accompanying examination of the stimulus. The important point to be emphasized here is that we again see that there are a number of similarities between humorous and nonhumorous reactions to the perception of incongruity. Because the context in which the incongruity is experienced plays an important role in determining whether an infant reacts positively or negatively, the stimulus itself cannot cause the infant to appreciate humor. Similarly, the fact that tension reduction (or a decrease in arousal) and the solution of moderately challenging cognitive tasks can produce smiling in both humorous and nonhumorous contexts suggests that the key to the essential nature of incongruity humor is not to be found in either of these directions.

Infant laughter has not been studied as thoroughly as smiling, although the available data do suggest that the developmental trends for laughter are comparable to those for smiling. Laughter first begins at about four months of age. Like those of smiling, the earliest causes of laughter have been found to be sounds in combination with active physical (tactile) stimulation (such as vigorously kissing the infant's stomach or "looming" toward the child while tickling the ribs and saying, "I'm gonna get you"). Visual and social forms of stimulation become increasingly effective throughout the first year.[10] By eight months of age, infants are most likely to laugh at such events as the "peek a boo"

---

[8]SROUFE and WATERS, Ontogensis of smiling and laughter.

[9]Ibid. KAGAN, Change and continuity in infancy.

[10]SROUFE, L. A., and WUNSCH, J. P. The development of laughter in the first year of life. Child Development, 1972, 43, 1326–1344.

game, in which either the mother's or child's face gets covered, or the mother shaking her hair or crawling on the floor. By one year of age, events like seeing the mother sucking a baby's bottle, sticking out her tongue, approaching with a mask on her face, or walking (waddling) like a penguin are most effective in producing laughter.

It is especially tempting to interpret a ten- or twelve-month-old's laughter at these highly incongruous activites of the mother as evidence for humor. After all, the infant is laughing, and these odd behaviors are even mildly amusing to older children or adults. It must be remembered, however, that the infant cannot be perceiving such incongruities as we do, because of its extremely limited intellectual capacities. It was pointed out in Chapter 1 that, as long as such incongruities occur in a familiar or safe (nonthreatening) context, accompanying arousal changes are expressed in the form of laughter. If they occur in an unfamiliar context, or one in which the infant feels uncomfortable for any reason, arousal takes on a negative character and leads to anxiety or crying. Clearly, the fact that the source of these incongruities lies in the mother's own behavior means that the situation must be a relaxed and safe one for the child. In short, the child's laughter can be accounted for without explaining it as a reaction to humor. Finally, according to the definition of humor offered in Chapter 1, such laughter could not be indicative of humor, because the infant has not yet developed the necessary cognitive prerequisites for humor; namely, the ability to engage in fantasy or make-believe behavior.

Development of Fantasy and Make-Believe

The development of fantasy and make-believe behavior will be discussed in some detail, because the capacity for such intellectual activity is considered to be a prerequisite for seeing incongruity as humorous. We have already seen that, as early as the first year of life, an infant has a strong sense of curiosity about objects and events in its world. Piaget emphasized that the "need" to explore novelty is built into a child's nervous system.[11] Earlier in this chapter, it was concluded that this tendency to-

---

[11]PIAGET, *Origins of intelligence in children.*

ward exploration is greatest when only moderate levels of novelty are encountered, with very high and low levels of novelty producing a relative lack of interest and reduced exploration. Numerous investigators have reminded us, however, that this natural curiosity in human beings occurs only when basic biological drives like sex and hunger are not aroused.[12] Given this novelty-seeking characteristic of children, it follows that newly developed capacities will be used to help maintain an environment with an optimal balance of new and familiar events. In fact, this may be one of the strongest motivating forces behind young children's tendency to spend great amounts of time engaged in fantasy activity. They can always create in fantasy a new and interesting set of circumstances simply by rearranging some aspect of reality as they know it.

Jerome Singer has made numerous important contributions to our understanding of young children's imaginative activities. In addition to studying fantasy and make-believe activities experimentally, he has suggested that make-believe activity can be viewed as resulting from a constant need of the brain for activity and stimulation:

> Let us consider the possibility that the very nature of the operation of the brain requires a constant recoding and rehearsal of stimulus material. . . . The brain is a system that involves constant activity and a replaying of the literally millions of images and verbal coding labels that have been experienced and stored. This seemingly tonic or continuous aspect of brain function is manifest in nocturnal sleep when we become aware of a great deal of mental activity.[13]
>
> . . . make-believe play can best be viewed as a normal outgrowth of the fundamental information-processing activity of the child. Such cognitive activity involves not only the external environment, but also requires the child to attend to the brain's processing of long term memory material. Such stimulation provides a novel and affectively positive environment for the child.[14]

The seemingly trivial make-believe play of the child grows essentially out of the very nature of the child's cognitive experience. It

---

[12]SCHACHTEL, E. G. Metamorphosis: On the development of affect, perception, attention, and memory. New York: Basic Books, 1959.

[13]SINGER, J. L. The child's world of make-believe: Experimental studies of imaginative play. New York: Academic Press, 1973, p. 194.

[14]Ibid., p. 199.

follows the assimilation and accommodation cycles and involves the seeking of moderate levels of increasing stimulation or reducing such moderate levels of stimulation to produce an experience of joy.[15]

It can also be argued that make-believe activities as manifested in children and presumably continued into adult life in the form of various types of daydreaming and imagery skills . . . have their own special value as part of living. In the case of young children, they provide a varied and interesting environment to which the child can respond irrespective of whether there may even be any later learning consequences. In addition, the ability to deal with unreality and to generate complex sensitivity to what is fantasy and unreal may have its own ultimate rewarding value in helping to enrich the overall awareness of discovering reality and human possibilities.[16]

I fully agree with Singer that it is a child's built-in tendency to be attracted toward moderate degrees of novelty that produces an early fascination with fantasy activity. In their fantasy world, children create experiences that they know cannot take place in reality. They love self-made incongruities and exaggerations because they offer endless strings of new ideas and events to explore. The knowledge that these events occur only in fantasy helps a child sort out what is real and what is not, as well as what is possible and what is not. A similar idea has been advanced by the Russian writer Chukovsky:

> Nonsense . . . not only does not interfere with the child's orientation to the world that surrounds him, but, on the contrary, strengthens in his mind the sense of the real; and it is precisely in order to further the education of children in reality that such nonsense verse should be offered to them.[17]
>
> One can sight any number of such verses which testify to the inexhaustible need of every healthy child of every era and of every nation to introduce nonsense into his small but ordered world, with which he has only recently become acquainted. Hardly has the child comprehended with certainty which objects go together and which do not, when he begins to listen happily to versus of absurdity.[18]

---

[15]Ibid., p. 207.   [16]Ibid., p. 37.

[17]CHUKOVSKY, K. *From two to five.* Berkeley: University of California Press, 1963. Taken from selected parts reprinted in Bruner, J. S., Jolly, A., and Sylva, D. (Eds.), *Play: Its role in development and evolution.* New York: Basic Books, 1976, p. 596.

[18]Ibid., p. 601.

Chukovsky notes that Russian folk rhymes for children are full of nonsense, absurdity, and incongruity and that children do not enjoy the tales as much if realistic or congruous events are substituted. The consistency of Chukovsky's views with those discussed in Chapter 1 dealing with the importance of prior mastery for children's humor is also evident in the preceding quotation. Children must understand the real order of things before incongruities and exaggerations become a source of pleasure. The incongruous events are enjoyed precisely because they are known to be at odds with reality.

We have described the preschool child's enjoyment of incongruities and other sorts of fantasy nonsense as if this were characteristic of all children. However, widespread individual differences can easily be seen in the extent to which children "lose" themselves in fantasy entertainment. Singer has argued that the following characteristic styles of thinking and feeling are related to strong dispositions to engage in fantasy: (1) divergent thinking (the tendency to produce more novel responses to problems or situations), (2) a greater quantity of ideas and more imaginative ideas, and (3) greater enjoyment of play.[19] Because of the apparent link between fantasy predisposition and divergent thinking, Singer believes that there is a close relationship between early make-believe activity and what later emerges as creativity. For example, he noted studies showing that college students classified as highly creative report more daydreaming and imaginary companions in childhood.

> To the extent that considerable make-believe activities are part of the growing child's repertory, these [activities] form links to a general attitude of "as if" or control over one's products, at least in the imaginary sphere. Such predispositions may next become the basis also for an artistic or scientific creative orientation in many young people.[20]

The notion of control over the maintenance of an optimally interesting internal environment is one that has not received much attention by writers interested in creativity. A great advantage of creating fantasy incongruities as a means of maintaining a

---

[19]SINGER, *Child's world of make-believe.*
[20]Ibid., p. 255.

stimulating environment is that a person can change fantasy events so as to maintain a level of stimulation that maximizes interest and enjoyment. External forms of stimulation could sustain comparable levels of interest, but they would be much more difficult both to initially arrange and to maintain.

Singer further suggested that the strength of a child's predisposition toward engaging in make-believe activity can be enhanced by a variety of circumstances, including the following:

1. An opportunity for privacy and for practice in a relatively protected setting where the external environment is reasonably redundant so that greater attention can be focused on internal activity. . . .

2. Availability of a variety of materials in the form of stories told, books and playthings. . . .

3. Freedom from interference by peers or adults who make demands for immediate motor or perceptual reactions. . . .

4. The availability of adult models or older peers who encourage make-believe activity and provide examples of how this is done. . . .

5. Cultural acceptance of privacy and make believe activities as a reasonably worthwhile form of play.[21]

Parents, then, can have a considerable influence on a child's fantasy orientation (and perhaps creativity) by arranging its physical and social environment along these lines. No data have yet been obtained linking genetic factors to individual differences in fantasy predisposition.

Reality Assimilation and Fantasy Assimilation

It has been argued that moderately novel and incongruous events are most interesting to infants and young children and are most likely to be sought out, in comparison with totally new or familiar events. This novelty-seeking extends to the realms of both reality and fantasy. In spite of this similarity, though, there are essential differences between the two—differences that are central to understanding the nature of cognitive development in children. When an infant or young child encounters any event in the real world that doesn't precisely fit (or match) the schema or concept that has been developed out of past experience with

---

[21]Ibid., pp. 198–199.

comparable events, an attempt is made to accommodate or stretch that schema to incorporate the additional qualities of the new event. We might call this process "reality assimilation," because it refers to the manner in which adaptation of the child's present way of making sense out of the real world takes place. According to Piaget, this is precisely how cognitive development occurs.[22] As long as the child is convinced that the incongruous event is a real one, an attempt will be made to incorporate it into existing knowledge. As the relevant schema is extended to include this new event, the incongruity disappears; that is, the event becomes part of the schema against which new stimulus events are compared. In this fashion, novelty is eliminated and the child's intelligence is expanded.

Reality assimilation, then, is the route by which cognitive development progresses throughout childhood, as well as adulthood. Throughout the first twelve to eighteen months, this is the only means children have of making sense out of incongruous events. Although infants frequently demonstrate smiling and laughter in this period, as we have seen, their approach to understanding the world is a more serious one. Whenever an object is encountered that is different from the child's experience with comparable objects, the process of accommodation and intellectual expansion is automatically initiated. At some point in the first half of the second year, however, infants begin to show a new form of behavior suggesting that they now have at their disposal a new and very different means of making sense out of incongruous events. For example, a child might vigorously rub an index finger back and forth across the teeth in a manner suspiciously similar to brushing with a tooth brush, or it might pull a pencil repeatedly over the hair "as if" combing or brushing the hair. Piaget describes numerous examples along these lines in his book *Play, Dreams, and Imitation in Childhood*.[23] His daughter Jacqueline first displayed such behavior at fifteen months when she reacted to a piece of cloth in a manner formerly reserved for her pillow. She also engaged in pretend washing at eighteen months, and pretend eating at twenty months. His other daughter, Lucien, first demonstrated this kind of behavior at twelve

[22]PIAGET, *Origins of intelligence in children.*
[23]PIAGET, *Play, dreams, and imitation in childhood.*

months of age. The common theme in these activities is that the child is reacting to one object *as if* it were another object. According to Piaget, this form of behavior is striking evidence that the infant's world has finally begun to be represented in the form of images. By having a memory image of an object or event available that can be conjured up at any time, the child is free to create incongruities by simply bringing the "wrong" image to bear on any given object. Thus, in the first example described above, the child presumably has an image of a tooth brush in mind while rubbing the index finger across the teeth.

> The child is using schemas which are familiar . . . but (1) instead of using them in the presence of objects to which they are usually applied, he assimilates to them new objectives unrelated to them from the point of view of effective adaptation: (2) these new objects, instead of resulting merely in an extension of the schema (as in the case of generalization proper to intelligence), are used with no other purpose than that of allowing the subject to mime or evoke the schemas in question. It is the unison of these two conditions— application of the schema to inadequate objects and evocation for pleasure—which in our opinion characterizes the beginning of pretense.[24]

Piaget described this type of behavior as symbolic play, because the child is playfully applying schemas to inappropriate objects without the usual accommodatory effort made in reality assimilation. The laughter that accompanies most of the examples of such behavior described by Piaget suggests that children derive considerable enjoyment from manipulating images in this way and proceed to engage in such manipulative play as soon as they develop the capacity to represent events by images. Because the object normally associated with the behavior exhibited by the child is present only in the child's imagination, we might refer to this peculiar form of attempting to "understand" the object as "fantasy assimilation." Fantasy assimilation differs from reality assimilation in that there is no accompanying attempt to change the schema into which the object is assimilated in order to eliminate the mismatch between the schema and the incongruous object. Thus, the schema for tooth brushing is not modified in a permanent fashion so as to include use of the fingers rubbing over

---

[24]Ibid., p. 97.

the teeth. Rather, the child temporarily dismisses the usual "rules" for determining which objects or events are appropriate for which schemas. In the child's fantasy, the new and incompatible object is treated as if it matched the image of some other object—even though the child is fully aware that it does not.

Playful Fantasy and the Beginnings of Humor

At the beginning of this chapter, it was suggested that fantasy assimilation is a necessary prerequisite for humor, although it is not sufficient to produce humor. It was also argued that the exploration of fantasy distortions of the real world is interesting and may be pursued for reasons having nothing to do with humor. It seems, then, that there are at least three ways in which incongruity may be experienced by a child. First, the child may have a "set" toward reality assimilation and will attempt to accommodate relevant schemas or concepts to fit the discrepant event. This is how learning and cognitive change occur. We have seen that stretching one's concepts to fit novel or incongruous events is experienced as pleasurable (as reflected in the smile), especially if an optimal amount of mental effort is exerted in the process.

The fantasy assimilation mechanism just described constitutes a second means of making sense out of incongruities. Within the operation of this mechanism, however, a child might have either of two opposing sets or attitudes toward dealing with incongruities. One set is similar to that characteristic of reality assimilation, in that exploration of the nature of the event and its relationship to previously obtained knowledge is serious. Existing schemas and concepts are not changed as a result of this process, but the primary orientation of the child is toward learning what happens when inappropriate objects or events are assimilated into different schemas. The creation of fantasy incongruities in this manner is interesting to the child. Some children spend hour after hour engaged in this make-believe activity. When in this more serious frame of mind, children are fascinated by the strange world that they are creating, *but they do not find it humorous.* An additional element must be present before the fantasy assimilation of incongruous events can be perceived as being funny: the crucial element of play or playfulness. The child who is in a playful frame of mind when attending to incongruous events at the fantasy level is not concerned with exploring the world of fantasy; rather, the prime focus is on acknowledging (to oneself or to others) the impossibility or absurdity of the events imagined. The events are humorous precisely because they are known to be at odds with reality. The same events would produce a different reaction if the child were not in this playful state. In a more serious mood, or with a stronger focus on the exploration of what happens when existing schemas are extended in fantasy to unusual or newly created events, the child's reaction might fluctuate between interest and puzzlement, but the humor would be lost. Humor in the young child, then, results from the playful contemplation of incongruity, exaggeration, absurdity, or nonsense only when the child realizes that the events exists in fantasy.

Numerous books have been written in the past two decades dealing with the nature and functions of play behavior.[25] The intent here is not to review this vast and growing literature, but to point out characteristics of play that seem to have an effect on the development of an appreciation of humor in young children. Most play can be divided into two broad categories: social play and play with objects. Although there may be incongruous relationships in the context of either form of play, it is object play that has the closest link to the kind of cognitive processes discussed in this chapter. In object play, a close relationship exists between the degree of novelty afforded by an object or situation and the amount of play behavior that is exhibited in connection with it.[26] Piaget and others have observed that curiosity and exploration generally precede play with novel or incongruous objects.[27] A child will visually examine and manipulate the object in an attempt to become familiar with it and to understand it. There is no play during this period, although some have referred to this initial behavior as exploratory play. The focus of attention is clearly on learning at this stage; that is, the child is in a serious mood,

[25]For a listing of these books, see BRUNER, J. S., JOLLY, A., and SYLVA, K. (Eds.), *Play: Its role in development and evolution.* New York: Basic Books, 1976.

[26]HUTT, C. Exploration and play in children. *Symposia of the Zoological Society of London,* No. 18, 1966.

[27]PIAGET, *Play, dreams, and imitation in childhood.*

not a playful one. It is only after the child learns the properties of the object and becomes less curious about it, that play activities are likely to begin. In most cases, these newly learned properties are incorporated into the ongoing play. This pattern is well illustrated by an example drawn from Catherine Garvey's research:

> A three-year-old boy saw a large wooden car in our playroom for the first time. (a) He paused, inspected it, and touched it. (b) He then tried to find out what it could do. He turned the steering wheel, felt the license plate, looked for a horn, and tried to get on the car. (c) Having figured out what the object was and what it could do, he got to work on what he could do with it. He put telephones on it, took them off, next put cups and dishes on it. These activities were a form of trying out ideas to see how they work. Finally, the car was understood, its properties and immediate usefulness reasonably clear. (d) He then climbed on it and drove it furiously back and forth with suitable motor and horn noises. We can readily accept the last activity as play.[28]

Other investigators have noted the mood changes that accompany this sequence:

> Investigative, inquisitive, or specific exploration is directional, that is, it is elicited by or oriented towards certain environmental changes. . . . Play, on the other hand, occurs only in a known environment, and when the animal or child feels he knows the properties of the object in that environment; this is apparent in the gradual relaxation of mood, evidenced not only by changes in facial expression, but in greater diversity and variability of activities. In play the emphasis changes from the question of "what does this object do?" to "what can I do with this object?"[29]

Play and exploratory behavior, then, are linked together in two distinct ways. First, exploratory investigations of new or incongruous situations provide the sense of understanding of the event that is a prerequisite for play. After play has been initiated with an object, however, the play activities themselves serve to further expand the child's understanding of the object: that is, even though the child's mood is not one primarily directed to-

---

[28]Garvey, C. *Play.* Cambridge, Mass.: Harvard University Press, 1977, p. 47.

[29]Hutt, Exploration and play in children (cited from Bruner, J. S., Jolly, A., and Sylva, K. (Eds.), *Play: Its role in development and evolution.* New York: Basic Books, 1976, p. 211).

ward learning, incidental learning does occur. The child discovers new properties of the object during play, even though learning is no longer of any concern. Not surprisingly, the exploratory phase of this sequence is shorter for simple stimulus events than it is for more complex ones.[30]

Earlier in this chapter, it was demonstrated that, when a child is in a reality mode of assimilation, interest and the probability of smiling are maximized when a new event is at a moderate level of novelty or discrepancy. A perfect match between the new event and existing knowledge results in immediate recognition or understanding of the event, a condition that typically produces boredom. But it is under this very condition that play is most likely to occur. This suggests that one of the most important functions of play may be to help maintain a stimulating and interesting environment. Regardless of whether play is strictly at the ideational level or also includes ongoing motor activity, a child does things with objects during play that it would not normally do in a nonplayful state. These unique play behaviors produce novel and surprising effects, which are in turn sources of interest and enjoyment to the child.

Humor develops as the child's playfulness extends to recently mastered ideas and images, as well as overt play with objects. The child in Garvey's example of the exploration-play pattern with a toy car (on p. 62), might have chosen to play only with ideas about the car instead of playing with the car itself once he felt that he understood the nature and function of the toy. For example, he might have imagined the car in a race, with himself as driver, or might have pretended that the car was a spaceship. Such fantasy play would remain humorless play as long as the child's attention was directed toward what he could do with the car in his make-believe world. The play would not trigger humor until attention was shifted toward the fact that the child is imagining the car to do something that he knows is nonsense, absurd, or impossible.

---

[30]Hutt, Exploration and play in children. Nunnaly, J. C., and Lemond, L. C. Exploratory behavior and human development. In L. P. Lipsitt and H. W. Reese (Eds.), *Advances in child development and behavior.* New York: Academic Press, 1973. Switzky, H. N., Haywood, H. C., and Isett, R. Exploration, curiosity, and play in young children: Effects of stimulus complexity. *Developmental Psychology,* 1974, 10, 321–329.

Social factors play a strong supporting role in a young child's perceptions of humor (see Chapter 6), but humor may be perceived during make-believe play when the child is either alone or in the presence of others. A child's earliest experiences of humor, as will be suggested in the next section, are private ones, because they are based on the manipulation of images of objects, and the child has not yet developed the langugage facilities that would permit sharing the experience. Singer has offered an opposing view, emphasizing the influence of social learning on children's early experiences of humor.[31] Although Singer believes that humor has its origin in make-believe play, the enjoyment derived from play does not take the form of humor, in his view, until the laughter or other forms of positive reaction of the adults or older children in the family are noted by the child. Presumably, this draws the child's attention to the nature of make-believe play that produces such reactions and instills a curiosity about what else might be done in order to reproduce them. The difficulty with this position is that it does not shed any light on either the cognitive prerequisites for humor or the processes that characterize a genuine experience of humor for the child. According to this position, a child might never develop a sense of humor, were it not for the reactions of others. In the view advanced in this book, the capacity for humor is built into the nervous system of human beings. As soon as underlying maturational processes permit a child to represent the world by images and to freely manipulate those images, the child will perceive humor from time to time. The importance of social factors stems from the fact that playful moods or attitudes are readily maintained through interaction with others, and it is only in the presence of such a playful set that humor can occur.[32] In the absence of any social contact, a child who developed in a highly stimulating environment would develop the capacity for humor, even though there might not be much to laugh at.

---

[31]SINGER, *Child's world of make-believe.*

[32]BATESON, G. The message "This is play." In B. Schaffner (Ed.), *Group Processes.* New York: Josiah Macy, Jr., Foundation, 1956. FRY, W. F., JR. *Sweet madness: A study of humor.* Palo Alto, California: Pacific Books, 1963. McGHEE, P. E. A model of the origins and early development of incongruity-based humour. In A. J. Chapman and H. C. Foot (Eds.), *It's a funny thing, humour.* Oxford, England: Pergamon Press, 1977.

An additional social influence upon humor results from the desire that most children (as well as adults) have to *share humor with others.* Although impossible or absurd make-believe creations may be enjoyed alone, the enjoyment is increased by sharing it. The urge to tell others our clever jokes and humorous insights is quite apparent in the following delightful example in which Chukovsky describes the details surrounding his daughter's first joke at twenty-three months of age:

> One day in the twenty-third month of her existence, my daughter came to me, looking mischevious and embarrassed at the same time—as if she were up to some intrigue. . . . She cried to me even when she was still at some distance from where I sat: "Daddy, oggie-miaow!". . . . And she burst out into somewhat encouraging, somewhat artificial laughter, inviting me, too, to laugh at this invention.[33]

This tendency to want to share one's humor with others remains a strong characteristic of most children into adulthood, especially among females (see Chapter 8). The earliness at which this occurs makes it tempting to conclude that it is a necessary condition for humor. Piaget, however, gave several examples of the vigorous laughter of children upon creating pretend incongruities when playing alone.[34] It seems then, that, although social conditions may have a considerable facilitating effect on the young child's humor, they are not necessary for humor.

Stages in the Development of Incongruity Humor

Once the capacity for make-believe or fantasy play develops in the second year, children progress through a series of stages in their humor. Although the ages at which children achieve a given stage vary considerably, the sequence of stages is the same for all children: that is, all children exhibit Stage 1 humor before Stage 2, Stage 2 before Stage 3, and Stage 3 before Stage 4. This regularity is not surprising, because the kind of humor of which a child is capable at any given point in development depends on the level of cognitive development achieved. Stages in humor de-

---

[33]CHUKOVSKY, *From two to five.* p. 601.
[34]PIAGET, *Play, dreams, and imitation in childhood.*

velopment, then, should closely correspond to general trends in cognitive development. The four humor stages described here correspond to specific cognitive acquisitions in the first seven or eight years, described initially by Piaget. This correspondence reflects the fact that, as children mature, they use newly developed cognitive capacities in play activities as well as in more serious forms of interchange with the environment.

Stage 1: Incongruous Actions toward Objects

A child first experiences humor in the context of playing with objects in the second year. This is made possible by the child's ability to represent objects with internal images. In effect, the maintenance and ready availability of images of objects directly leads to make-believe. Initially, pretend activities are restricted to the invention of objects in their absence:[35] that is, eighteen-month-olds treat an image of a toy as if it were that toy, being fully aware of the difference between the two. It requires only a minor extension of this basic ability for the child to assimilate objects into a schema that does not actually match those objects. By keeping the image of the appropriate object in mind while acting toward the new and inappropriate object, the child treats the new object as if it were compatible with the current image-based schema. Given a playful set, it is this incongruous juxtaposition of object, image, and action that is at the heart of the child's first experience of humor. A number of examples typical of this stage of humor development have already been noted. An example from Piaget follows:

> At 1:3 (12) Jacqueline ... saw a piece of cloth whose fringed edges vaguely recalled those of her pillow; she seized it, held a fold of it in her right hand, sucked the thumb of the same hand and lay down on her side, laughing hard. She kept her eyes open, but blinked from time to time as if she were alluding to closed eyes.[36]

In another example, one of Piaget's children picked up a leaf and held it up to her ear, talking to it as if it were a telephone. Laughter usually accompanies this type of behavior. It is impossible to

---

[35]GARVEY, *Play.*

[36]PIAGET, *Play, dreams, and imitation in childhood.*

determine whether any particular activity is related to humor, but vigorous laughter and other cues indicating a generally playful mood are highly suggestive of humor. As stated earlier, it is the very knowledge of the inappropriateness of the action executed toward an object that leads to humor and its accompanying laughter when the child is in a playful frame of mind. Throughout each of the stages described here, *laughter reflects the pleasure derived from creating in fantasy play a set of conditions known to be at odds with reality.*

The first two stages of humor overlap considerably because each one relies on the manipulation of images of events. Stage 2 is characterized by the use of words to create incongruities, but the inconsistency between verbal label, the real object (or action initiated toward the object), and the image brought to bear on that object combine to supply the source of humor. Because children begin to master language soon after they develop primitive representational capacities, verbal statements may, at times, accompany the incongruous actions that constitute Stage 1 humor. For example, a girl may say "comb" or "comb hair" while going through hair-combing motions with a ruler. This example is categorized as Stage 1 humor because of the importance of the activity directed toward the ruler. Overt physical activity is central to incongruities created at this first stage. The same basic notion might be manifest at Stage 2 some months later when the child simply describes the idea of combing her hair with a ruler in the absence of hair-combing motions.

An observation made by Piaget affords an additional example of Stage 1 humor that includes verbal components. Piaget noted that at twenty-two months of age his daughter "put a shell on the table and said *'sitting,'* then put it on top of another, adding delightedly: *'Sitting on pot.'*"[37] In this example, again, there is a strong reliance on the feedback provided by overt action toward objects. If she had simply said "sitting on pot," and then broke up laughing, an observer would have difficulty knowing what the child was laughing at, but the event would clearly be an example of Stage 2 rather than Stage 1 humor.

The playful manipulation of images of objects that characterizes a child's earliest humor begins with simple single trans-

[37]Ibid.

formations of objects, as in the foregoing examples, and proceeds to multiple and more complex transformations. Any given object may have numerous features that the child might utilize to create incongruous action-object-image juxtapositions. With increasing age, the child becomes dissatisfied with one-dimensional incongruities and strives for more complexity in humor by either distorting several properties of an object simultaneously or drawing on more abstract features of the object. Again, it is essential to note that this pattern in humor development results from underlying basic cognitive developmental changes along similar lines.[38] A related pattern may be found in the kinds of objects that enter into Stage 1 incongruities. More often than not, the one-and-a-half to two-year-old will direct incongruous actions toward objects that have some similarity to the appropriate object. From the second year on, there is a decreasing reliance on such resemblances in make-believe play, regardless of whether the play is of an exploratory or humorous nature.

Stage 2: Incongruous Labeling of Objects and Events

Piaget observed that a new form of symbolic play begins to emerge toward the end of the second year, in which the child either identifies one object as another or identifies its own body as another person or thing.[39] For example, Jacqueline at twenty-seven months "pointed to a big rough pebble: *'It's a dog.'* Where's its head?' *'There'* (a lump in the stone). 'And its eyes?' *'They've gone!'"* On another occasion, at twenty-four months of age, Jacqueline "opened the window and shouted, laughing: *'Hi boy!'* (a boy she met on her walks and who was never in the garden). Then, still laughing, she added: *'Over there!'"* The laughter in the last example suggests that humor is more likely to have been experienced here than when the pebble was imagined to be a dog. This is only a guess, though, based on the appearance of a playful mood in the second example. It is impossible to be certain that a child has experienced humor simply by examining the child's behavior or the degree of affect displayed. Humor is a private ex-

---

[38]Fein, G. A transformational analysis of pretending. *Developmental Psychology,* 1975, 11, 291–296.

[39]Piaget, *Play, dreams, and imitation in childhood.*

perience, and we can only make an educated guess regarding humor perceptions on the basis of behavioral cues.

Although the presence of real objects may play an important role in the humor of Stage 2, as in the foregoing examples, it is the *absence of action toward objects* that epitomizes humor at this stage. Physical activity may occur, but it is not central to Stage 2 humor. The verbal statement alone creates the incongruity and leads to laughter. This marks the first step in the child's humor toward increased abstraction, which continues to increase as new cognitive abilities are acquired during childhood and adolescence. Stage 1 humor does not simply disappear, however, as the capacity for Stage 2 forms of incongruity is established. Rather, everyday humor experiences are composed of various combinations of Stage 1 and Stage 2 incongruities. Some may be purely one or the other, but most are likely to consist of both discrepant actions toward objects and inaccurate descriptions of those actions or objects.

In the most common occurrence of Stage 2 humor, children simply give names to objects or events that they know to be incorrect. Thus, a child may find it endlessly amusing to call a dog a cat, a hand a foot, an eye a nose, and so forth. Having a sense of mastery over a word seems to be the critical factor in determining when a child begins to find it funny to change names of objects: that is, once the child learns the correct name for an object or part of the body, a playful frame of mind may lead to calling it every word but the right word. (In the next chapter, it will be suggested that apes that have learned sign language show an identical tendency to play with signs once the correct sign has been mastered.) Any parent can attest to the fact that all objects are fair game once the humor of name-changing is discovered. The duration of this form of humor varies among children, but it usually lasts until other, more interesting forms of humor are discovered. Typically, children maintain some enjoyment of name-change humor until the late preschool years. So this primitive form of joking is also characteristic of the early phase of Stage 3. Stages 2 and 3 differ with respect to such humor, however, in that joking in the former is likely to take the form of substituting an incorrect real word for the correct real word, whereas joking in the latter may also include the substitution of nonsense words for the correct word.

The fact that the Stage 2 child uses verbal labels readily understood by other children or adults provides for the beginnings of social influence on both the production and the enjoyment of humor. From the very beginning, however, children differ widely in the extent to which they seek social outlets for their humor. Most children prefer to share humorous fantasy play with others once they discover the mutual enjoyment to be derived from such sharing. Others may prefer to restrict their humorous creations to their own imaginations.

There seem to be two principal means by which experiences of humor in the early preschool years become interwoven with social interaction in general. The first is typified by Chukovsky's daughter (described earlier), whose first known joke was "Daddy, oggie-miaow." In this case, it seems that the child took the initiative of wanting to share what must have been a thrilling insight; namely, that it is a lot of fun to think of a dog making a cat sound. It is likely that children who share their earliest verbal humor in this fashion have already developed a close social bond with the person with whom it is shared. A child who has already developed a pattern of maintaining close proximity to the parent(s), or frequently approaching the parent(s) for affection and other forms of positive contact, may be especially likely to use such simple jokes as a means of gaining positive reactions (see Chapter 7).

A second, and probably more common, means by which humor becomes primarily a social phenomenon derives from parents' (or others') reactions to the child's early name-changing and other pretend games (see Chapter 6). Some parents pay very little attention to their children's fantasy play, viewing it as "childish" and a "waste of time." If their son or daughter seems to be especially prone toward fantasy play, whether with objects or words, they may tell the child to stop being silly or foolish. Under these conditions, the child eventually gets the message that humor and other forms of fantasy play are not viewed positively and either reduces the amount of time spent in such play or develops a pattern of avoiding others when engaged in it. Other parents may be delighted by the same play creations, reacting with delight and affectionate attention. Assuming that such reactions are typical, the child would be expected to seek out occasions for sharing humorous creations with parents as well as others.

If a child has brothers and sisters or friends who are relatively close in age, they, too, might influence the extent to which humor is produced. Other children are likely to share a genuine sense of enjoyment of the same kinds of fantasy distortions of reality. Regardless of which child "makes the first move" in sharing humorous fantasies, each soon discovers the mutual enjoyment of such play. Each learns that it is just as much fun to listen to someone else's joke as to make up one's own. In preschools or nursery schools catering to two- to three-year-olds, children can often be seen taking turns at mislabeling objects or initiating other forms of fantasy distortions. In this fashion, a regular pattern of social reinforcement for joking is established.

Play signals have an important role in humor experienced in a social context. Even though two-year-olds have made considerable progress in their understanding of the world, their confidence about the nature of objects and the word labels given to them is easily shaken. In name-change humor, for example, the toddler's reaction depends on who issues the statement and how it is done. If an adult calls a cat a dog, the child may simply look puzzled, because the animal is obviously a cat. This reaction is especially likely if the adult typically does not joke with the child, usually making only serious, reality-based statements. Apart from the normal mode of interaction between adult and child, however, the child's reaction will be heavily influenced by cues in the adult's behavior. For example, if the adult is smiling or laughing, or says "this is only pretend," at the time of the misnaming, the child will know that the statement was meant as a joke (or meant to be "silly"). Given the limited mastery of language between the ages of two and three years, such play signals are essential if incongruities are to be perceived as funny. In later years, as the child's internal sense of mastery in understanding the world increases, humor may (at least on some occasions) be experienced in the complete absence of play signals. Even if all available cues were to suggest that the incongruity is a real one, the child would be so certain of the impossibility of the event that it would be assumed to be make-believe or an error of some type. If the evidence favoring reality is sufficiently strong, however (such as when you hear your own dog speak to you in English), the confidence of even the older child or adult might be reduced to the point that humor would be interfered with.

For the toddler, the only way to be sure of the fantasy nature of any given incongruity is to be the one who makes it up. The child who originates the idea of calling a cat a dog or of using a stick as if it were a comb can be very confident that it is only make-believe. There is no need for play signals telling us how to interpret events when they originate in our own fantasy play. Accordingly, the majority of the toddler's humor is self-generated. Only in the midst of a clearly playful interaction will the name-changing games of others be experienced as humorous.

Stage 3: Conceptual Incongruity

The activites described in connection with Stages 1 and 2 continue to be sources of humor throughout a child's preschool years. But, when the child is about three years old, they are extended by a newly developed capacity for conceptual thinking. It is only at this time that children begin to realize that the words they are using actually refer to classes of objects or events that have certain key defining characteristics, and yet differ in other nonessential respects. For example, in addition to simply using the word cat upon seeing cats, the distinctive features of cats are noted (e.g., a head, a tail, four legs, fur, whiskers, a characteristic sound, etc.); all of a child's knowledge about cats becomes organized into a single concept of "cat." This basic cognitive acquisition serves the very important function of boosting the child's confidence in understanding the world. This increased confidence makes it easier to assume that any given incongruous event should be fantasy-assimilated rather than reality-assimilated.

Incongruity-based humor during Stage 3 may occur when any one or more aspects of a concept are violated. Whereas the Stage 2 child laughs when a cat is referred to as a dog, the Stage 3 child laughs upon imagining or seeing a drawing of a cat that has two heads, but no ears, and that makes a "moo" sound instead of a "miaow" sound. A two-year-old finds it funny to call a ball an apple or a pumpkin, whereas a three-year-old finds it funny if the ball has ears and a nose or says "ouch" when kicked. Stage 3 humor is more complex than that of Stage 2, in that many different characteristics may be involved (even though the child has difficulty keeping all these characteristics in mind at once). The number of characteristics that may enter into the humorous depiction of an object is limited only by the number of different ones that define the concept formed with respect to that object. Although humor is an all-or-nothing affair for the two-year-old (either the correct or incorrect name is given for an object), the three- or four-year-old is capable of perceiving varying degrees of incongruity. Up to a point, the greater the number of characteristics of the object violated, the more incongruous it is (it is not yet clear whether funniness increases directly as a function of the number of incongruous elements).

Beyond this unspecified point, so many elements have been distorted or changed that the child has difficulty recognizing the object; rather than becoming an incongruous depiction of a familiar object, the extremely discrepant depiction of the object is simply perceived as a totally novel and unfamiliar object. This eliminates the funniness, and is likely to produce curiosity and attempts at reality-assimilation. Whether fantasy- or reality-assimilation occurs, however, depends on the strength of the cues surrounding the event: that is, whether they are more playful than serious. As long as the strange cat is seen as a drawing, or described in a joking context or with a smile on the teller's face, the child knows that a playful fantasy interpretation is called for. But if an unusual looking cat walks in front of the child, or is described by someone with a "straight" face or in a serious context, a genuine attempt will be made to make sense out of this strange creature—to explain it in relation to past experiences.

Advances in language development play a central role in determining the onset of Stage 3 humor, and much of the preschooler's humor includes language in one way or another. The use of words, however, does not necessarily enter into all of the humor experienced at this point. It makes no difference whether the cat described above is experienced visually or verbally. The important point is that the child knows that cats have two ears, only one head, and do not make "moo" sounds. Given a playful set of circumstances, this knowledge is sufficient to make the imagination of such a cat funny.

Martha Wolfenstein emphasized, in a psychoanalytically oriented book on children's humor written twenty-five years ago, that three- and four-year-olds take great delight in distorting familiar concepts.[40] She argued that it is just about this time that children are beginning to understand the idea of a person "having a name," instead of being that name. As a result, a boy might find

---

[40]WOLFENSTEIN, M. *Children's humor.* Glencoe, Illinois: Free Press, 1954.

it very funny to call another boy by someone else's name—especially a girl's name. Gender changes are especially intriguing because the three- or four-year-old is likely to be struggling with the question of what it means to be a boy or girl. Once a child has definitely categorized himself or herself to be a boy or girl, and has begun to separate others according to their sex, he or she may laughingly call another child by the label for the opposite sex, or by the name of a particular person of the opposite sex ("Ha, ha, you're a girl," "You look just like a boy," "Hi girl," "Hi Sally," etc.). A child who has not yet mastered gender-related concepts will be threatened by such statements in most cases, although the circumstances in which they are made have a strong influence on the reaction. Of course, it is funnier to call someone else these names than to have them directed at oneself. When someone else says "you're a boy" (if the child is actually a girl) and does not seem to be joking or playing, this is likely to be upsetting rather than funny.

One of the most striking features of Stage 3 humor derives from the strong perceptual orientation in a child's thinking during the preschool years:[41] that is, the preschool child understands objects and events primarily on the basis of their appearance. Because of this perceptual "centeredness," a child between the ages of three and six forms concepts of objects from their prominant perceptual features. Much of the humor of this period, then, is based on the incongruous appearance of things. Thus, a child might laugh at a picture of a bicycle with square wheels without having a well-developed sense of awareness of the effect this would have on trying to ride it. A drawing of an elephant sitting on a tree limb looks funny because the child knows that elephants do not climb trees. Again, though, it might not occur to the child that a limb would not actually support an elephant and that there is no way in which an elephant could climb up a tree even if it were strong enough to support such weight. A cartoon showing a television set with a fish bowl on top, in which a man's face is in the fish bowl and a fish is swimming around on the television screen, would be funny because "they're backwards," but there would be little awareness of the notion that there is no means by which such a reversal could actually occur. Only by Stage 4 can a

---

[41]PIAGET, *Origins of intelligence in children.*

child step beyond the appearances of things and begin to think in a logical manner about what could and could not happen, and why. When asked to explain why such an event is funny, the preschooler cannot advance beyond a purely descriptive account and indicate why the situation described makes it funny. A Stage 4 child, on the other hand, is capable of at least three types of interpretive explanations, including (1) pulling together and contrasting the incongruous elements of the situation, (2) comparing the incongruous situation with the normal or expected one, and (3) giving a motivational interpretation of some character of the cartoon or joke.[42]

A new form of language play develops during Stage 3 in addition to simple name substitutions. Both repetitious rhyming of words and the creation of nonsense words are common sources of humor during the three- to six-year period. A child may begin with a familiar word and continue to slightly alter its sound with each repetition, as in "itsy, bitsy, mitsy, pitsy," "happy, dappy, sappy, bappy," "Tommy, bommy, lommy," and so on. Consistent with the strong perceptual orientation of this period, it is the sound change that is funny, not the altered meaning of the word. Similarly, the generation of such nonsense words as "squidzel," "zwimpy," "glorkel," and "vorp" are funny simply because they do not sound like any word the child has ever heard before.

Stage 4: Multiple Meanings, or the First Step toward Adult Humor

Children's humor first begins to resemble the humor of adults when they begin to realize that the meaning of words is often ambiguous. Much adult humor has as its basis the fact that two or more meanings are applicable to a particular key word in a joke or story. Puns are a classic example of this form of humor. In order to appreciate the humor in puns, a child must be simultaneously aware of the two meanings and realize that the obvious one provides for a normal set of circumstances, whereas the less probable one creates some sort of incongruous situation. For example, consider the following classic joke: "Hey, did you take a bath?" "No! Why, is one missing?" The Stage 3 child understands both usages of the word "take" in this joke, but cannot keep both in mind at the same time. The normal interpretation of "take a bath" refers to the act of bathing, and the preschooler cannot get beyond this to consider the second meaning as well. So, there is no sense of incongruity for the younger child, and the joke is described as making no sense. By the age of about seven (on the average), children begin to be able to detect linguistic ambiguity[43] and realize that there are two ways in which the key word makes sense. A child then understands that, although this second meaning does make sense in one respect, it nonetheless creates an incongruous set of circumstances—which, of course, is exactly what makes it funny. Stage 4 children understand the following joke, then, whereas Stage 3 children do not: "Order! Order in the court!" "Ham and cheese on rye, your honor."[44]

The child's entrance into Stage 4 can be easily demonstrated by presenting riddle-type questions that have two possible answers, instead of the usual one.[45] One of the answers should be a joking one derived from double meaning, whereas the other should be a straightforward factual answer. The child is then

---

[43]SHULTZ, T. R., and PILON, R. Development of the ability to detect linguistic ambiguity. *Child Development*, 1973, 44, 728–733.

[44]SHULTZ, T. R., and HORIBE, F. Development of the appreciation of verbal jokes. *Developmental Psychology*, 1974, 10, 13–20.

[45]McGHEE, P. E. Development of children's ability to create the joking relationship. *Child Development*, 1974, 45, 552–556.

asked to simply indicate which answer is the funnier of the two. Here are two examples:

> "Why did the old man tip-toe past the medicine cabinet?"
> Serious answer: "Because he dropped a glass, and didn't want to cut his foot."
> Joking answer: "Because he didn't want to wake up the sleeping pills."

> "Why did little Mary hit an egg against the table when she made a cake?"
> Serious answer: "To crack the egg, so she could dump it in the bowl."
> Joking answer: "Because the recipe said to beat the egg."

If several examples like this are presented, a preschooler will choose the serious and joking answer with approximately equal frequency. Because there is no awareness of the double meanings on which the riddle depends, one answer seems just as reasonable as the other. From about age seven on, children get increasingly better at choosing the joking answer. More abstract or complex ambiguities are the last to be understood.

In addition to achieving an understanding of puns and other jokes based on multiple meanings, the elementary school-aged child is able to understand other forms of abstract humor. The perceptual basis for incongruity that was required for humor in Stage 3 is no longer necessary in Stage 4. Stage 4 children understand the following joke, whereas Stage 3 children do not: "Well, I see you have a new dog. I thought you didn't like dogs." "I don't! But my mother bought a lot of dog soap on sale, so we had to get a dog to use it up."[46] As the child imagines what is happening in this story, there are no inconsistencies with perceptual experience. The perception of incongruity only occurs at the more abstract level of behavioral inconsistency. Thus, it makes no sense to buy a product that you don't need just because it is on sale. It is also illogical to buy a dog that you don't want in order to use up a product that you don't need. This is the first sign of logic entering into the humor process.

Stage 4 humor is achieved as a direct result of the acquisition of a series of cognitive abilities referred to by Piaget as con-

---

[46]McGHEE, Cognitive development and children's comprehension of humor.

crete operational thinking.[47] The reduced perceptual centeredness characteristic of the transition to concrete operational thinking has a tremendous influence on a child's thinking, in that it allows the child to consider relationships between events rather than simply focusing on the end states or outcomes of events. Concrete operational skills also allow "reversibility" of thinking: that is, they permit one to go back and replay events, examining in the process the relationship between beginning points, middle points, and end points. In the context of a joke, reversible thinking enables a child to go back and forth between several different meanings of key words; and this is precisely what is required for comprehension of jokes based on double meanings. It is also concrete operational thinking that permits a child of elementary school age to go beyond purely descriptive explanations of jokes toward more interpretive explanations.

A final influence of concrete operational thinking on children's humor is that it permits comprehension of qualities of humor beyond simple incongruous relationships. The Stage 4 child is less egocentric than the preschooler. The young child's egocentrism makes it impossible to take another person's point of view, and this has a major effect on reactions to humor. In short, younger children seem to be more cruel in their humor because they laugh directly at another person's limp, unusually shaped nose, distorted speech, and so forth. It simply does not occur to them that they might be hurting the feelings of people in such conditions. Because of the reduction of egocentricity during Stage 4, however, the eight-year-old is more likely to refrain from laughter until the deformed person is out of sight. Similarly, humorous events in which one person receives damage to possessions or personal harm from another are funny to a Stage 4 child only if the damaging act is perceived as accidental or unintentional. For a Stage 3 child, intent is irrelevant to how funny such a joke is perceived to be. Rather, more damaging outcomes are funnier than less damaging ones, apart from any other issues.[48]

It is impossible to place an upper age limit on Stage 4 humor. Adolescents do develop more sophisticated forms of humor and tend to favor anecdotes and spontaneous wit rather

---

[47]PIAGET, Origins of intelligence in children.

[48]McGHEE, P. E. Moral development and children's appreciation of humor. *Developmental Psychology*, 1974, 10, 514–525.

than memorized jokes, but the characteristics of Stage 4 humor remain to some extent into adulthood. For example, puns are generally less funny to adolescents and adults because of the simplistic nature of their play on words. Yet, all of us have at some time laughed at an especially clever pun. It is during late childhood and early adolescence that preferences for particular types of humor begin to be firmly established. After Stage 4, then, individual differences in patterns of humor appreciation become more prominant than any changes related to the child's age or developmental level.

Development of Tendentious Forms of Humor

The views presented in this chapter have been restricted to humor based on incongruous relationships. Attention has been given to incongruity-based humor in the absence of sex, aggression, and other tendentious qualities described by Freud.[49] This approach has been taken because incongruities seem to be the basic building blocks for most occurrences of humor. In the everyday world of cartoons, jokes, and humorous incidents, though, incongruous relationships probably typically form only the bare bones of humor. The real meat or substance of the event that makes us laugh is the emotional investment we have in the situation. For example, if a child hears a joke in which a teacher is put down, the child's relationships with teachers generally (or with a specific teacher) will probably be more important in determining the funniness of the joke than any incongruities depicted. As described in Chapter 1, a hostile feeling toward teachers may be suddenly released in the "safe" context of a joke. Clearly, then, the dynamics behind appreciation of hostile and sexual forms of humor are different from those behind appreciation of humor based on emotionally neutral incongruities. The overall pleasure derived from a specific joke or cartoon will depend on the combined operation of both sets of dynamics. An especially clever joke that allows a release of sexual or hostile feelings or tensions will always be funnier than a joke that is simple and emotionally neutral. But if an emotionally neutral clever

---

[49]FREUD, S. *Jokes and their relation to the unconscious.* New York: Norton, 1960.

joke is compared with an emotionally charged simple joke, which will be funnier? There is no clear answer to this question, because different people react in very different ways in this situation. If the joke taps an area of special sensitivity in either children or adults (as most sexual jokes do), most people will laugh more at it—regardless of how clever it is! A smaller number of people seem to derive more enjoyment from incongruities and ironies that are not overly sexual or aggressive.

The earliest form of tendentious humor involves the execution of some action or the saying of a word that is perceived as taboo by the child. In a more general sense, the first humor can be expected in connection with any aspect of the child's experience that becomes a focus of tension or special concern. For many children, initial tendentious humor centers on urination or defecation. In addition to the usual trials and tribulations of bladder and bowel training, children soon learn that these behaviors are somehow different from other behaviors. Parents seem to be very concerned about just when and where these acts occur, and become very upset when they occur at the wrong place or the wrong time. Even the most easy-going parents may be embarrassed or angered at untimely messes. As toilet-related activities increasingly become sources of emotional tension, children may make a game out of them or verbally joke about them. As mentioned in the last chapter, psychoanalysts feel that this gives the child a means of coping with the distress related to toilet training.

Once a child masters the functioning of bladder and bowels, joking about them may begin to wane. Yet, because most parents continue to stress the importance of proper toilet habits, children usually continue to derive enjoyment from toilet-related words (poo-poo, ka-ka, pee-pee, etc.). Humor in connection with these activities should show signs of change, however, because the child is making great advances in cognitive abilities. It becomes boring to simply say the taboo words, so more complicated and interesting ways of expressing "toiletness" are created. This pattern continues throughout the child's development: that is, new ways of joking about sources of tension are developed as new intellectual capacities evolve. The underlying conflict may be the same, but children generally prefer intellectually challenging ways of joking about conflicts at all ages. A child who jokes about toilet activities in a manner characteristic of a younger child may be laughed at by peers precisely because of this sign of immaturity. So there are strong incentives—both internal and social—for children to engage in joking in a manner consistent with their own developmental levels.

The tendentious aspects of humor development, then, reflect children's common tensions, conflicts, and anxieties.[50] As preschoolers become aware of and concerned about physical differences between the sexes, this becomes a popular topic for joking. Because most people continue to have some form of conflict or stress in regard to sexual activity on into adulthood, it is not surprising that sexual jokes remain popular throughout childhood. Similarly, it is safe to assume that most children experience high amounts of frustration during their early years. The very process of becoming socialized holds regular occasions for frustration for the preschooler. New sources of frustration confront the child in school and in social relationships. So joking about sources of frustration should also continue into adulthood. The fact that frustration often leads directly to aggression (or aggressive feelings, once the child has learned to curb aggressive impulses) helps account for the widespread popularity of aggressive forms of humor throughout development.

Beginning in the preschool years, and continuing into adolescence, a common focus of children's joking is the possession of knowledge and giving the right or wrong answers.[51] The fact that the increase in riddles and other forms of joking about who has knowledge and who doesn't is sharpest at about age six suggests that the emphasis placed on learning in school may be a major motivating force behind such joking. In school, it is very important to have the right answers, and children are evaluated and rewarded in accord with their ability to come up with the right answers. This is a source of anxiety to many children, especially those who feel some pressure from parents to do well in school. Joking is especially popular in its own right during this period, because children have just learned to understand double meanings. The content of much of the joking at this time, though, suggests that jokes are being used to help cope with the conflict surrounding learning and having knowledge.

The general dynamics behind tendentious forms of humor do not seem to change throughout development. The basic unifying principle at all ages is the one initially emphasized by Freud.[52]

---

[50]WOLFENSTEIN, *Children's humor.*

[51]Ibid.

[52]FREUD, *Jokes and the unconscious.*

Humor affords a *sense* of the release of tension in conflict by allowing an indirect release of the energy that has built up because of the conflict. Whether there is, in fact, a physical transfer of energy is not the most important question here. What matters is that people seem to feel as if there is an energy release and that there is relaxation, or arousal reduction, as a result of the joking. Regardless of the physical changes going on within our bodies, we do seem to enjoy jokes in connection with sources of emotional arousal—as long as the tension is not too great. Young children joke about sources of conflict in a very direct way, but the basic process is similar to that taking place in adults. The development of the joke facade (see Chapter 1) is the greatest single change that occurs in connection with tendentious forms of humor. By the time children reach first grade, they begin to see the importance of disguising the sexual or aggressive content of their jokes. To an extent, this results from the greater intellectual challenge offered by more sophisticated jokes whose true nature is somewhat disguised. Most important, though, the disguise enables a child to deny the sexual or aggressive nature of the joke if necessary. Once the basic concept of establishing the joke facade is acquired, it is the child's general progress in cognitive development that determines how cleverly and indirectly sexual or hostile ideas are expressed.

The Humor of Real Incongruities

Incongruities have been discussed throughout this chapter as if children find them funny only when they are seen as make-believe; that is, as occurring in fantasy. It has been argued that it is a child's knowledge that a given event cannot occur in reality that makes it funny (assuming the presence of a playful frame of mind). But humor is not restricted to the world of fantasy. Children begin to experience humor in connection with unusual or incongruous events in the real world as early as age two or three. For example, they may laugh at a person with a very large or unusually shaped nose, at "making a face," at unusual vocal sounds, or at inappropriate or otherwise incongruous actions. Fantasy may contribute to the funniness of these events, but it is not necessary for the events to be perceived as humorous, as is the case for occurrences known to be impossible. Because of the strong perceptual orientation in a child's thinking, this early humor based on real incongruities always depends on the appearance or sound of objects and events. When children say that something looks funny or silly, they are acknowledging that it is very different from what one usually sees. Although preschoolers are gradually gaining confidence in their ability to discern what is possible and what is not possible in the world of objects, for the most part anything is possible in their view. They are very aware that certain events shouldn't happen, because they have never happened in the past, but there is no sense of logical necessity that outcomes occur in one way or another. For example, three-year-olds know that people don't have fur all over their bodies, yet seeing someone covered with fur would be sufficient to prove that it can happen. As progressive cognitive development produces a greater sense of certainty about the range of possibilities for objects and events, the observation of events formerly assumed to be impossible should begin to interfere with humor rather than cause it. If an older child does see a person whose body is covered with fur, that child is likely to laugh only if the situation is perceived as a joking one. If the fur were discovered to be real, curiosity and puzzlement would replace humor, and the child would initiate reality assimilation in an attempt to understand such an unusual event.

A more abstract form of reality-based incongruity is irony. It is not uncommon for events in everyday living to somehow turn out opposite to what is expected or normal. We see such situations as ironic and incongruous. No attempt has been made to study the development of appreciation of irony, but the highly abstract nature of most ironic occurrences suggests that children do not begin to appreciate this form of humor until early adolescence and the beginning of formal operational thought. As in earlier forms of humor in real incongruities, the humor of irony results from the fact that something that really should not occur (although its occurrence is possible) has happened. The humor of irony is usually further fueled by related embarrassments or awkward situations accompanying the unexpected reversal of events. Again, though, humor will be seen in such situations only if the person is able to see the light side of them: that is, to approach them in a playful frame of mind.

Photograph by Sheldon Woodward

3 Humor and Evolution

Fantasy production was considered in the preceding chapter to be a natural outcome of the basic tendency of the human nervous system to seek out novel forms of stimulation, and of a child's tendency to utilize recently developed capacities. It is the advanced level of development of the human brain that permits the symbolic functioning required to experience humor. We have always assumed that the human brain was unique in this respect, because no other species has developed a form of communication sufficiently complex to be classified as a language system. But, if the capacity to manipulate images of objects is the bare cognitive prerequisite for humor, it may be that human beings are not alone in their capacity to experience humor. We have known for some time that chimpanzees and gorillas (and other higher primates) do have primitive representational capacities. Man may be the only creature who tells jokes, but joke-telling is actually a highly developed form of humor. No serious attempt has yet been made to obtain evidence for humor in animals, perhaps because no one has known exactly what to look for. Certainly, smiling and laughter cannot be used as criteria for humor, because they are not convincing evidence even among human beings. The present chapter will address the issue of animals' capacity for humor, contrasting the behavior of apes in a natural habitat with that of apes who have achieved a high level of mastery of a language system employing manual signs. Positive evidence of humor in signing apes will be presented, and the implications of this evidence for the evolution of humor in human beings will be considered.

Humor in Animals

Writers from varied disciplines have tried to come to grips with the question of whether any other animals are capable of the human experience of humor. Those who attributed humor to animals other than human beings seem to have drawn their conclusions from the fact that certain primates show a reaction that is very similar to laughter and smiling in humans.[1] Charles Darwin noted this similarity more than a century ago.[2] Most writers who have struggled with this problem, however, have not been convinced by this parallel. They have typically drawn a negative conclusion on the basis of the differences between human beings and other primates—not the similarities. William McDougall, a well-known early social psychologist, simply proposed that humor is a higher-level instinct not possessed by other animals.[3] On the other hand, it has also been argued that human beings have no instincts and that this is precisely why they had to develop a sense of humor; only with the capacity for humor could they cope with the contradictions and absurdities that their superior intellects allowed them to witness.[4] One investigator has observed that a smilelike social grimace is exhibited by chimpanzees and gorillas while playing, along with laughter when tickled, but these reactions were considered to have no meaningful connection to the cognitive experiences we call humor.[5] The most convincing argument that lower animals do not experience humor stresses their limited intellectual abilities, relative to those of human beings. Arthur Koestler has recently advanced this view, arguing that

> two conditions had to be fulfilled before *homo ridens*, the laughing animal, could emerge: first a relative security of existence, which called for new outlets for excess energies; second and more important, a level of evolution had to be reached where reasoning had

[1]CRILE, J. W. *Man an adaptive mechanism.* New York: Macmillan, 1916.

[2]DARWIN, C. *The expression of the emotions in man and animals.* London: Murray, 1872.

[3]McDOUGALL, W. Why do we laugh? *Scribners*, 1922, 71, 359–363.

[4]BLISS, S. H. The origin of laughter. *American Journal of Psychology*, 1915, 26, 236–246. SHAW, F. J. Laughter: Paradigm of growth. *Journal of Individual Psychology*, 1960, 16, 151–157.

[5]FRY, W. F., JR. Laughter: Is it the best medicine? *Stanford M. D.*, 1971, 10, 16–20.

gained a certain degree of autonomy from the "blind" urges of emotion; where thought had acquired the independence and nimbleness which enable it to detach itself from feeling—and to confront its glandular humors with a sense of humor. Only at this stage of "cortical emancipation" could man perceive his own emotions as redundant, and make the smiling admission "I have been fooled". . . . Beneath the human level there is neither the possibility nor the need for laughter; it could only arise in a biologically secure species with redundant emotions and intellectual autonomy.[6]

All of these views are speculative, of course. No attempt has yet been made to search for parallels to children's humor in the behavior of animals. It has been impossible to make such comparisons because of the lack of development of a language system in animals below human beings. Fortunately, however, recent efforts to teach sign languages to apes have now afforded the opportunity for such comparisons, such that a better-founded position can be established regarding the uniqueness of human beings in the realm of humor. Before turning to this research, though, such behaviors as smiling, laughter, and play must be ruled out as indices of humor in animals.

Smiling and Laughter

Charles Darwin wrote a detailed description of the physical and physiological properties of laughter, suggesting that in its original form laughter indicated a state of joy and high spirits.[7] This accounts for the frequent observation of laughter during young children's play, according to Darwin. Half a century later, McComas agreed with this view, emphasizing that, before primates developed complex language systems, laughter and weeping constituted essential signals regarding an animal's mood, emotions, and physical state.[8] Laughter expressed the positive state that the animal was in and served as an invitation to others to share that state. McComas further assumed that laughter became highly developed in human beings because of their long dependency status. The long period of infancy required the de-

[6]KOESTLER, A. *The act of creation.* New York: Dell, 1964.
[7]DARWIN, *Expression of emotions in man and animals.*
[8]McCOMAS, H. C. The origin of laughter. *Psychological Review,* 1923, 30, 45–55.

velopment of powerful signals that could release and control the care-taking efforts of parents and other members of the adult community. (Every parent knows that both smiling and laughter serve this function very well.) McDougall, on the other hand, suggested in the 1920s that laughter developed in human beings as a biological mechanism for protecting them against the danger of "excessive sympathy" for the problems and misfortunes of others.[9] Without this outlet, a person's psychological burden would become unbearable. According to McDougall, "the perfectly happy man does not laugh, for he has no need for laughter." This view is similar to the psychoanalytic one emphasizing the coping functions of humor.

Two decades later, Rapp proposed that ridicule constituted one of the earliest sources of laughter. "In earliest times . . . when a man saw for the first time some other person, not connected with him by strong ties, and observed that this person was crippled, ugly, or in any way malformed, for some inexplicable reason he burst into laughter."[10] Rapp subsequently suggested that feelings of superiority were responsible for this initial laughter. Hayworth emphasized the fact that primitive people encountered many dangers, and that "laughter was originally a vocal sign to other members of the group that they might relax in safety."[11] This laughter was considered to have been, in effect, a shout of triumph, and a form of mockery of a defeated enemy. This suggests that early laughter was very hostile in nature.

More recently, Fry has suggested that both laughter and "social grimacing" in apes tend to be exhibited when an animal is faced with some kind of threatening situation: that is, a situation in which elements of both threat and security are present.[12] He viewed the social grimace as a form of "appeasement display." In the presence of such a grimace, a second animal is more likely to

[9]McDougall, W. The theory of laughter. *Nature*, 1903, 67, 318–319.

[10]Rapp, A. Toward an eclectic and multilateral theory of laughter and humor. *Journal of General Psychology*, 1947, 36, 207–219.

[11]Hayworth, D. The social origin and function of laughter. *Psychological Review*, 1928, 35, 367–385.

[12]Fry, W. F., Jr. A comparative study of smiling and laughter. Paper presented at meeting of the Western Psychological Association, San Francisco, April, 1971. Fry, W. F., Jr. The appeasement function of mirthful laughter: A comparative study. Paper presented at the International Conference on Humour and Laughter, Cardiff, Wales, July, 1976.

respond in a playful manner than in an aggressive one. The fact that smiling in human infants has been traced to an experience of conflict by some investigators[13] led Fry to suggest a link between the social grimace in apes and the smile in human infants.

Recent observational studies in naturalistic settings by ethologists, comparative biologists, and psychologists have provided a sounder basis for speculation about the evolution of smiling and laughter than was available to early writers on the subject. Robert Hinde noted that many expressive behaviors, including smiling and laughter, are common to every culture investigated so far.[14] Although experiential factors certainly cannot be ruled out as causes of this consistency, Hinde concluded that the bulk of evidence suggests that similarities in affect displays and expressive movements must be "regarded as indicators of their evolutionary origin, rather than, or as well as, their development in the individual." In support of this view, he observed that the form and context of smiling and laughing are similar not only between human cultures, but also, though to a lesser degree, between animals and man.

The most extensive study of the phylogeny of laughter and smiling to date was completed by van Hooff.[15] He examined primate facial displays with the aim of discovering phylogenetic precursors or "homologues" of human smiling and laughter. He suggested that two displays are especially strong possibilities: (1) the silent bared-teeth display, and (2) the relaxed open-mouth display. The silent bared-teeth display, referred to by others as the grin face[16] or social grimace,[17] "is characterized by: fully retracted mouth corners and lips, so that an appreciable part of the gums is bared; closed or only slightly opened mouth; absence of vocalization; inhibited body movements and eyes that are widely

[13]AMBROSE, J. A. The development of the smiling response in early infancy. In B. M. Foss (Ed.), *Determinants of infant behavior*. London: Methuen, 1961.

[14]HINDE, R. A. *Biological bases of human social behavior*. New York: McGraw-Hill, 1974.

[15]VAN HOOFF, J. A. R. A. M. A comparative approach to the phylogeny of laughter and smiling. In R. A. Hinde (Ed.), *Non-verbal communication*. Cambridge, England: Cambridge University Press, 1972.

[16]ANDREW, R. J. The origins and evolution of the calls and facial expressions of the primates. *Behaviour*, 1963, 20, 1–109.

[17]FRY, Comparative study of smiling and laughter; Appeasement function of mirthful laughter.

or normally open and can be directed straight or obliquely towards an interacting partner."[18] This behavior seems closely linked to a larger category of vocalized bared-teeth displays that occur when an animal is threatened. Van Hooff concluded that

> in the ascending scale of the primates leading to man, there is a progressive broadening of the meaning of the element of baring the teeth. . . . Originally forming part of a mainly defensive or protective pattern of behavior, this element becomes a signal of submission and non-hostility. In some species the latter aspect can become predominating, so that a reassuring and finally a friendly signal can develop.[19]

The relaxed open-mouth display is similar to the "play face" described by other investigators. According to van Hooff,

> In the majority of primates, it has much in common with the aggressive *staring open-mouth* display. . . . It is often accompanied by a quick and shallow rather staccato breathing. In some species, the breathing may be vocalized (e.g., the chimpanzee). The vocalizations then sound like "ahh ahh ahh."
> In all the primates in which it occurs the *relaxed open-mouth* display typically accompanies the boisterous mock-fighting and chasing involved in social play. . . . It may function as a meta communicative signal that the ongoing behavior is not meant seriously, but is to be interpreted instead as "mock-fighting". . . . In the chimpanzee the *relaxed open-mouth* display can easily be elicited by tickling. . . .[20]

Van Hooff studied fifty-three different types of social behavior in chimpanzees and found that the silent bared-teeth display was most strongly related to a category of behaviors he described as "affinitive." The relaxed open-mouth display was most strongly related to playful forms of behavior. Bared-teeth displays in connection with play were rare. On the basis of these and other findings, van Hooff offered an evolutionary explanation of laughter and smiling. He suggested that a phylogenetic link exists between the "friendly" silent bared-teeth display in chimpanzees and human smiling, and between the relaxed open-mouth display

---

[18]van Hooff, Comparative approach to phylogeny of laughter and smiling, pp. 212–213.
[19]Ibid., p. 217.   [20]Ibid., p. 217.

and human laughter. He found that, although these responses are quite distinctive in chimpanzees, they tend to merge together in other primates.

> Human laughter and smiling also appear to shade into each other quite smoothly. They are undoubtedly highly associated temporally, and they are at least to a certain extent contextually interchangeable. From a purely morphological viewpoint our laughter can roughly be considered as an intermediate of the classical primate *relaxed open-mouth* display and the *silent bared-teeth* face . . . and the smile as a weaker form of it.
>
> So if the proposed homologies are correct, this means that laughter and smiling, though being of a different phylogenetic origin, must have converged and started to overlap considerably. Nevertheless . . . it might be possible to find situations where laughter and smiling are not interchangeable, and where specific causal and functional aspects which are in agreement with their different origins manifest themselves. Thus, smiling might typically be used in the expression of sympathy, reassurance of appeasement . . . while laughter occurs typically in the free and easy atmosphere of a comradely relationship where jokes come easily and everything is fun . . . Smiling in the latter context might be low-intensity laughter which, by causation and function, and perhaps also in form . . . differs from the affinitive smiling. . . .[21]

Some support for van Hooff's position has been obtained in studies of children. For example, in a study of a large number of social behaviors of preschool children, four clusters of behavior were found ("rough and tumble play," "aggression," "crying," and "social") that closely paralleled the clusters found by van Hooff for chimpanzees.[22] Moreover, children tended to laugh in the context of rough and tumble play, whereas they tended to smile in connection with less vigorous social behavior.

If the facial displays described by van Hooff are linked to human smiling and laughter in the manner he suggested, it might be argued that the perceptions that adult humans have of smiling and laughing should be consistent with the behavior that accom-

---

[21]Ibid., p. 226.

[22]BLURTON-JONES, N. G. An ethological study of some aspects of social behavior of children in nursery school. In D. Morris (Ed.), *Primate Ethology*. Chicago: Aldine, 1967. BLURTON-JONES, N. G. Non-verbal communication in children. In R. A. Hinde (Ed.), *Non-verbal communication*. Cambridge, England: Cambridge University Press, 1972.

panies those displays in primates. To test this possibility, he presented ninety-nine adjectives referring to social moods or attitudes to one hundred adults and asked them to place each in one of four categories: (1) aggressive, (2) submissive or fearful, (3) affinitive, and (4) playful. Additional groups were asked whether each of the ninety-nine words indicates an attitude typically (or possibly) accompanied by smiling or laughter. Consistent with van Hooff's model, smiling was more strongly identified with the affinitive category of behavior than was laughing, whereas laughing was more strongly identified with the playful category than was smiling.[23]

It has also been proposed that the primate grin had its primitive origins both as a protective response and as a response to startling stimuli. With respect to the former, "drawing back the lips is a preliminary either to biting or to throwing out something noxious that has been taken into the mouth."[24] In more advanced monkeys, the grin is commonly used as a defensive gesture designed to show friendly intent (as is the human smile). According to this view, the human social smile can be traced in a direct line of evolution to the more primitive primate grin. The smile of pleasure, on the other hand, is assumed to have its origins in smiling as a reaction to startling stimuli. This reaction has gradually evolved into the smile that indicates pleasure derived from the processing of small and pleasant changes in stimulation (support for this interpretation of the human smile was given in Chapter 2).

A more recently advanced view has presented a similar line of evolutionary development of smiling and laughter, outlining the following sequence: (1) protective reflex grimace related to various types of vocal warnings in response to primarily threatening situations, (2) silent grimace in response to situations that are threatening but secure (3) socially conditioned smile accompanied by laughter (or prelaughter grunting or chortling) in response to contrasting stimuli in a generally secure environment.[25]

---

[23]VAN HOOFF, Comparative approach to phylogeny of laughter and smiling.
[24]ANDREW, Origins and evolution of expressions of primates.
[25]FRY, Appeasement function of mirthful laughter.

Animal Play

The fact that animals play comes as no surprise to anyone who has had a pet cat or dog. Playful forms of behavior have been observed in all mammals and in many species of birds. For any given species, it is the younger animals that spend the greatest amounts of time in play; adults tend to play only under special circumstances, such as after persistent playful approaches by a younger animal. A general rule of thumb suggests that play becomes more frequent, more complex, and more organized at progressively higher phylogenetic levels. The flexible play shown by primates contrasts sharply with the highly stereotyped play of lower organisms.[26] It is especially important to note that the frequent play characteristic of the young extends over a longer period in more advanced species. In fact, it has been suggested that play continues to be an important behavior for human beings throughout the life span.[27]

Animals, like humans, engage in both social play and object play. Most investigators, however, have been primarily interested in social play, attempting to determine the functions of such play in a broad adaptive sense. The most common interpretation of social play is that it serves to "develop strengths and skills in the young in preparation for emergency life-and-death behaviors. . . ."[28] A more modest position would suggest that, for the immature members of a species, play simply serves to develop and polish skills that will be needed later for successful social interaction. On one point there is clear agreement, however: play occurs only in relaxed circumstances; that is, in the absence of physiological pressures (such as hunger or sex drives) and threats from the environment.[29]

It was noted in Chapter 2 that play signals serve to communicate to others participating in the social interaction that "this

---

[26]BEACH, F. A. Current concepts of play in animals. *American Naturalist*, 1945, 79 (785) 523–541.

[27]HERRON, R. E., and SUTTON-SMITH, B. *Child's play.* New York: Wiley, 1971.

[28]ALDIS, O. *Play fighting.* New York: Academic Press, 1975.

[29]Ibid. RENSCH, B. Play and art in apes and monkeys. In E. W. Menzel (Ed.), *Precultural primate behavior.* Vol. 1. *Symposia of the Fourth International Congress of Primatology.* New York: S. Karger, 1973.

behavior is not to be taken seriously." Such signals are also essential to the maintenance of playful forms of behavior. It is interesting to note that the most common play signal among both human
beings and apes is found in a cluster of reactions related to smiling or laughter (e.g., the play face or social grimace).[30] The fact
that this play signal is related to humor in human beings makes
the temptation to assume apes capable of humor extremely great.
We have seen, however, that the occurrence of smiling or laughing is no guarantee that a child has found an event to be humorous; so we certainly could not accept it as an index of humor for
chimpanzees. The importance of such signals, though, cannot be
denied. Without some such signal in mock-fighting, biting, and
chasing activities, the recipient of these behaviors would take
them to be serious attacks and would prepare to defend itself.
Some play signals are common among several species, but each
species may also have its own distinctive set of signals. In children,

> there are involuntary signals (such as smiling or a twinkle in the
> eye); there are simulated signals in which the pretence is indicated
> in some gestural way, by an exaggeration of action or appearance;
> there are stock play signals in which the individual is invited or
> challenged to play; and there are postplay signals when one indi-
> vidual assures the other that he was only joking, etc. In animals,
> likewise, there may be particular signals for the onset of play. . . .
> Howling monkeys trigger off play with twittering squeaks to each
> other, and dog mothers do the same by rubbing faces, gently biting,
> mouthing or pawing at the pup. . . . Dogs may signal to each other
> similarly by wagging their tail[s], which is perhaps the canine
> equivalent of a smile.[31]

It seems, then, that most animals that engage in social play
have at their disposal one or more behavioral signals that communicate to others that the behavior of the moment is an incon-
sequential one. We have seen that strong parallels exist between

---

[30]ALDIS, *Play fighting.* BATESON, G. The message "this is play." In B. Schaffner (Ed.),
Group processes, second conference. New York: Josiah Macy, Jr., Foundation, 1956.
BRUNER, J. S., JOLLY, A., and SYLVA, K. (Eds.) *Play: Its role in development and evolu-
tion.* New York: Basic Books, 1976. HERRON and SUTTON-SMITH, *Child's play.*
LOIZOS, C. An ethological study of primate play. *In Proceedings of the Second Inter-
national Congress of Primatology.* New York: S. Karger, 1969. VAN HOOFF,
J. A. R. A. M. The facial displays of Catarrhine monkeys and apes. In D. Morris
(Ed.), *Primate ethology.* London: Weindenfeld and Nicolson, 1967.

[31]HERRON and SUTTON-SMITH, *Child's play,* pp. 186–187.

human smiling and laughing and the facial/vocal responses of other higher-order primates such as the chimpanzee. Vocalizations similar to laughter have been observed to accompany play in such varied species as chimpanzees, gorillas, orangutans, dogs, baboons, entellus langurs, and rhesus macaques.[32] Although laughter and smilelike behaviors do serve to maintain playful behavior, however, there is no reason to interpret the play behavior of any of these species as indicative of humor. As defined in this book, primitive humor experiences require symbolic play, which in turn requires the manipulation of images of objects rather than manipulation of the objects themselves. To resolve the question of animals' capacity for humor, then, we must seek evidence indicative of apes' (or other animals') capacity for symbolic representation. More specifically, we must obtain evidence suggestive of make-believe behavior in apes.

Make-Believe Play

In order to experience humor in the perception of incongruous relationships, a child in Stage 1 must impose an image of one object upon another object, being fully aware that the behavior directed toward the latter is only appropriate for the former, and does not make sense in connection with the latter. Given a playful frame of mind, acknowledgement of this inappropriateness may be experienced as humorous. The most convincing evidence for animal humor, then, would be the demonstration of such inappropriate behaviors toward objects in the presence of a play signal. Exploratory or curiosity-related behavior could best be ruled out if the "inappropriate" behavior consisted of a sequence of behaviors not previously observed to be directed toward the object in question. In the absence of such evidence, some support might be claimed for animal humor if it could be demonstrated that a given animal has the cognitive prerequisites for humor; that is, is capable of representing objects in terms of images, and of purposefully manipulating these images in the absence of the original object. It was concluded in the preceding chapter that it is impossible to determine in any particular situation whether an event was perceived as humorous by a young child. Given our

---

[32]ALDIS, *Play fighting.*

knowledge of the child's cognitive capacities, the presence of an apparently playful state, and the observation of behavior of the types described in connection with the four stages of humor listed, we can only make an educated guess that the event was considered funny by the child. Similarly, it is clear that nothing that an animal could do would constitute unequivocal proof of a humor experience. But, granted the observation of the three conditions just described for children, we would be safe in concluding that the animal has met all of the necessary prerequisites for experiencing humor.

In the classic early work on animal play, Karl Groos argued that many higher species are capable of make-believe:

> Only the fact that animals cannot speak prevents us from proving the existence of "make-believe". . . . The animal which knows that it is engaged in a pseudo-activity (e.g., mock-fighting) and continues to play reaches the deliberate make-believe, *"enjoyment of pretense"*. . . .[33]

Unfortunately, although Groos has appropriately conceptualized an activity such as mock-fighting as a "pseudo-activity," he does not make a convincing case that such activities do, in fact, include make-believe or pretense. It is tempting to anthropomorphize in interpreting such behavior. There is no doubt that animals in play often exhibit highly contradictory behaviors (such as slowing down or failing to take an obvious short cut when being chased) and, therefore, do behave *as if* they were pretending. But this does not necessarily mean that the animal is capable of the kind of image manipulation required for humor at its most primitive level. Piaget has described such play activities in apes as "merely patterns of behavior begun, but not carried through."[34]

If evidence of pretend behavior is to be found among animals, it should be most likely to occur in more intelligent species, such as chimpanzees and gorillas. After a thorough search of the primate literature, and numerous discussions with individuals engaged in primate research, I have located only one convincing example of pretend behavior in apes. This example is provided by Cathy Hayes, who, along with her husband, raised the chimpan-

---

[33]Gross, K. *The play of animals.* New York: Appleton, 1898.

[34]Piaget, J. *Play, dreams, and imitation in childhood.* New York: Norton, 1962.

zee "Viki" as if she were their own child. This example is cited at length, both because it is convincing and because of its rarity in the published literature.

> The singular events which I am about to relate find no parallel in chimpanzee literature or in the experience of my friends who work with apes. . . .
>
> On the sunny afternoon our story begins. . . suddenly I became aware that Viki's monkey-jungle activity had stopped. She seemed to be absorbed in a brand new game. Very slowly and deliberately she was marching around the toilet, trailing the fingertips of one hand on the floor. Now and then she paused, glanced back at the hand, and then resumed her progress. . . .
>
> Watching her cautiously so as not to be apprehended, I thought at first that she might merely be enjoying the vibrations of her fingertips as they scratched along the linoleum. But gradually I remembered where I had seen her act this way. Viki was at the pulltoy stage when a child is for ever trailing some toy on a string, when everything with a string attached becomes a pulltoy. Dragging wagons, shoes, dolls, or purses, her body assumed just this angle. She trudged along just this busily on two feet and one hand, while the other arm extended backward this way to pull the toy. Viki had an imaginary pulltoy!
>
> No sooner had I arrived at this amazing deduction than she interrupted the sport one day in turn and made a series of tugging motions. That is, they would have been called tugging had there been a rope to tug, which of course there was not. . . . Eventually there was a little jerk and off she went again, trailing what to my mind could only be an imaginary pulltoy. This incident had convinced me that my hypothesis was correct.
>
> Still I was reluctant to believe what I had seen until Viki found a new game to play with her imaginary toy. She dearly loved to "fish." Standing on the furniture, she pulls up from the floor any plaything with a string tied to it. Now from the potty she began to raise the "pulltoy" hand over hand by its invisible rope. Then she lowered it gently and "fished" it up again. . . .
>
> Late in the afternoon I was combing my hair before the bathroom mirror when Viki dragged the unseen pulltoy around the toilet. I was scarcely noticing what had become commonplace, until she stopped once more at the knob and struggled with the invisible tangled rope. But this time she gave up after exerting very little effort. She sat down abruptly with her hands extended as if holding a taut cord. She looked up at my face in the mirror and then she called loudly, "Mama! Mama!". . . .
>
> Acting out an elaborate pantomime I took the rope from her hands and, with much pulling and manipulation, untangled it from the plumbing. I dared not meet her eye until I held out to her the

rope which neither of us could see (I think). "Here you are, little one," I said.

Then I saw the expression on her face. In a human mute it might have been called a look of sheer devotion, of appreciation for understanding. In addition a tiny smile played on her lips. And her whole face reflected the wonder in children's faces when they are astonished at a grown-up's enthusiastic escape into make-believe. . . .

Then her funny little face crinkled into a grin and she tore off around the toilet faster than ever before, dragging her imaginary toy behind her. . . .

After this I decided to get into the fun. One day as she played on the couch in a confusion of toys, I began to walk up and down the room, trailing a ghostly pulltoy of my own. But my toy had sound effects. It went "clackety clackety" on the bare floor, had to be hoisted on to the rug, and there it went "squush squush." In a little while Viki began to stare at me. She jumped off the couch and came running, not to me but to my toy. I stopped and she stopped also, at exactly the spot my invisible rope met my imaginary pulltoy. She stared transfixed and then uttered her awestruck "Boo!"

The final episode occurred the very next day. Once again I was pulling my toy across the floor while Viki played on the couch. She noticed me and seemed about to come down. Then she began to worry, flopping prone on the couch and rocking nervously. I went on walking, glancing back, and going "clackety clackety" and "squush squush." Finally her eyebrows came together in great anxiety and she cried, "Oo oo, oo oo," as distressed as I have ever seen her. When I passed close by, she made a flying leap into my arms. . . . on that day the imaginary pulltoy disappeared from our home never to be played with again.[35]

At the very least, this example seems to firmly establish that chimpanzees do have the capacity for pretend or make-believe. Given her grin during part of the play activities, in combination with the generally playful state characteristic of most of her activity with the "pulltoy," this is the most convincing kind of evidence of humor that an animal without a language system could provide. On the other hand, perhaps more impressive than this single documented example of pretend behavior is the fact that

---

[35]HAYES, C. *The ape in our house.* Gollancz, 1952. Taken from selected material reprinted in Bruner, Jolly, and Sylva, *Play*, pp. 534–536. (Copyright © 1951 by Catherine Hayes. Reprinted here by permission of McIntosh and Otis, Inc.)

not one published report has described comparable behavior among apes in their natural habitat. Jane Goodall, for example, has never observed this type of behavior among chimpanzees in the wild.[36] Admittedly, it may be difficult to know when such pretend activities are actually occurring. The observer must be intimately acquainted with an animal's daily activity in connection with a broad range of objects and events. Yet, when behavior such as Viki's does occur, it is very striking because of its contrast with the animal's usual behavior pattern. It may be, then, that Viki's demonstration of pretend behavior resulted in some way from her very unusual upbringing. The Hayeses undertook their project to determine the extent of a chimpanzee's capacity to learn to speak English. Physical restrictions imposed by the nature of her vocal apparatus made it impossible for Viki to speak more than a few simple words, but she did achieve a considerable ability to understand spoken English. Thus, it may be that Viki's constant contact with language enabled her to develop her own representational capacities to the point at which pretend behavior was possible. The relationship between language and humor development will be elaborated upon in a later section of this chapter.

We must conclude, then, that apes do not have the experience we call humor—at least when raised in their natural environment. They do not behave in a manner that makes a convincing case that they are capable of pretending one object to be another—an essential prerequisite for humor. This is a puzzling conclusion, in light of the fact that it has been known for some time that chimpanzees and gorillas are capable of manipulating images of objects.[37] Piaget examined Wolfgang Kohler's early work with gorillas and concluded:

> It is therefore clear, that, prior to any language, more or less complex systems of representations can be formed which imply something more than the mere perceptive "index." It is the case of "signifiers" which are differentiated from the "signified" to which

---

[36]Personal communication, May, 1976.

[37]Kohler, W. *The mentality of apes.* New York: Harcourt, 1925. Hayes, K. J., and Nissen, C. H. Higher mental functions of a home-raised chimpanzee. In A. M. Schrier and F. Stollnitz (Eds.), *Behavior of nonhuman primates.* New York: Academic Press, 1971.

they refer, whether it be a matter of "symbolic objects" like the tokens, which must be considered to be half-way between the index and the symbol proper, or of "representation," to use Koehler's term, i.e., of memory-images.[38]

It seems, then, that apes achieve a level of representational capacity at least equivalent to that of an eighteen-month-old human infant. And yet, only the human behavior leaves no doubt about the occurrence of pretense. Given comparable capacities for image manipulation, should we not expect similar forms of pretend behavior in the two species? Again, our attention must be drawn to the fact that the human infant is exposed to the frequent and systematic use of a language system, whereas the ape is not. It may be that the very early learning of language that coincides with the acquisition of image-manipulation skills plays a crucial role in facilitating the manipulation of images by human infants. Even though a child has not yet spoken the first meaningful word, early exposure to language may aid separation of the signifier from the signified. This may account for the contrast between Viki's behavior and the behavior of other chimpanzees that have not been exposed so frequently to language.

If language does play the key role in transforming an animal into a creature capable of seeing the humorous side of events, then any chimpanzee or gorilla raised in an environment in which some form of language is used should show an increased frequency of pretend behavior of the type shown by Viki and human infants. In the past decade or so, several projects have been initiated with the aim of determining the extent of chimpanzees' and gorillas' capacity to learn a language system that employs manual signs. Because apes in the wild have developed a primitive system of gestural communication, this form of language system—granted that they are able to master it to a degree—should enable them not only to understand language communications, but to initiate them as well. Before reviewing the evidence from the first generation of signing chimpanzees and gorillas, however, we will consider the playful nature of humor in more detail.

---

[38]PIAGET, *Play, dreams, and imitation in childhood*, p. 69.

Humor and Intelligence: The Evolution of Abstract Forms of Play

Incongruity-based humor might best be conceptualized as a form of playing with ideas that automatically resulted from the evolution of higher levels of intelligence—levels permitting the easy manipulation of symbols for events. This conclusion seems inevitable in light of what is currently known about animal play and the phylogeny of play: (1) play occurs with increasing frequency at progressively higher phylogenetic levels; (2) as more advanced levels of motor and intellectual capacity evolved, they tended to be used in connection with play activities as well as in the service of more serious adaptive interchanges with the environment; (3) play is especially characteristic of the immature members of a species; (4) playful forms of behavior tend to occur only when an animal is confronted with neither a high biological drive state nor a perceived threat to safety; (5) early play activities typically provide some adaptive advantage for the animal as an adult. It follows that any newly developed form of play within a given species should be consistent with this pattern.

If we assume that the behavior of primitive people did not violate this pattern, some qualitatively different form of play must have appeared as a result of acquiring the ability to represent the external environment by image-symbols. There are only two logical candidates for such early play with symbols: (1) conjuring up an image of an object in the absence of that object, and (2) conjuring up an image of one object in the presence of a second object. A simple incongruous or nonfitting relationship is produced in each case. Action consistent with the image of the absent object may or may not have accompanied such early image play, although its appearance must have considerably increased the pleasure derived from the production of simple object-image discrepancies.

It was emphasized in Chapter 2 that children's playful manipulation of images and language symbols may take on two quite distinctive forms: (1) an exploratory form, accompanied by a serious focus of attention, in which learning about the relationship between fantasy and reality and maintaining an optimally novel and stimulating environment are the primary concerns:

and (2) a playful form, characterized by a lack of serious exploratory interests, in which the primary concern is creating in fantasy a set of conditions known to be at odds with reality. Strictly speaking, both types of activity may be called play. But only the second is characterized by what Nina Lieberman and others have called *playfulness*.[39] An incongruous juxtaposition of image, object, and action may be produced in each case, but only in the second will that incongruous relationship be perceived (possibly) as humorous. Other factors combine to determine the overall funniness of the event, but at least the necessary conditions for humor are met in the playful condition.

When primitive people first developed an image-based representational capacity, both exploratory activities and playful ones must have occurred in connection with images. The playful production of incongruities between action, image, and object should have led to the first humor experience of *Homo sapiens*. Although this evolutionary sequence should have occurred, the finding of a lack of pretend behavior among chimpanzees and gorillas in the wild suggests that it may not have occurred. If it is true that only an ape that has mastered some form of language system demonstrates behavior suggestive of a capacity for humor—in spite of the fact that all apes appear to possess the capacity to represent objects in terms of images, which should be sufficient to produce humor—then it is likely that primitive people also did not begin to experience their early incongruous fantasy creations as humorous until some progress had been made in the development of language.

It is difficult to account for the lack of humor among apes that have not had considerable exposure to a language system. One important factor, however, may be the ease and speed with which representations of objects are manipulated. A more abstract representational system, such as a gestural or vocal language system, may increase the flexibility of fantasy manipulations until a threshold that is required for humor is reached. On the other hand, it does not seem likely that the fourteen- or sixteen-month-old human infant who exhibits the kind of pretend behavior that apes lack would have made sufficient progress in

---

[39]Lieberman, N. *Playfulness: Its relationship to imagination and creativity.* New York: Academic Press, 1977.

learning a language for an abstract representational system to be responsible for such increased flexibility. For the time being, then, the issue must remain unresolved. We can only conclude at this point that apes that were not capable of humor before heavy exposure to some form of language begin to exhibit behavior suggestive of a humor capacity after such exposure. Evidence in support of this conclusion will be presented later in this chapter.

An Adaptive Function of Humor?

So far in this book, the origin of humor has been dealt with only in the context of cognitive development and language acquisition; animals begin to playfully manipulate their representations of the real world soon after these representations are available. This kind of playful manipulation is transformed into humor once progress has been made in learning a language system that does not rely solely on images. *Humor is the logical result of an extension of playful forms of behavior to the more abstract intellectual sphere of ideas.* If humor is a form of intellectual play, it should be possible to demonstrate some adaptive function of humor. It was noted in an earlier section that animal play activities are most commonly considered to afford an opportunity to develop and polish the physical and social skills that will be needed for satisfactory functioning as an adult. Although humor's usefulness for enhancing physical adaptation to the environment is questionable, a strong case can be made for its role in facilitating social adaptation. In everyday human affairs, humor often serves as a social "lubricant." It is used to ease social tensions, to indicate friendly intent, and to strengthen social bonds. For an animal with highly developed social relationships, these are most important accomplishments. It is impossible to determine, however, whether humor served primitive people in this fashion.

It was pointed out in Chapter 1 that a number of early philosophical and psychological theories of humor emphasized humor's ability to reduce existing tension in the body. Civilization has brought with it endless daily sources of stress that increase anxiety, tension, and so forth. Laughter, according to these views, allows tension to escape the body, leaving the person laughing more relaxed and better equipped to deal with the environment. Anybody feeling tense who has reflected on his or her bodily state before and after hearty laughter has probably sensed the tension reduction or relaxation that these theorists were describing, but physiological studies do not yield clear evidence in support of this view. Such physiological data are not essential for making a case for humor's adaptive significance, however, if people *feel* less tense and upset as a result of humor. Tension, frustration, anger, and other states of high arousal are likely to interfere with smooth and effective social interaction. A person who feels more relaxed and less frustrated or angry following a humorous episode should be better equipped to deal with the social as well as nonsocial demands of his environment.

It might also be argued that extended periods of more serious forms of adaptation to the physical or social environment produce a need for increased play activity. Organisms capable of fantasy activity may use it as a means of achieving a temporary respite from the more rigorous demands of serious information processing. Assuming that the effort required for the kinds of cognitive change taking place in reality assimilation eventually leads to mental fatigue, we would expect a reduction of cognitive activity geared toward learning and cognitive change and an increase in more effortless forms of activity. Fantasy play provides such an opportunity. Thus, humor might serve the essential function of readying a mentally fatigued individual (animal or human) to engage anew in the intellectually demanding process of cognitive growth and learning.

The Emergence of Humor in Signing Chimpanzees and Gorillas

Animals have developed communication systems with varying degrees of complexity. Human beings have long been assumed to be unique, however, in their development and use of a communication system sufficiently complex and abstract to be called a language. Although there is no reason to question the assumption that only human beings have developed such a communication system, the efforts of the past decade to teach the American Sign Language for the Deaf to chimpanzees and gorillas have permanently dismantled our conception of at least some animals' capacity to learn a language system. It has been more than ten years since Allen and Beatrice Gardner first began teaching sign language to Washoe, a chimpanzee.[40] Washoe's (and other apes') mastery of the signing system has been astonishing and has obliged us to carefully reconsider the intellectual capacities of apes.

As already noted, early attempts to teach language to chimpanzees were based on a vocal language system.[41] These efforts met with little success, adding credence to the view that human beings alone possess the capacity for language. It is now widely known that the failure of these projects was due to the structural limitations of the chimpanzee's vocal tract, not to intellectual limitations.[42] The reader will recall that Viki achieved a high level of comprehension of English, even though her word production was limited to a few "rough" words. A gestural medium should be much better suited for determining apes' language-learning capacities, because they commonly use gestures in their own spontaneous communications. It is interesting to note in this connection that it has been speculated that human language evolved from a primitive system of gestural communication.[43]

The Language Question: What Have They Learned?

There has been considerable controversy in the past ten years over whether the signing that apes have learned qualifies as language. The answer to this question depends on how language is defined. The language-learning accomplishments of chimpanzees and gorillas meet the requirements of some definitions, but not others. Unfortunately, resolving the question is beyond the scope of this book. There is no doubt that chimpanzees and gorillas achieve an astonishingly high level of mastery over the vari-

---

[40]GARDNER, R. A., and GARDNER, B. T. Teaching sign language to a chimpanzee. *Science*, 1969, 165, 664–672.

[41]GARNER, R. C. *Apes and monkeys: Their life and intelligence.* Boston, 1900. HAYES, *The ape in our house.* HAYES and NISSEN, Higher mental functions of a home-raised chimpanzee.

[42]LIEBERMAN, P. Primate vocalizations and human linguistic abilities. *Journal of the Acoustic Society of America*, 1968, 44, 1574–1584.

[43]HEWES, G. W. Pongid capacity for language acquisition: An evaluation of recent studies. In E. W. Menzel, Jr., (Ed.), *Precultural primate behavior.* Vol. 1. *Symposia of the Fourth International Congress of Primatology.* New York: S. Karger, 1973.

ous language systems to which they are exposed. The main concern here is to determine whether the achievement of such a level of mastery leads to the appearance of new forms of behavior suggestive of a capacity for humor, regardless of whether what has been learned qualifies as language.

Summaries of the language-learning accomplishments of apes are now widely available;[44] so their achievements will be only briefly reviewed here. Generally speaking, chimpanzees and gorillas who have spent several years learning a language system reach a level of intellectual and language functioning at least equivalent to that of a three- to four-year-old child. In a project begun more than ten years ago, David Premack created a synthetic language using plastic tokens of various shapes, colors, and sizes. Sarah and three other chimpanzees have demonstrated the capacity to learn complex syntactical relationships, including negation, conjunction, and the conditional ("if-then"), along with questions and dimensional concepts.[45] Premack has demonstrated that a chimpanzee is capable of distinguishing the physical properties of a token from the object it signifies. For example, the arbitrarily selected symbol for "apple" in this language system is a blue plastic triangle. On different occasions, Sarah was asked to describe the features of an apple and of the plastic symbol for apple. In each case, she mentioned such qualities as "round" and "red" but did not refer to the color or shape of the symbol itself.[46] This and other experiments demonstrated the capacity

---

[44]FOUTS, R. S. Acquisition and testing of gestural signs in four young chimpanzees. *Science*, 1973, 180, 978–980. GARDNER, B. T., and GARDNER, R. A. Two-way communication with an infant chimpanzee. In A. Schrier and F. Stollnitz (Eds.), *Behavior of nonhuman primates*. Vol. 4. New York: Academic Press, 1971. GARDNER, B. T., and GARDNER, R. A. Evidence for sentence constituents in the early utterances of child and chimpanzee. *Journal of Experimental Psychology: General*, 1975, 104, 244–267. GILL, T. V., and RUMBAUGH, D. M. Mastery of naming skills by a chimpanzee. *Journal of Human Evolution*, 1974, 3, 483–492. LINDEN, G. *Apes, men, and language*. New York: Saturday Review Press/Dutton, 1974. PATTERSON, F. The gestures of a gorilla: Language acquisition in another pongid species. In D. Hamburg, J. Goodall, and E. McCown (Eds.), *Perspectives in human evolution*. Menlo Park, California: W. A. Benjamin, 1978. PREMACK, D. On the assessment of language competence in the chimpanzee. In A. M. Schrier and F. Stollnitz (Eds.), *Behavior of nonhuman primates*. Vol. 4. New York: Academic Press, 1971. PREMACK, D. *Intelligence in ape and man*. Hillsdale, New Jersey: Lawrence Erlbaum Associates, 1977.

[45]PREMACK, Assessment of language competence in the chimpanzee; *Intelligence in ape and man*.

[46]Ibid.

for displacement and the ability to disregard the physical properties of objects in describing them. Sarah showed equal facility
at forming judgments (such as "same" versus "different") about
the relationship between objects and between representations
of objects. More impressively, she could make such judgments
about the relationship between two statements about objects,
judging them to have either the same or different meanings. This
capacity would be essential to any experience of humor derived
from such statements.

Although Sarah's accomplishments in using the language
system designed by Premack have been impressive, a system
based on the physical manipulation of plastic tokens does not appear to be conducive to play behavior that requires a language.
Premack does describe a number of interesting "error" responses,
including choosing the wrong token, placing the correct tokens in
an incorrect order, and simply refusing to answer or respond. He
does not clarify whether these responses tended to be made while
Sarah engaged in playful behavior, but it appears that they did in
some cases and not in others. This approach, then, has little
promise for determining the humor capacities of language-using
apes.

Duane Rumbaugh and his associates in Georgia used a com-
puter to teach the chimpanzee Lana a language based on symbols
arranged on a console keyboard.[47] Her achievements in learning
this language ("Yerkish") have been nearly as impressive as
those of Sarah, but Rumbaugh has noted that Lana rarely engages in playful forms of communication using this language system.[48] It may be, then, that neither of these two approaches allows for the kind of spontaneity in using language that seems to
be so important for humor in human beings. A gestural system of
language, on the other hand, does allow for such spontaneity. If
this does have an important bearing on humor, we should see
both more "signs" of playfulness in signing apes and more evidence of behavior suggestive of humor.

Washoe, the first chimpanzee taught sign language by the
Gardners, could reliably use 132 signs after fifty-one months of
training. It is interesting to note that the early babyish versions of

---

[47]GILL and RUMBAUGH, Mastery of naming skills by a chimpanzee.

[48]RUMBAUGH, DUANE, personal communication, April, 1976.

Washoe's signs were very similar to the early signs of human children.[49] Her expressive vocabulary was also comparable to that of preschool English-speaking children. In response to questions (who, what, where, and whose), she replied with "appropriate sentence constituents" 84 percent of the time after fifty-one months of training, placing her at a "relatively advanced level of linguistic competence," compared with a preschool child.

Washoe demonstrated very early that she could use signs to refer to classes of objects (rather than specific objects), in that she applied signs appropriately regardless of various irrelevant characteristics of the object. Thus, the sign for "ball" might be used irrespective of the color or size of the ball or the context in which it was found. As was noted in Chapter 2, children do not begin to apply English words in this fashion until about age three. Roger Fouts, who currently works with Washoe and other signing chimpanzees at the Institute for Primate Studies in Oklahoma, systematically tested Lucy's (another chimpanzee) use of signs to represent class concepts. Lucy was given twenty-four different fruits and vegetables to classify at a point at which her food-related vocabulary included "food," "drink," "fruit," "candy," and "banana." Certain signs were appropriately used to designate generic classes (fruit was called "fruit" and vegetables were called "food"), whereas others were used in reference to specific objects only (banana). She had no sign except the general term "fruit" with which to refer to citrus fruits, and so she isolated the most obvious characteristic of citrus fruit and made up her own name, calling them "smell fruits." Similarly, the term "drink fruits" was coined to describe watermelons. Most important, once Lucy learned specific signs within a general class (which also had a sign), she did not apply the new sign to any other object within the general class of objects. For example, once she learned the term "berry" for cherry (which she had known previously only as "fruit"), she did not refer to any other kind of fruit as "berry."[50]

In most respects, then, it is safe to conclude that chimpanzees and gorillas that have been taught a complex language sys-

---

[49]GARDNER and GARDNER, Sentence constituents in early utterances of child and chimpanzee.

[50]LINDEN, Apes, men, and language.

tem of some form over a long period achieve a level of intellectual and language functioning comparable to that of a preschool child. Even Viki (described earlier), who had a rich comprehension of spoken English but virtually no vocal productive capacities, performed at a level comparable to that of a three-year-old child when tested at age three on those items of the Gesell, Merrill-Palmer, and Kuhlman tests that do not require language.[51] Other investigators have similarly concluded that apes' "ability to abstract such dimensions as size, form, color, brightness, and the like certainly seems to be on a par with that of a human child of two or three."[52]

If, as suggested earlier, newly developed capacities tend to be used in both playful and nonplayful forms of interaction with the environment, the newly acquired signing system should be incorporated into an ape's playful behavior long before a three- or four-year-old level of human functioning is achieved. Unique forms of play within the language system should emerge. Before considering the evidence regarding such activities, attention must be given to the criteria to be used for determining whether any new developments within play can be categorized as humor.

Behavioral Criteria for Humor in Apes

The study of humor in children is done by observing both the reaction to events judged in advance to have a high potential for humor (e.g., jokes) and the production of statements or actions "designed" to evoke laughter in others. Laughter is the most commonly accepted index of whether or not a child finds something humorous. We assume that an event must have been funny to the child or laughter would not have occurred. The difficulty here is that even young children learn very quickly that laughter is the expected or appropriate response under certain circumstances. A child knows that most formal humor stimuli, such as cartoons or jokes, are designed to be laughed at. Thus, laughter may or may not indicate a genuine experience of humor. Furthermore, as noted in Chapter 2, there are other genuine causes of

[51]HAYES and NISSEN, Higher mental functions of a home-raised chimpanzee.

[52]MASON, W. A. Environmental models and mental modes: Representational processes in the great apes and man. *American Psychologist*, 1976, 31, 284–294.

smiling and laughter that have nothing to do with humor. Like the laughter of children, a grin or grimace, a "bared-teeth response," or a "relaxed open-mouth display" of an ape cannot be considered conclusive evidence of the animal's capacity for humor. These responses are already known to accompany playful forms of behavior; so their occurrence cannot be taken as an index of the peculiar subset of play we call humor.

One approach to the study of humor in animals might be to rely on an animal's ability to form its own judgments regarding whether or not something is funny: that is, we might teach an ape a sign for funny and then observe the circumstances under which the sign is used. The difficulty here is determining how to initially define the usage of the sign for "funny." Certainly a chimpanzee or gorilla would be able to learn to discriminate future conditions having the same properties as the event(s) used to define the meaning of the sign. But what would this tell us about the animal's capacity for humor? The idea of simply asking a chimpanzee what it "thinks" is funny is an appealing one, but it may tell us more about the trainer's conception of humor than the chimpanzee's. Washoe, for example, seems to use the sign "funny" to refer to playful activities or "having fun." She uses the sign when playing games (especially tickling and chasing) and when being pursued after some "mischief."[53] So when she signs "funny tickle," "funny peekaboo," "funny you," and so forth, it is probably something closer to enjoyment than humor that is being expressed. The problem is that we really don't know what is being expressed.

In contrast with Washoe's use of the sign for "funny," other signing primates at the Oklahoma Institute for Primate Studies use it to refer to human behavior that is silly, unusual, or out of context.[54] This is very close to the way in which children use the term and may prove useful in sorting out the differences between the sense of humor of a chimpanzee or gorilla and that of a child. Given the close parallel to children's usage of the term, the accompaniment of a play signal would suggest that an experience comparable to that of children might be occurring. A systematic

[53]GARDNER and GARDNER, Sentence constituents in early utterances of child and chimpanzee.

[54]FOUTS, ROGER, personal communication, April, 1976.

analysis of the conditions under which this sign is used would be required before any conclusions might be drawn regarding its significance as an index of apes' capacity for humor.

The production of playful incongruities by the animal itself would be the strongest evidence possible for humor among signing chimpanzees and gorillas. By comparing the fantasy productions of animals that have learned a signing language system to those of children who have begun to learn English, we can at least determine whether such apes are capable of producing the kinds of incongruities that children enjoy. Given that the available evidence suggests that the level of intellectual and language functioning achieved by signing chimpanzees and gorillas is comparable to that of a three- or four-year-old child, plus the fact that each of these species engages in frequent play activities during immaturity, plus the assumption that all playful species use newly acquired capacities as a source of new forms of play, it would seem inevitable that these apes would show some form of new play that makes use of the enhanced representational capacity afforded by the signing system. Whether this new form of play will qualify as humor will, of course, be open to debate. In this book, this determination will be made on the basis of the same criteria used in interpreting young children's incongruous fantasy productions. Most important, any incongruous event created by an animal must be perceived as being incongruous *by that animal*, not just by the human observer. We can make this assumption only if there is strong evidence that the animal "knows" the expected or normal relationship between the events in the incongruous relationship: that is, evidence that the animal has mastered the stimulus elements and knows their relationship to one another. For example, if an ape has given the correct sign for apple consistently for several months, and one day gives an inappropriate or distorted sign, it is safe to assume that this is not an "error" in the usual sense of the term. The animal in this circumstance must be quite aware (at some level) of the nature of the discrepancy it has created. Finally, there must be evidence of the presence of play cues to make the strongest case for any given incongruity being experienced as humorous. At the risk of being repetitious, the position adopted in this book will be restated here. Humor is considered to be most essentially a cognitive or intellectual form of experience, although it has predictable (to a

degree) physiological, behavioral, and subjective emotional correlates. Accordingly, the level of cognitive development achieved by
a given species, or by an individual member within a species at
an early point in development, is the prime determinant of
whether humor experiences are possible—given that the species
is disposed toward using newly developed capacities in a playful
fashion. The existing evidence suggests that chimpanzees and
gorillas have both the necessary cognitive prerequisites and a
highly playful nature. There is every reason to expect, then, that
they will engage in the playful production of fantasy incongruities, deriving the same sort of pleasure experienced by young
children when they have created in their own fantasy a set of
conditions known to be at odds with reality.

Judging by the developmental pattern shown by children,
apes should begin to distort actions toward objects before they
begin to use the signing system to distort familiar relationships.
Stage 2 humor (incongruous labeling of objects) should occur
once the animal has made considerable progress in mastering
sign language. This might take either of two forms. First, the signing chimpanzee or gorilla might simply give a (correctly executed) wrong sign for an object or event, just as children take
great pleasure in misnaming events. Again, this must be a previously mastered sign and it must be given in the presence of a play
signal to be considered humor. Otherwise, it might be argued that
the animal is simply "lying"; that is, seriously intending to deceive the human examiner. A second means of creating incongruous or distorted relationships through the use of sign language is
to distort the signs being used. Children demonstrate this form of
humor by rhyming, combining words, making up new nonsense
words, and so forth. In sign language, meaning is communicated
by means of a particular configuration of the signing hand, a distinctive movement of the hand, and direction of that movement
toward a specific area of the body. Altering any one of these three
components changes the meaning of the sign. Thus, there are
three ways to create an incongruous communication by altering
the sign itself. We might speak of degrees of incongruity in this
respect, depending on whether one, two, or three components of
the correct sign are changed. This would seem to be a more complex form of humor than simply giving the wrong sign for an ob-

ject; so apes should not begin to demonstrate this form of language distortion until some time after they have demonstrated simple name-change distortions.

Evidence Suggestive of Simian Humor

The bulk of evidence reported here concerns Koko, a female gorilla that has been learning sign language at Stanford University for the past several years. All of the behavioral examples in the discussion that follows were provided by Francine Patterson and others who work with Koko. Most of the examples described for chimpanzees were provided by Roger Fouts, director of the Institute for Primate Studies at the University of Oklahoma. It should be noted at the outset that all of the researchers studying language acquisition by apes are exclusively interested in language issues and do not share the concerns raised here. Accordingly, all of the examples reported here are anecdotal, based on recall of incidental observations. No investigations designed to determine the frequency of occurrence of humor-related behavior have been initiated. Play signals were reported to have occurred in connection with some of the examples reported, but not with others. All of the researchers working with signing apes, however, were quick to point out that, because they were not looking for such play cues, their failure to observe them cannot be taken as assurance that they were not there. The strongest conclusion that we can reach, then, is that such signals are often present when incongruities are produced using the signing system. Finally, it will be noted that there are more examples of Koko's behavior than there are examples of chimpanzees' behavior. This is not intended to imply that such behaviors are more typical of gorillas than chimpanzees.

Pretend Play with Objects Observations of behavior in signing apes comparable to that designating Stage 1 humor in children have been relatively rare, although there is no doubt that such behavior does occur. The clearest example is provided by Washoe, the original signing chimpanzee. One day Washoe picked up a toothbrush and called it a hair brush, whereupon she raised it to her head and completed a sequence of motions identical with those that would correspond to the correct use of a real hair brush.[55] Washoe had never before been seen using any object but a hair brush in this fashion. This would seem to be a clear-cut case of pretense with objects.

Koko often shows two related forms of pretense involving eating behavior. She goes through the motions of eating food without actually eating it. By itself, this behavior would not be convincing, but she frequently shows the same behavior with nonedible objects, such as scarves, dirt, sticks, and rocks.[56] She especially enjoys offering these objects to people to eat. Again, a generally playful mood has been reported to coincide with some of these offerings, but not with others. Koko also commonly "talks" to her dolls as if they were real people or gorillas. During one play sequence, when Koko thought no one was watching her, she told one doll that it was "bad" and asked it to "kiss" the other doll. After having one doll ask the other to tickle it, she asked them to play with each other. After the two dolls wrestled with each other, she told them that they were both "good." On another occasion, Penny (a person) asked Koko to feed the doll (which she is quite capable of doing correctly). Koko promptly signed "eye," and put the bottle in the doll's eye instead of the mouth. In many cases, this kind of behavior is accompanied by close observation of the human in attendance, as if the animal were looking for a reaction to the behavior.

The relative infrequency of occurrence of behavior along these lines may be due to the fact apes do not remain in this "stage" for a very long period. Children show exclusively Stage 1 humor for only a few months. Assuming that a signing chimpanzee or gorilla would similarly pass through this stage very quickly, we would expect most forms of fantasy play to take advantage of the language system in some way. Children who have progressed to Stage 2 or 3 humor sometimes display examples of Stage 1 humor, but the more recently developed forms of humor seem to be more exciting and challenging. It is not surprising, then, that Stage 2 examples were most frequently observed among apes. This level of fantasy play is more consistent with their current level of cognitive and language functioning.

---

[55]Fouts, Roger, personal communication, September, 1977.

[56]Patterson, Francine, personal communication, September, 1977.

This type of pretend behavior has not been observed among chimpanzees or gorillas in the wild. The closest example is from Jane Goodall's observations of a chimpanzee holding a doll in the same manner that a real infant is held.[57] This behavior cannot be considered evidence of pretense, however, because of the high degree of perceptual similarity between the doll and a real infant.

Giving the Wrong Sign   All investigators working with signing chimpanzees or gorillas have found that these animals seem to enjoy the "game" of mislabeling objects. Koko, for example, consistently uses the correct sign for objects when she has not been asked for a particular sign. When asked to identify an object she has just spontaneously named, however, she may either not give the sign at all or give an incorrect sign. For example, Koko spontaneously signed "bird" upon seeing Penny pick up a picture of a bird while preparing for a test session. When Koko was subsequently asked what the picture was, she signed "flower."[58] According to Penny Patterson, Koko often plays a teasing game in which she will do everything but what she is asked to do. This holds equally well for signing and nonsigning behavior. During such games, she may give numerous wrong signs before finally grudgingly giving the correct sign. In behaving overtly, she frequently does the opposite of what has been requested of her. For example, if she has been asked to smile, she frowns.

The parallel of these behaviors to those of preschool children is startling. Rare, indeed, is the child who has not played the game of "doing everything but . . ." with parents or peers. It has already been noted (see Chapter 2) that early preschoolers find it very funny to give objects odd-sounding or simply incorrect names. As with children, apes sometimes grin or laugh in connection with this type of behavior, but such evidence of playfulness may also be lacking. Can an ape's (knowingly) incorrect response be called a "lie" if there is no evidence of playfulness? It is difficult to answer this question at present, but it seems that apes do use their mislabeling capacities in the midst of varying emotional states. In a playful state, this misnaming may be experienced as funny. In a more negative emotional state, the animal

[57]GOODALL, JANE, personal communication, May, 1976.
[58]PATTERSON, FRANCINE, personal communication, September, 1977.

may minimize play cues in order to genuinely deceive; or it may call a person by another name as a means of expressing anger. Thus, Koko referred to Penny as "dirty toilet" upon getting upset at her. Koko also frequently substitutes the sign for "bug" (the signs for "bug" and "rotten" are the same) for a person's name, apparently as a means of insulting that person.

Washoe also developed the use of the sign for "dirty" to express negative emotional states. She began to sign "dirty" plus the handler's name one day when confined by the handler.[59] Another chimp, Lucy, frequently used the sign for "dirty" when referring to objects or animals she didn't like (e.g., "dirty leash," "dirty cat"). "Dirty cat" was first signed following an argument with a local cat. In each case, the learned usage of this sign had been restricted to events having to do with toilets, including defecation, urination, soiled items, and so forth. It would seem, then, that apes are capable of "stretching" the meaning of a word (sign) to apply to an event not normally identified with it. One writer has pointed out that the use of the term "dirty" in these cases "exploited a purely descriptive term for pejorative associations. ... By putting her feelings into words, Lucy was also bending words to suit her feelings."[60] Clearly, this is a capacity that might serve the animal's humor experiences as well.

In a related example, the chimpanzee Ally made repeated requests to a visitor to be tickled ("you tickle Ally"). When the visitor ignored the request, Ally signed this over and over again, poking the person on the chest when signing "you." Eventually, he became more insistent, signing "you!" "you!" "you!" When these efforts continued to be ignored, Ally finally signed "You tickle Ally, you nut!" In this case, Ally had already learned this term to refer both to nuts and to himself (he is often called a "nut" by his handlers).

Distortion of Signs   In addition to simply giving the wrong sign for objects and events, apes enjoy changing parts of a sign, while leaving the rest of the sign intact. This is not to be confused with "sloppy" signing, in which the animal gives the correct sign, al-

---

[59]LINDEN, *Apes, men, and language.*
[60]Ibid.

*"You know why it takes three gorillas to change a light bulb?
It takes one to hold the bulb and two to turn the ladder."*

beit in an abbreviated form. As with mislabeling, the production of distorted signs is often preceded by signs of playfulness or a refusal to cooperate. A common form of distortion is simply to reverse some component of the sign. The sign for "tiger," for example, consists of bringing the fingers across the face in a forward direction. On one occasion when Koko was asked to give the sign for "tiger," she gave the sign backwards by reversing the direction of the hand movement, again following an initial reluctance to give the sign at all.[61]

On another occasion, Koko refused to give the sign for "drink," in spite of the fact that it had long ago been mastered. After repeated requests, she finally gave the sign, but with one basic modification. The correct sign consists of thumb-at-mouth, with the hand in a fist position. The hand is moved upward, in imitation of drinking from a bottle. When she finally did give the sign, Koko placed her thumb in her ear instead of her mouth. The incongruity here, then, results from the fact that the configuration and movement of the hand were accurately executed, but the location of the movement was altered. There can be no doubt that Koko was intentionally giving an altered sign.

The sign for "cigarette" consists of two fingers (index and middle) extended (as if holding a cigarette) and moved toward the mouth. Again, it is essential to note that this is a sign Koko had

---

[61]HILLER, BARBARA, personal communication, March, 1976.

mastered some time ago. When asked to give this sign, she gave the appropriate movement and location, but with only one finger instead of two. She persisted in giving the sign in this way until her handler finally reminded her that it was two fingers, not one. At that point, she used two hands to make the sign, extending one index finger from each hand. This example is especially pertinent, because Koko spontaneously grinned when she extended one index finger from each hand. This grin indicates the playful nature of the distortion and strongly suggests that she was quite aware of what she was doing. This is precisely the kind of evidence that can be expected if signing apes are producing their own humorous fantasy incongruities.

Use of the Sign "Funny"   As noted earlier, the sign "funny" is used to refer to mischievous activities and to "out of context" behavior, and it is used in the context of game playing (such as chasing or tickling). We cannot, then, equate an animal's use of this sign with the experiencing of humor. Although it may be paired with humor in some cases, it seems that it is used more often in relation to "having fun." For example, in the context of ongoing play, Koko offered Penny a kitchen scrub brush and asked her to eat it. She then asked for it back and promptly asked Penny for the "funny red wiper" (bib).[62] In this case, Penny had also previously used the sign "funny" in referring to the wiper; so Koko may have been simply imitating an earlier communication.

A delightful example of Washoe's use of the sign "funny" is provided by Roger Fouts.[63] Washoe urinated on Roger one day while riding on his shoulders. Immediately after this act, she signed "funny" in a self-congratulatory way. This example is especially interesting because of the repeated snorts (breathing through the nose with a snoring sound) made by Washoe while repeating the "funny" sign. Whether this was a humorous occurrence to Washoe is debatable, but the closeness to children's behavior under similar conditions is undeniable. Washoe seemed to have thoroughly enjoyed the incident. It may also be, of course,

---

[62]Patterson, Francine, personal communication, September, 1977.
[63]Fouts, Roger, personal communication, April, 1976.

that Washoe's reaction was comparable to the nervous laughter of human beings. Assuming that she was aware that she had done something inappropriate or unacceptable, she may have been trying to make the best of a bad situation. This interpretation seems unlikely, however, because most of her behavior closely parallels that of preschool children. A preschooler would show no inhibition of laughing at such an event unless the threat of punishment were imminent. So far, signing apes have not been asked "why?" when they refer to something as being funny.

Reactions to Incongruous Statements by Human Beings   Most investigators have carefully avoided issuing statements to signing apes that are not "straightforward" or linguistically correct. This is understandable, because their sole concern is to maximize the opportunity for language learning. The fact that chimpanzees and gorillas initiate their own incongruities using sign language is all the more notable because of the lack of modeling by humans. This must be taken to mean that apes derive pleasure from creating language distortions once they have begun to master the language: in this sense, they are very much like children. One handler has, upon occasion, made nonsensical or incongruous statements to Koko. Interestingly enough, Koko's reaction has consistently been to call these statements "stupid."[64] But this is not surprising, in light of the fact that no effort was made to give Koko some sort of play signal. There is no way of knowing how she might react if the attempt to communicate playfulness were successful, but under the existing conditions she was right: the statement made no sense at all.

Rumbaugh and his associates have presented Lana the chimpanzee with linguistically incorrect statements and found (predictably) the reaction to be one of puzzlement.[65] All available cues suggested that this communication was a straightforward one, as had always been the case in the past. It is much more difficult for a young child (and a chimpanzee or gorilla, presumably) to know whether to assimilate as reality or fantasy an exter-

---

[64]PATTERSON, FRANCINE, personal communication, September, 1977.

[65]RUMBAUGH, DUANE, personal communication, April, 1976.

nally produced incongruity. As long as the incongruity originates in one's own imagination, there can be no doubt about its pretend nature. This suggests that, even when researchers do begin to present "joking" material to signing apes, evidence should be greater in connection with self-initiated jokes. In this regard, it is interesting to note that preschool children habitually complain that jokes are "stupid" or "silly."' They are often annoyed at so-called jokes because they make no sense. Thus, apes and children seem to share this sentiment until they both understand the meaning of the incongruous relationship and realize that it must be interpreted in a playful or pretend fashion.

Reinforcement of Incongruity Production   Koko does not engage in playful or joking behavior with equal frequency with all of her handlers. Penny finds the kinds of distortions and incongruities that have been described only infrequently directed toward her, whereas they are directed toward other handlers with greater regularity. The handler who seems most strongly convinced of apes' capacity for joking, interestingly enough, is the recipient of the greatest amount of teasing and practical joking. It may be that a person who has an interest in these irregular forms of behavior notices them more often simply because of that interest. On the other hand, if such a person reacts more to the incongruities produced by Koko, this may be sufficient reinforcement to lead Koko to increase them in that person's presence.

Language and the Evolutionary Origin of Humor

Given the definition of incongruity humor offered in this book, the behavioral examples just discussed strongly suggest that signing chimpanzees and gorillas experience humor, whereas members of the same species in the wild do not. The playful nature of apes in the wild cannot be questioned; there is considerable room for questioning their ability to engage in make-believe activities, however. There is no evidence of the one form of humor that does not directly utilize a more formalized language system: that is, untrained chimpanzees and gorillas do not show any evidence of pretending one object to be another. This is surprising, because they do seem to possess an image-based representational capacity and have developed a primitive form of communication system.

The expansion of apes' capacity to assign specific meanings to hand and arm gestures by giving them a ready-made sign language, then, has the pivotal effect of transforming these animals from humorless (although playful) creatures to organisms capable of simple forms of incongruity humor. This phenomenal achievement appears to be an inevitable outcome for a species in which playfulness is already a prominant characteristic. If a given species uses important adaptive capacities (physical and intellectual) for play and enjoyment under conditions that lack biological urgency and outside threats from the environment, any newly acquired skills should be used in a similar fashion. As already suggested, if an animal is capable of achieving a reasonably high level of mastery over a language system, play within the language will automatically result. It was further suggested that the most primitive kind of such play should take the form of imposing the image of one object on another, while engaging in activity appropriate to the former, but not the latter. Signing apes exhibit such behavior, but nonsigning apes do not. The one exception to this conclusion is Viki, the chimpanzee raised like a human child in a highly verbal environment. The level of understanding of spoken English achieved by Viki seems to have been sufficient to permit such representational play. It is impossible to determine whether Viki was capable of higher forms of ideational play, comparable to Stage 2 or 3 humor for children. But there can be no doubt about signing apes' capacity for such higher orders of play.

Throughout Chapters 2 and 3, the distinction between play and humor has been emphasized. It has been argued that a playful state or "frame of mind" is a necessary prerequisite for humor and that the same activity may lead to humor or some other experience or reaction depending on whether a playful or more serious state prevails. Children generate incongruous relationships in their own fantasy simply out of curiosity and a desire to "see what happens" when nonfitting elements or ideas are brought together. The emergence of a playful state eliminates this learning focus and transfers the child's attention to the nature of the inappropriateness of the event imagined. It is this playful consideration in fantasy of an event known to be at odds with reality that is the essence of primitive humor. The available evidence regarding signing apes' intellectual capacity, in combination with the high degree of similarity between apes' language and nonlanguage pretend play and that of children, suggests that the subjective experience of apes may be similar to that of young children. Stage 1 and Stage 2 incongruities exhibited by signing chimpanzees and gorillas are sometimes accompanied by play signals (or a playful state), and sometimes not, suggesting that apes may simply enjoy the results of producing such events in the same manner that children enjoy doing so. Such distortions of the real world are interesting to explore when in a serious state, and funny when in a playful state.

It should be remembered that, although apes have not yet been found to display behavior suggestive of humor above Stage 2, they may be capable of more advanced forms of humor. Research on how to raise chimpanzees or gorillas so as to maximize their language-learning opportunities is still in its infancy. We do not yet know the limits of the linguistic capacities of these animals. It is probably safe to assume, however, that, if apes are exposed to more optimally stimulating early environments, they will show more sophisticated levels of humor as they achieve higher levels of intellectual and language functioning.

The conclusion that the acquisition of language enables apes to experience humor has clear implications for the evolutionary origin of the humor experiences of human beings. Humor must have been first appreciated soon after the early stages of development of a propositional language system. Only at this point would the necessary ease of manipulation of representations of the environment have been achieved. If the development of language had its origins in a gestural communication system, it might even be argued that early human humor was similar to that experienced by Koko and Washoe. The anthropologist Gordon Hewes has suggested that language did develop in this fashion:

> For a long time before the evolutionary emergence of articulate vocal language, the early hominids probably communicated propo-

sitionally by means of hand and arm gestures, supplemented both by other nonverbal signs and by primate vocal calls not yet deserving of the term speech.[66]

Regardless of whether initial human communication was vocal or gestural, the question of timing of the evolutionary origin of humor seems to be reducible to the question of the timing of the beginning of language.

---

[66]HEWES, Pongid capacity for language acquisition.

4 Age Differences

It was argued in Chapter 2 that children do not become capable of experiencing humor until the second year of life, when they begin to acquire primitive symbolic capacities. The reader should refer to that chapter for a discussion of infants' smiling and laughter and their significance to humor. It is assumed here that the ability to engage in pretend or make-believe fantasies is a prerequisite for humor, and children do not demonstrate such imaginative activities until early in the second year. Accordingly, the discussion of age differences will begin with the humor of the two-year-old. Detailed consideration will not be given to humor in the adolescent period, because very little is known about developmental changes in humor past the age of eleven or twelve. Surprisingly, researchers who study children's humor have almost totally neglected the adolescent period.

The Preschool Years

3 - 5 yrs.

The most obvious characteristic of humor initiated by preschoolers is that it is closely connected with ongoing play activity. Although language plays a key role in much of the young child's humor, "acting funny" is also typical of the preschool years. It was noted in earlier chapters, though, that children often laugh in situations that are not humorous. For example, the sheer enjoyment and excitement of ongoing play activities may produce endless bouts of laughter, even though nothing is really "funny." Care must be taken, then, to distinguish between age differences in laughter and age differences in humor. It is safer to say that laughter (rather than humor) usually accompanies young children's play. There is some evidence that laughter reaches a peak at about age three, and declines thereafter,[1] although children laugh at an increasing variety of situations as they get older.[2] Also, they laugh more in the presence of other children than when alone,[3] and laugh more with friends than in the presence of strangers.[4]

Detailed consideration of developmental changes in preschoolers' humor was given in Chapter 2. Accordingly, this section will not be exhaustive, but will include details not presented in Chapter 2. In that chapter, it was argued that the earliest form of humor centers on pretend activity toward objects: that is, it may be funny to a one-and-a-half-year-old to suck on a piece of cloth *as if* it were a bottle. The child has an image of the bottle in mind while sucking on the cloth, which provides the awareness that this is the wrong kind of activity for this object. It is precisely this awareness that makes it funny. This kind of activity sets the stage for much of the child's humor up to age five: that is, early humor commonly has as its basis the child's doing something to produce an incongruous event or relationship.

Laughter during Motor Play

Given that laughter usually accompanies vigorous play[5] and that physical activity toward objects is central in early experiences of humor, it is tempting to conclude that laughter during play is an indication that children have found something humorous. But even a brief observation of three-year-olds at play suggests that laughter is a highly contagious reaction that may suddenly erupt in the midst of rough and tumble play, running, jumping, chasing, and so forth. In these situations there is noth-

---

[1]DING, G. F., and JERSILD, A. T. A study of laughing and crying in preschool children. *Journal of Genetic Psychology*, 1932, 40, 452–472. ENDERS, A. C. A study of the laughter of the preschool child in the Merrill-Palmer nursery school. *Papers of the Michigan Academy of Science, Arts, and Letters*, 1927, 8, 341–356.

[2]JUSTIN, F. A genetic study of laughter provoking stimuli. *Child Development*, 1932, 3, 114–136.

[3]KENDERDINE, M. Laughter in the preschool child. *Child Development*, 1931, 2, 228–230. ENDERS, Laughter of the preschool child in the Merrill-Palmer nursery school.

[4]DING and JERSILD, Laughing and crying in preschool children.

[5]GESELL, A., and ILG, F. *The child from five to ten.* New York: Harper and Brothers, 1946. DING and JERSILD, Laughing and crying in preschool children. KENDERDINE, Laughter in the preschool child.

ing that is actually funny to the child. The laughter is simply a spontaneous manifestation of the pleasure and excitement of the play activity itself. It may be that much of this laughter is a form of "release" from the tension or excitement that the child has built up. This interpretation is supported by the frequent observation that children are especially likely to laugh following the successful completion of an activity viewed as dangerous, threatening, or "scary."[6] For example, exaggerated laughter is likely after jumping off a high platform, going down a big slide, or climbing a "difficult" tree, if the child had some anxiety about doing it beforehand. Children enjoy new challenges to their developing physical skills but may experience considerable discomfort if they have doubts about their ability to complete an act successfully. Laughter serves both to reduce this tension and announce triumphantly to others that the source of concern has been mastered.

This source of laughter has a clear connection with infant laughter (see Chapter 1). An incongruous or otherwise arousing event produces laughter in infants as long as the arousal occurs in a familiar or "safe" context. If the arousal gets too high, or the immediate context is perceived to be threatening in some way, crying will replace laughter. Although similar arousal changes occur in humor (see Chapter 1), the occurrence of this chain of events does not assure that something is humorous.

Lawrence Sherman recently suggested the expression "group glee" to describe a form of mirth long known to nursery school observers.[7] Group glee refers to the spontaneous wave of animated laughter that quickly spreads through a group of children engaged in ongoing play activity. In addition to laughter, there may be screaming, running, jumping, hand-clapping, or other forms of loud and frantic activity. Because of the social support of these activities, they often do not seem to have the arousal-reducing effect that they do when a child is alone or with

---

[6]BLATZ, W. E., ALLEN, K. D., and MILLICHAMP, D. A. *A study of laughter in the nursery school child.* Toronto: University of Toronto Press, 1936. JACOBSON, E. The child's laughter: Theoretical and clinical notes on the function of the comic. *Psychoanalytic Study of the Child,* 1946, 2, 39–60. ENDERS, Laughter of the preschool child in the Merrill-Palmer nursery school.

[7]SHERMAN, L. W. An ecological study of glee in small groups of preschool children. *Child Development,* 1975, 46, 53–61.

only one other child. Again, although these reactions often result from a humorous event (such as saying a "taboo" word, describing a teddy bear as a "teddy dog," etc.), they may also stem from such nonhumorous sources as seeing something scary (in a pretend sense), being chased, or hearing that "its okay to go outside."

Vocal and Verbal Humor

Playful vocalizing begins with babbling in the first year but does not become associated with humor until vocal sounds acquire meanings in the second year. It was noted in Chapter 2 that real words may accompany an incongruous act toward an object in the earliest language-related humor. Thus, a child may say "bottle" while sucking on a cloth or other object. Between two and three years of age, children begin to use the "wrong" word for objects and events in the absence of any incongruous act toward them. In this sense, the three-year-old is capable of more abstract forms of humor than is the two-year-old. The older child might simply call a cloth a "bottle" without sucking on it. This mislabeling of objects and events remains popular until the age of five or so. In addition to giving wrong names for familiar objects and actions, children of this age take great pleasure in renaming each other or in saying to a boy: "you're a girl" (and vice versa).[8] During the three- to five-year age period, children seem to be especially intrigued by the fact that objects have particular names and can be called some names, but not others. Once they become confident of the correct name of something, it becomes very funny to either misname it or distort the correct name in some way. Thus, a three-year-old may call a shoe a "floo," or a "poo," or a "shoop."

Once they begin to find humor in the misnaming of objects and activities, preschoolers begin to enjoy simple riddle-type questions and guessing games. It is especially funny when adults enter into the fun and give inept answers. Catherine Garvey observed that children of this age also frequently make up "non name words," like "Mrs. fool-around," or "Johnny out-in-the grass."

[8]WOLFENSTEIN, M. *Children's humor.* Glencoe, Illinois: Free Press, 1954.

They use outrageous names, juxtapose improbable elements, invent unlikely events, retaining just enough sense of the real world to hold the fabrication together. In several cases the nonsense is produced as if it were serious sense and *marked as play only by laughter after the performance*. With gestures and dramatic delivery, and a straight face, one boy (3:5) told another a story about his Thanksgiving turkey, which was caught, patched up with a band-aid, and cooked. It thereupon flew out the window. Both giggled happily after the narrative.[9]

This example points out the importance of play signals for humor, as described in the two preceding chapters: that is, even though the child knows that a turkey that has just been taken out of the oven cannot fly away, a cue is needed from the other child to be sure that the statement was only meant as a joke (as pretend). (Preschool children need such cues more than do older children and adults, because of their very limited level of cognitive mastery over their world.) An older child would be more likely to *assume* that a joking interpretation is called for, because of absolute certainty of the impossibility of the event. Finally, this example demonstrates an additional way in which language may be used in the service of humor; namely, by postulating an event, or a relationship between events or objects, that is known to be at odds with reality.

An additional form of language-based humor develops in the second and third years in which the sounds of words, rather than their meanings, are distorted. A child may begin with a real word and gradually change it to the point that it has little resemblance to the original word (e.g., "watermelon, fatermelon, schmaterbelon") or may simply add a nonsensical ending or beginning to a word (e.g., "pajoodles" instead of "pajamas," or "rhinoceropiple" instead of "rhinoceros"). One very popular form of sound play humor is "silly" rhyming. Three- and four-year-olds love to produce such rhymes as "itsy, bitsy, mitsy," "teenie, weenie, beenie," "shoe, boo, foo, poo," and so forth.[10] Either real words or nonwords may be used in such rhyming. Garvey noted that another form of humor in the alteration of familiar words can be found in the systematic distortion of a whole communication, such as "try-

[9]GARVEY, C. *Play*. Cambridge, Massachusetts: Harvard University Press, 1977, p. 71.

[10]GESELL and ILG, *The child from five to ten*.

ing to speak with the lips held spread wide and rigid or talking in a squeaky or gruff voice. . . ."[11]

Nonlanguage sounds may be imitated by the child in a distorted fashion also. Thus, a child might find it very funny to make a cow's "moo" sound in a very low voice, with odd variations in pitch, in a stuttering fashion, and so forth. The sound of a fire engine might be similarly modified by either distorting the familiar sound or substituting an entirely inappropriate sound (such as a "moo"). The distortion of a known sound, then, has the same effect as the distortion of meanings related to a (verbal or nonverbal) sound. In both cases, the child is introducing elements known to be incongruous or inappropriate, and it is this playful acknowledgment of their inappropriateness that makes each funny.

Scatological, sexual, or other "taboo" words have probably been sources of humor for young children for as long as parents have shown signs of concern about their expression. Wolfenstein and other psychoanalytic writers (see Chapters 1 and 2) have insightfully noted that this form of humor is initially very direct, often consisting of little more than saying a taboo word or describing a taboo act.[12] For example, a three-year-old may simply approach another child or an adult and say "poop" or "kaka." Not surprisingly, the content of such "jokes" depends on the child's concerns at the time and on the kinds of prohibitions or concerns expressed by parents. Elimination jokes are popular among preschoolers because of the special taboos related to urination and defecation at the time. By the time sexual matters become a strong source of curiosity for the child, considerable progress has already been made in the child's awareness of the development of a "joke facade." Most children have learned to use the playful context of a joke to express sexual or aggressive ideas, always having at their disposal the claim "I was only joking." It is at about the age of six or seven that children become capable of understanding jokes based on the simultaneous awareness of two meanings. Thus, the elementary-school child can always argue that "the other" meaning was the one intended, if necessary. As children approach the end of the preschool years, they become

---

[11]GARVEY, *Play*, p. 63.

[12]WOLFENSTEIN, *Children's humor.*

increasingly aware of the social impropriety of the direct expression of scatological, sexual (to a limited extent), and aggressive ideas or statements. The pleasure derived from expressing these ideas does not diminish, however (at least, not for sex and aggression); so the child learns that jokes afford an ideal way of expressing them without upsetting people.

The same trend exists for any socially unacceptable behavior. One investigator found this to be the second most common source of all nursery school children's laughter and to be the most common source among three-year-olds.[13] A simple depiction of a child engaging in a forbidden act was sufficient to produce laughter in many three-year-olds. Even the depiction of children engaging in activities incompatible with traditional sex-role behavior is sufficient to cause laughter in three- to five-year-olds.[14]

It should be noted that, when preschoolers do initiate verbal humor, it is spontaneous and original and often has a rambling quality. They do not memorize jokes or riddles as school-aged children do, nor do they seem as preoccupied with repeating the same joke or riddle over and over. This may be simply because preschoolers have poorer memories, but it more likely indicates their tendency to focus thought more exclusively on the current real or imagined situation. In either case, their humor tends to have a closer connection to ongoing behavior and the current general stimulus context than is the case for older children.

Finally, it should be remembered that most preschoolers' humor is based on the perceptual properties of objects and events. Exaggerations or distortions of the appearances and sounds of familiar events are central components of humor up to the elementary-school years. This aspect of early humor was discussed in Chapter 2 and will not be further discussed here.

The Elementary-School Years

By the age of seven or eight, most children have become aware of the fact that many words are ambiguous in meaning and

---

[13]KENDERDINE, Laughter in the preschool child.

[14]McGHEE, P. E., and GRODZITSKY, P. Sex-role identification and humor among preschool children. *Journal of Psychology*, 1973, 84, 189–193.

that this ambiguity creates a whole new world of possibilities for humor. This sets the stage for the elementary-school child's favorite form of humor—the riddle. Riddles are first understood in the first or second grade and remain popular until about the fifth grade.[15] Brian Sutton-Smith has defined riddles as follows:

> The riddle is a puzzling question with an answer made arbitrary by the fact that the subject was expecting to react to meaning A and was given meaning B, but made systematic by the fact that meaning A and B share another systematic relationship.[16]

One of the most interesting features of the early enjoyment of riddles is that many children begin to memorize and repeat riddles before they fully understand them. As noted in Chapter 2, this lack of comprehension can be easily demonstrated by presenting first-graders with both joking and serious answers to riddle-type questions. When asked to choose the funnier answer, first-graders are as likely to choose one as the other—a clear indication that they do not understand the double meaning responsible for the humor.[17] From grade two on, though, children get increasingly better at distinguishing between the funny answer and the serious one.

When first- and second-graders make up their own riddles, the answer tends to be either realistic or completely nonsensical. Sutton-Smith has referred to such riddles as "preriddles," because the answer does not possess the qualities of a true riddle, as defined above. Initially, the child seems to view riddles as puzzling questions that have arbitrary answers. The answers are not really arbitrary, of course, but seem to be to the child, who cannot discriminate between the joking and the nonjoking answers.

→ QUESTION: "Why should you always wear a watch in the desert?"
ANSWER: "Because a watch has springs in it."

Even if a first grader is familiar with the fact that water bubbles up from the earth in something called a "spring," this joke can be understood only if there is a simultaneous awareness of both this

---

[15]SUTTON-SMITH, B. A developmental structural account of riddles. In B. Kirschenblatt-Gimblett (Ed.), *Speech, play and display.* Hague, Netherlands: Mouton, 1975.

[16]Ibid.

[17]McGHEE, P. E. Development of children's ability to create the joking relationship. *Child Development,* 1974, 45, 552–556.

meaning and the notion of a spring being used to wind watches and make them run. Without this awareness, a six-year-old might also consider the following answers to be acceptable and funny: "Because then you'll always know what time it is," "Because the desert gets hot," or "Because camels live in the desert." Such answers may or may not have a meaningful connection to the riddle question; the important point is that they lack the second meaning, which is essential to creating ambiguity in interpretation.⟩

Between grades three and five, children may be endlessly preoccupied with riddles and may laugh over and over again at the same answer each time a riddle is repeated. Although different riddles include different forms of linguistic ambiguity, Sutton-Smith has noted that nearly all require some kind of "implicit reclassification":[18] that is, "a word, term, letter, etc., is presented in one way, but then implicitly reclassified in some other way. . . ." In the riddle just presented, it is the term "spring" that must be reclassified to understand the point of the riddle. It will be suggested later in this chapter that particular underlying cognitive changes are occurring between grades one and two that permit children to reclassify events in their thinking, thereby enabling them to appreciate the multiple meanings of riddle humor.

After the age of ten or eleven, children become increasingly bored with riddles, which rely on simple ambiguities of key words, and begin to prefer jokes with more sophisticated meanings. Incongruous forms of humor at this point are likely to center on social or other behavioral expectations, illogical behavior or events, and so forth.[19] Jokes outside of the familiar question-answer format become increasingly popular, and humor beings to take on more of the spontaneously creative qualities demonstrated by the preschooler. Spontaneous wit becomes more evident in the adolescent, who tells humorous anecdotes rather than memorized riddles (although memorized jokes continue to be popular into adulthood).

---

[18]SUTTON-SMITH, Developmental structural account of riddles.

[19]McGHEE, P. E. Cognitive development and children's comprehension of humor. *Child Development*, 1971, 42, 123–138. SUTTON-SMITH, Developmental structural account of riddles.

Most children develop an interest in riddles during the first grade, but the practice of asking a question and giving a funny answer develops three or four years earlier. Thus, three-year-olds are engaging in much the same practice when they make up nonsense answers to questions or give the wrong name when asked the name of a familiar object. If a cooperative peer or adult is available, the preschooler may ask a question that gives the responder an opportunity to give a playful wrong answer. These riddle-type questions begin at about the same time that children begin asking endless strings of questions aimed at learning about the object or event in question. It may be, then, that more playful forms of question-answer activities similarly indicate an underlying interest in learning and a concern (perhaps even an anxious one in some children) about having knowledge, having the right answers, being right or wrong, and so forth. Along these lines, two investigators recently found that

> riddles exist in cultures where rote learning from authority figures is emphasized, as well as oral interrogation by those figures. In addition, there is evidence of high compliance training of the children, and of highly developed sensitivity to ridicule.[20]

Because our own culture is a very knowledge-oriented one, both within and outside school classrooms, it may be especially conducive to producing a preoccupation with riddles in the early grade school years. Along these lines, Sutton-Smith has suggested that

> the fun of the riddles on this account derives from the fact that their incongruities model, in a safe way, the larger process of adult interrogation and ambiguity. As a model of this process, the riddle appears to be a contest in which one central person competes with another or others for possession of the role of arbitrary authority. The key part of this process is the fact that one person exercises control over the other.[21]

The thematic content of many riddles is consistent with this view. In many cases, a "moron" or otherwise stupid person exhibits some bumbling or dumb behavior. Also, the child who cannot answer the riddle question is put into the position of hav-

---

[20]ROBERTS, J. M., and FORMAN, M. L. Riddles: Expressive models of interrogation. *Ethnology*, 1971, 10, 509–533.

[21]SUTTON-SMITH, Developmental structural account of riddles.

ing to admit his or her stupidity for not knowing what turns out to be a very easy answer once the appropriate (although improbable) interpretation of a key word or phrase is discovered.

Some riddles based on double meanings are more easily understood than others. Thomas Schultz noted that linguistic ambiguity can occur at any of four different levels: lexical, phonogical, surface structure, or deep structure.[22] Lexical ambiguity refers to the kind of double-meaning humor already commented on, in which a single word is open to two different interpretations. Thus, in W. C. Fields well-known statement that he believes in "clubs for children," the basis for the humor is the possibility that he is referring to big sticks to be used for hitting children rather than organizations to promote social interaction. Such ambiguous words come up very frequently in everyday communication, but we are usually able to determine which meaning is appropriate from context. In a joke, however, cues indicating the correct interpretation are purposefully removed so as to sustain the possibility of the (unlikely) humorous meaning. Children who complain that jokes of this type make no sense have not yet achieved a simultaneous awareness of the two meanings that apply.

Phonological ambiguity occurs when a given sound (or phonological) sequence (not necessarily a single word) can be interpreted in two or more ways. Shultz gives the following examples of such ambiguity: (1) "I have enough for eighty (eight tea) cups"; (2) "He saw three pears (pairs)"; (3) "The doctor is out of patience (patients)." Clearly, the ambiguities here arise from the fact that the two alternatives sound the same in each case. These examples also demonstrate that ambiguities are not necessarily funny in their own right. There is no humor in these examples because each is a reasonable statement, regardless of how it is interpreted. They would become funny only if one of the meanings were clearly impossible, improbable, inappropriate (under the circumstances), or associated with information giving it an additional connotation.

The distinction between surface-structure and deep-structure ambiguity is more complicated, in that it draws on syn-

---

[22]SHULTZ, T. R., and PILON, R. Development of the ability to detect linguistic ambiguity. *Child Development*, 1973, 44, 728–733.

tactical relationships between words within a sentence. According to Shultz,

> Surface-structure ambiguity results when the words of a sentence can be grouped or bracketed in two different ways with each bracketing expressing a different semantic interpretation. For example, the sentence "He sent her kids story books" can be bracketed as ((He) ((sent) ((her kids) (story books)))) or as ((He) ((sent) ((her) (kids story books)))). In the former case, the woman's kids are being sent story books; in the latter case, the woman is being sent kids' story books. In surface-structure ambiguity two slightly different deep structures are mapped onto a single surface structure. Here the two deep structures specify two different sets of structural relations between the key words in the sentence. For example, in the sentence "The duck is ready to eat," "duck" can function as either the logical subject or the logical object.[23]

The following jokes used by Shultz in his research are typical of some of the jokes that elementary-school children enjoy:

Lexical ambiguity
Order! Order in the court!
Ham and cheese on rye, please, Your Honor.

Phonological ambiguity
Waiter, what's this?
That's bean soup, ma'am.
I'm not interest in what it's been, I'm asking what it is now.

Surface-structure ambiguity
I saw a man eating shark in the aquarium.
That's nothing. I saw a man eating herring in the restaurant.

Deep-structure ambiguity
Call me a cab.
You're a cab.[24]

The next examples used by Shultz demonstrate the same types of humor in the form of riddles:

Lexical ambiguity
Why did the farmer name his hog Ink?
Because he kept running out of the pen.

Phonological ambiguity
Why did the cookie cry?
Because its mother had been a wafer so long.

---

[23]Ibid. p. 728.

[24]SHULTZ, T. R., and HORIBE, F. Development of the appreciation of verbal jokes. *Developmental Psychology*, 1974, 10, 13–20.

"Order! Order in the court!"
"Ham and cheese on rye please, Your Honor."

Surface-structure ambiguity
Tell me how long cows should be milked.
They should be milked the same as short ones, of course.

Deep-structure ambiguity
What animal can jump as high as a tree?
All animals—trees cannot jump.[25]

Shultz's research findings using these kinds of jokes and riddles suggest that phonological ambiguity is the first form of linguistic ambiguity to be considered funny by a child, beginning at

[25]SHULTZ, T. R. Development of the appreciation of riddles. *Child Development*, 1974, 45, 100–105.

about age six or seven (although a child can appreciate other forms of humor derived from the distortion of familiar sounds several years earlier). Appreciation of lexical forms of ambiguity soon follows. Jokes and riddles based on deep- and surface-structure ambiguity, on the other hand, do not seem to be understood by a child until about eleven or twelve years of age. The fact that this is just about the time most children begin to lose interest in riddles suggests that most children enjoy and repeat riddles based on phonological and lexical forms of ambiguity.

As noted earlier, much of the preschooler's humor is of a perceptual nature and deals with concrete aspects of the child's experience. Things that look or sound "wrong," "backwards," or "funny" are humorous to the child because they are inconsistent with the way in which the child has experienced them in the past. The fact that children begin to enjoy humor based on linguistic ambiguities by the first grade or so indicates that this perceptual emphasis in humor begins to change at this time. The school-aged child begins to be less concerned with the perceptual qualities of things and becomes more concerned with underlying meanings. This is not to say that perceptual distortions make no contribution at all to the older child's humor. This quality continues to add to humor into adulthood. It is simply that, for an older child, the emphasis is on more abstract features.

Once children can appreciate more abstract forms of humor, they begin to find it funny when people are illogical in their behavior.[26] For example, a joke might easily be developed around the idea of a person's having bought fifty pounds of bananas simply because they were selling at a good price. A child older than eight immediately realizes the absurdity in this. In effect, to fully appreciate the joke, the child must realize that in most cases it does make sense to stock up on things when they are on sale. This logical rule does not apply, however, to products that have a very short period of usability. In the same fashion, social expectations for certain forms of behavior may become humorous to a child— especially if they are depicted in a way that demonstrates that (at least in some respects) they really make no sense. On the other hand, part of the funniness of absurd or illogical behavior to the

---

[26]McGHEE, Cognitive development and children's comprehension of humor.

elementary-school child lies in the child's awareness that some people actually do show such nonsensical forms of behavior.

From age seven on, children show an increasing tendency to spontaneously reflect on what they are laughing at, and why.[27] The increase in reflectiveness is due to a general improvement in children's analytical skills with age. Thus, older children are better at listening to a series of a given type of joke and then making a general statement about what is required for funniness within that type of joke.[28] Similarly, when asked to explain why a given joke or cartoon (this is always a challenging—and sometimes irritating—task, even among adults) is funny, older children are likely to give interpretive explanations whereas younger children are likely to give descriptive explanations.[29] In commenting on the purchase of fifty pounds of bananas, a ten-year-old would probably be able to point out that buying large quantitites when they are on sale usually makes sense, although it doesn't in this case. In general, an older child is likely to probe further than the concrete events described in the joke in order to support his or her view of the absurdity of the situation. A six-year-old, on the other hand, is more likely to react to the fact that fifty pounds of bananas really is a lot of bananas and that they could never eat that many bananas at one time. Or an image of trying to carry all those bananas may be funny in its own right. In some respect, the child's answer would be very concrete and descriptive of the event in accord with the child's own experience with bananas.

One of the most consistent findings from research on children's humor indicates that comprehension of cartoons or jokes is greater as children get older.[30] The degree to which a child com-

---

[27]LAING, A. The sense of humour in childhood and adolescence. *British Journal of Educational Psychology*, 1939, 9, 201.

[28]McGHEE, Development of children's ability to create the joking relationship.

[29]McGHEE, Cognitive development and children's comprehension of humor. McGHEE, P. E. The role of operational thinking in children's comprehension and appreciation of humor. *Child Development*, 1971, 42, 733–744.

[30]McGHEE, Cognitive development and children's comprehension of humor. BRODZINSKY, D. The role of conceptual tempo and stimulus characteristics in children's humor development. *Developmental Psychology*, 1975, 11, 843–849. PRENTICE, N. M., and FATHMAN, R. E. Joking riddles: A developmental index of children's humor. *Developmental Psychology*, 1975, 11, 210–216. SHULTZ, *Development of the appreciation of riddles*. SHULTZ and HORIBE, Development of the appreciation of verbal jokes. WHITT, J. K., and PRENTICE, N. M. Cognitive processes in the de-

prehends a joke or cartoon is usually determined by asking the child to explain why it is funny (or what is supposed to make it funny, if the child happens not to find it so). There is little agreement on just how comprehension should be defined, but most approaches attempt to determine the extent to which the explanation "zeros in" on the elements of the joke considered by an independent group of adult judges to form the central core of the humor. Children who are sidetracked by incidental aspects of a cartoon or joke, without pointing out the central incongruity (or other basis for humor) in some way, would get low comprehension scores. In most scoring systems, children who draw immediate attention to the key sources of humor, without being sidetracked by less important aspects, would generally receive high comprehension scores. Thus, for the riddle "Why did the cookie cry?", a child would be given a high comprehension score only if direct mention were made of the fact that "away for" sounds just like the cookie called "a wafer." A low comprehension score would be given for statements to the effect that the cookie missed it's mother, because the cookie was crying, because the cookie had a mother, and so forth. Not surprisingly, children's explanations grow increasingly similar to those of adults as they get older.

One of the difficulties with this approach is that it uses an adult level of responding as a norm of the highest explanation (although many adults do not achieve the highest possible comprehension score). In comparison, a child's answer or explanation is likely to seem incomplete or inadequate. A child who argued that the preceding riddle was funny because "cookies do not have mothers" would probably be given a middle-range comprehension score, because the explanation did, in fact, focus on a genuine incongruity. Clearly, though, it is not the highest level of incongruity represented in the riddle; that is, the riddle is not mainly about whether or not cookies have mothers. But the fact that children miss the "main point" of the riddle may be less interesting than the fact that they do find simpler incongruities in the riddle and respond to those. In short, we need to pay closer

velopment of children's enjoyment and comprehension of joking riddles. *Developmental Psychology*, 1977, 13, 129–136. ZIGLER, E., LEVINE, J., and GOULD, L. Cognitive processes in the development of children's appreciation of humor. *Child Development*, 1966, 37, 507–518.

attention to the *quality* of children's understanding of humor events, rather than exclusively focusing on the degree to which the child's understanding approximates some standard that has been set up in advance.

Unlike comprehension, appreciation of different types of humor does not seem to be a function of age. There is support for the views that appreciation decreases with age,[31] increases with age,[32] is not related to age,[33] and increases up to a point, after which it decreases with age.[34] This inconsistency is not surprising, because the relationship obtained should depend on complexity and other factors serving to influence how well jokes or cartoons are understood (see Chapter 5). Although some studies use very simple cartoons, riddles, jokes, and so forth, others use very complex ones, or a combination of varying levels of difficulty. Humor researchers are just beginning to understand *what* children find humorous at different ages; we still know very little about *why* the things they find humorous are funny to them.

Age Six to Eight: A Period of Transition

It was noted throughout the preceding section that the first or second grade seems to consistently mark a period of transition from humor preferences similar to those of a preschooler to those of a school-aged child. It is during this period that children first begin to understand and appreciate the ambiguous meanings of words—a necessary condition for understanding the humor of older children and adults. It is also during this period that most children's humor becomes less perceptually oriented and begins to center on abstract qualities of behavior and thought. Simple

---

[31]BRODZINSKY, Conceptual tempo and stimulus characteristics in children's humor development. PRENTICE and FATHMAN, Joking riddles. SHULTZ, T. R. The role of incongruity and resolution in children's appreciation of cartoon humor. *Journal of Experimental Child Psychology*, 1972, 13, 456–477. WHITT and PRENTICE, Cognitive processes and children's enjoyment and comprehension of joking riddles.

[32]McGHEE, Cognitive development and children's comprehension of humor. McGHEE, Operational thinking and children's comprehension and appreciation of humor.

[33]McGHEE, Cognitive development and children's comprehension of humor.

[34]ZIGLER, LEVINE, and GOULD, Cognitive processes and children's appreciation of humor.

violations of logic in behavior and decision-making finally begin to be funny. Children's increased capacity for reflection and analysis at this point also enables them to go beyond the simple act of "verbally pointing" to the funny event. Simple descriptions are replaced by more generalized interpretations of the incongruities spotted.

Thomas Shultz has suggested that the six- to eight-year period is a time of transition from seeing humor only in "pure incongruity" to the appreciation of incongruities that are somehow resolvable.[35] Presumably, children less than six years of age simply do not understand (and, therefore, do not appreciate) information in a cartoon or joke that serves to make sense out of the incongruity. Because the older child does understand (depending on the complexity of the joke) that there is information in the joke that helps restore (in a fashion) congruity, pure, unresolved incongruity is no longer very funny. The studies completed by Shultz seem to support his view, although its validity has been recently been challenged (see below). Perhaps the most intriguing aspect of Shultz's position is that he is suggesting that the humorous incongruity does not have to make sense in the end in order to be funny to younger children. As long as the event is incompatible with what the child has come to expect through past experience, this inconsistency is enough in its own right to make it funny. There is no need for an additional surprising twist that somehow enables the apparent incongruity to wind up being appropriate and meaningful in an unexpected way. This view is consistent with the conclusion stated earlier that young children's humor centers on the perceptual qualities of objects and events and that incongruous events are funny to a young child because they look "wrong," "backwards," and so forth.

Shultz tested his two-stage theory of humor development by carefully preparing altered versions of jokes and riddles, such that the information needed to resolve the incongruity was removed. Resolution-removed versions of the jokes presented in the last section are given below:

1. Silence! Silence in the court!
   Ham and cheese on rye, please, Your Honor.

---

[35]SHULTZ, Development of the appreciation of riddles. SHULTZ and HORIBE, Development of the appreciation of verbal jokes.

2. Waiter, what's this?
   That's tomato soup, ma'am.
   I'm not interested in what it's been, I'm asking what it is now.
3. I saw a ferocious shark in the aquarium.
   That's nothing, I saw a man eating herring in the restaurant.
4. Call a cab for me.
   You're a cab.[36]

As in the original versions of these jokes, the second statement is incongruous in relation to the first statement. In contrast to the original versions, though, there is no information in these jokes that enables us to eventually resolve the incongruity. These jokes strike adults as nonsensical incongruities, and are not funny because, as Jerry Suls,[37] Shultz, and others have noted, the ultimate resolution of incongruity is essential for adults to appreciate humor. The controversial part of Shultz's research concerns his finding that first graders considered the resolution-removed versions of jokes and riddles just as funny as the original versions. From grade three on, the original versions were consistently seen as funnier than the resolution-removed versions.

According to Shultz, the lack of a preference for the original versions is convincing evidence that it is the incongruity alone that is funny to younger children (below grade two). The problem with this conclusion is that Shultz himself has found that it is not until the second or third grade that children begin to understand the ambiguities in the kinds of riddles and jokes he used.[38] Because first graders undoubtedly failed to understand the ambiguity in such words as "Order!," "bean," and "man eating," it is not surprising that they did not prefer the original versions. The importance of this lack of comprehension is further seen in Shultz's finding that first graders considered riddles in which the incongruity was removed to be just as funny as the original versions. A more convincing case would be made for younger children's appreciation of only pure incongruity if the same kinds of findings were obtained for humor that is easier to understand.

---

[36]SHULTZ and HORIBE, Development of the appreciation of verbal jokes.

[37]SULS, J. A two-stage model for the appreciation of jokes and cartoons: An information-processing analysis. In J. H. Goldstein and P. E. McGhee (Eds.), *The psychology of humor: Theoretical perspectives and empirical issues.* New York: Academic Press, 1972.

[38]SHULTZ and PILON, Ability to detect linguistic ambiguity.

Diana Pien and Mary Rothbart recently completed a study that tested this view. They presented original and resolution-removed versions of simple cartoons to children and found that even four- and five-year-olds considered the original versions to be funnier than the resolution-removed versions.[39] If there is a stage during which children are not capable of appreciating resolution aspects of humor, then, it must occur before age four. As noted in Chapter 1, it may be that some form of resolution is always needed before incongruities are seen as funny—even by a two-year-old. We may eventually discover that the ways in which children are able to resolve the incongruities they perceive become more complex and abstract as they get older. Two- and three-year-olds may experience a sense of resolution simply through their awareness of the normal or expected relationship between elements composing the incongruous event. The utilization of resolution information to mentally transform the incongruous relationship into a congruous one may only be a more complicated form of resolution that evolves as children acquire more sophisticated intellectual skills. Unfortunately, we must await further research along these lines before this issue can be resolved.

The Role of Cognitive Development

It has become increasingly apparent that the major changes occurring in children's humor between six and eight years of age are not merely accidental. Jean Piaget demonstrated long ago that important changes in intellectual capacity are occurring at precisely this time.[40] We cannot fully treat Piaget's theory of child development here, but a brief review of the cognitive transitions he described should demonstrate the close connection between the child's developing cognitive skills and the qualities of humor appreciated.

According to Piaget, children less than about seven years of age are very egocentric and perceptually oriented in their thinking. In forming judgments about events, they are heavily

[39]PIEN, D., and ROTHBART, M. K. Incongruity and resolution in children's humor: A reexamination. *Child Development*, 1976, 47, 966–971.

[40]PIAGET, J. *The psychology of intelligence.* New York: Harcourt and Brace, 1950.

influenced by appearances and less influenced by what they may otherwise know to be true. When knowledge comes into conflict with appearances, they tend to rely more on the latter than the former. It is precisely this "perceptual centeredness" that accounts for the heavy emphasis on perceptual features of events in preschool children's humor. Their thought tends to be intuitive, and there is no sense of logical necessity that objects or events must relate to one another in a particular way. Piaget referred to thought in this period as "preoperational," in that the child does not yet possess the capacity for the kinds of mental operations demonstrated after the age of seven or eight.

Several specific cognitive abilities lead to the onset of concrete operational thinking. Most important, the elementary-school child has lost much of the earlier preoccupation with the appearance of things and has become much more interested in relationships. Rather than being interested only in the end-state or final product of a chain of events, the concrete operational child is also interested in the nature of the transition; that is, the process by which the end-state is achieved. The best example of this is the well-known conservation experiment, in which a child must decide whether there is more, less, or the same amount of material in a mass of plasticene after a ball of it has been flattened into a pancake or hot dog shape. Most five-year-olds think that there is more material in the altered plasticene because it looks longer, wider, and so forth. Most eight-year-olds realize, however, that, although it may look as though there is more in one shape than the other, there must be the same amount as long as none was removed. A child who has learned to conserve quantity knows that they must be equal. The ability to keep two things in mind at the same time enables the older child to draw the correct conclusion in conservation tests: that is, the child must be able to simultaneously think about what it looked like initially and what it looks like at present. Although the child is fully aware that they appear to be different, the knowledge that the altered product could be changed back to its original shape instills confidence that the two shapes must contain equal amounts. The ability to bring information about a prior state of affairs to bear on one's thinking about the present situation is referred to by Piaget as "reversibility." Reversibility is similar in many respects to running a film backward in order to examine the starting frame. Reversibility and the ability to think about relationships rather than end-states seem to be central to the appreciation of humor based on double meanings: that is, to understand the kinds of jokes and riddles presented earlier in this chapter, the child must shift attention from the obvious meaning of some key word and consider one or more additional meanings in connection with the obvious one. The joke is not understood until both (or all) of the meanings have been realized. The peripheral meanings that create the incongruity are likely to make sense only in a limited manner, but it is precisely this (perhaps out of context) meaning that makes the joke funny. In short, then, the capacity for reversibility and various other mental operations (which will not be discussed here) enable the child to go back and forth in thought between different ideas, meanings, and relationships; and this is a necessary prerequisite for a genuine appreciation of the riddles and jokes enjoyed by elementary-school children.

The acquisition of concrete operational thinking by seven- and eight-year-olds has been found to be positively related to the ability to detect hidden meanings,[41] comprehension and appreciation of riddles based on homonyms (e.g., pear versus pair and patience versus patients),[42] comprehension of behavioral incongruities (in the absence of accompanying violations of perceptual qualities of events),[43] interpretive rather than descriptive explanations of jokes and cartoons,[44] and comprehension of sequential cartoons.[45] Children whose cognitive development is more advanced have more confidence in their expectations about what is possible and what is not, and this confidence seems to help them see certain incongruous events as either impossible or improbable, except in a fantasy sense—a condition already noted (see Chapter 2) as playing a major role in perceiving incongruities as

---

[41]SHULTZ, T. R., and BLOOM, L. Concrete operational thought and the appreciation of verbal jokes. Unpublished manuscript, cited by Shultz, T. R., A cognitive-developmental analysis of humor. In A. J. Chapman and H. C. Foot (Eds.), *Humour and laughter: Theory, research, and applications.* London: Wiley, 1976.

[42]WHITT and PRENTICE, Cognitive processes and children's enjoyment and comprehension of joking riddles.

[43]McGHEE, Cognitive development and children's comprehension of humor.

[44]Ibid.

[45]McGHEE, Operational thinking and children's comprehension and appreciation of humor.

humorous.[46] In most of these studies, separate controls were exercised for general intelligence level, so that a child who is more advanced in a Piagetian sense does not necessarily have a higher measured IQ. Thus, the specific cognitive acquisitions related to operational thinking, rather than the child's general intelligence level, lead to changes in humor between age six and age eight.

An important outcome of newly emerging cognitive capacities between six and eight concerns the child's thinking about moral issues. Piaget noted that the moral thinking of younger children leads them to conclude that misdeeds must always be punished and that more extreme levels of punishment are always "more just" than less extreme levels.[47] Five- and six-year-olds hold this view regardless of the motivational circumstances in which the misdeed is committed. But eight-year-olds do not automatically make this kind of judgment. Their feelings about a misdeed are likely to depend on whether it was intentional or accidental, and they are likely to argue that the punishment should in some way fit the nature of the misdeed.

Such moral judgments are closely related to a child's reactions to certain cartoons and jokes, because a common theme in many forms of humor concerns a "bad guy," an injustice, or an evil force that is subsequently overcome by a hero or other positive force. One investigator studied the relationship between humor and moral development by presenting seven- and eight-year-olds with a fairy tale in which a "bad prince carried out an evil plot to deprive his brother of his right to share the rule of the kingdom. The bad prince, having gained the upper hand over his brother by devious means, declared his supremacy."[48] In three different endings to the story, the good prince gained the upper hand in the end and administered a mild, extremely harsh, or equitable punishment to the bad prince. Children whose moral development was less mature liked the version depicting extreme retaliation for the misdeed, whereas children whose moral de-

[46]McGhee, P. E., and Johnson, S. F. The role of fantasy and reality cues in children's appreciation incongruity humor. *Merrill-Palmer Quarterly*, 1975, 21, 19–30.

[47]Piaget, J. *Moral judgment of the child.* New York: Harcourt and Brace, 1932.

[48]Zillman, D., and Bryant, J. Viewers' moral sanction of retribution in the appreciation of dramatic presentations. *Journal of Experimental Social Psychology*, 1975, 11, 572–582.

velopment was more mature liked the ending in which the retaliation was equitable. It seems, then, that for both younger (morally less mature) and older (morally more mature) children, a sense of justice in what happens to the bad guy is an important element for full enjoyment of the humor depicted. The funniness of different jokes differs for these two groups, however, because they have opposing views about just and unjust outcomes.

Another aspect of younger children's moral thinking leads them to feel that it is the objective or quantitative aspects of an event that determine how naughty or wrong it is perceived to be. These children are very egocentric, and so they are unaware of the intentions behind a hostile act. In their view, the greater the harm or damage done, the naughtier the behavior. Children older than seven or eight, on the other hand, tend to believe that an act is wrong only if the resulting damage was intentional. This aspect of children's views about morality has also been shown to be closely related to differences in humor appreciation. Children less than six or seven years old tend to find joking events funnier if the outcomes are more damaging.[49] The accidental versus intentional nature of the damage does not influence funniness for these children. For older children, highly damaging outcomes are most likely to be funny when they are accidental. In the example below, then, the first version would be funnier to most younger children, whereas the second would be funnier to most older children.

> *Intentional High Damage.* Helen was only a little girl who often didn't get along well with her mother. Her mother always made her dry the dishes and she didn't like drying dishes. One day when her mother asked her to help with the dishes, she got mad and decided to mess up the table. She got a bunch of eggs and started beating her hand up and down on the eggs. The eggs made a big mess, with eggs and shells all over the table. When her sister walked in, Helen gave a sly smile and said, "I'm baking a cake and the recipe said to beat the eggs."

> *Unintentional Low Damage.* Helen was only a little girl and had never baked a cake before. But, she decided she would surprise her mother by making a delicious cake for her mother's birthday. When Helen's sister came into the kitchen, she found Helen beating her hand up and down on an egg. The egg cracked and the yoke spilled

---

[49]McGHEE, P. E. Moral development and children's appreciation of humor. *Developmental Psychology,* 1974, 10, 514–525.

on the table. Helen turned to her sister and said innocently, "I'm baking a cake and the recipe said to beat the eggs."[50]

Younger children's enjoyment of humorous jokes and stories including high amounts of damage can also be demonstrated in older children, simply by making the messier high-damage situation unintentional (drawings depicting these scenes were used in order to help draw attention to the differences in size of mess).

These findings help to explain the conviction held by most adults that young children seem to be very cruel and heartless in their laughter and humor. For example, most of us have seen three- to six-year-olds laugh at the deformity or odd behavior of another person, showing no awareness of the effect such laughter might have on the person who must live with the affliction. The cognitive changes that produce the higher level of moral development described enable the seven- or eight-year-old to begin to take another person's perspective. This leads the child to begin to be more discrete in openly expressing laughter under such conditions. Both older and younger children may find humor in an ungainly walk or other oddities of behavior, but the older child is more likely to either leave the scene or wait for a more opportune moment in which to release the impulse to laugh. It was noted earlier that it is also about age seven or eight that children begin to use the "joke facade" as a means of disguising the aggressive or sexual aspects of jokes. It seems likely that the awareness that leads a child to suppress laughter at another person in that person's presence also generates the feeling that the true nature of jokes sometimes needs to be disguised.

Although writers and performers have been producing humor for children for centuries, we still know very little about the reasons why children's preferences for humor change as they get older. There can be no doubt about the fact that progressive changes in cognitive development have a strong bearing on the kinds of humor a child can understand (and there must be some level of comprehension before the humor can be appreciated), but not all children show the same changes in preferences as they get older. This means that other important personality or experiential factors must also have a strong influence on the developing sense of humor. These additional influences will be discussed in the remaining chapters of this book.

---

[50]Ibid.

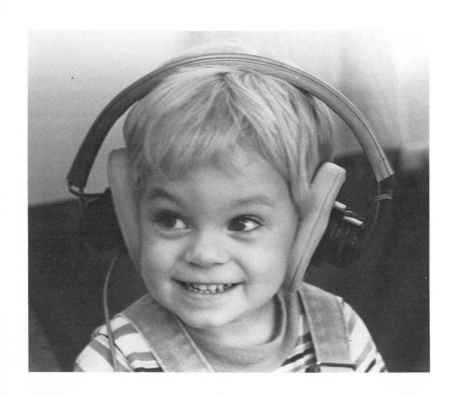

5 Cognitive Factors and Humor

Humor has been conceptualized in this book as a particular kind of cognitive event. It has been noted that it is a specific cognitive acquisition in the second year of life, namely the ability to represent things symbolically (with images), which first enables the infant to experience humor. Also, new cognitive abilities during development typically allow for the understanding and appreciation of new forms of humor. Humor has been defined as a form of intellectual play; even animals may experience humor if they can learn a prearranged language system that allows for the easy manipulation of ideas. The general importance of fantasy and play activity for humor has been discussed, including the argument that in most cases incongruities will not be considered funny by younger children unless they are viewed in a playful and fantasy sense. Finally, it has been seen that humor appreciation seems to involve two distinct mental activities; we must first identify the nature of the incongruous event, and then set out to resolve or make sense of it. In this chapter, other cognitive factors that have an important bearing on children's appreciation and production of humor will be discussed.

The Importance of Intellectual Challenge
(Or: The Problem with Puns)

All of us have had the experience of faking laughter at jokes that we do not find very funny. In many cases, we are not amused because of the offensive nature of the material in the joke. Psychoanalytic writers remind us that jokes with sexual, aggressive, or other types of offensive themes must cleverly disguise the true nature of the joke in order for us to fully appreciate the humor. In other cases, the mere lack of familiarity with the content of the joke will prevent us from understanding the humor that may have others laughing hilariously. Two other detractors from full appreciation of humor concern the level of difficulty of the joke; we tend not to be very amused by jokes or cartoons that are either too simple or too complex. Simple jokes are not very funny because we immediately understand the punch line. No real mental effort on our part is required to "get the point." Other jokes seem to be so long, or to have so many interconnected things happening, that we have trouble understanding the point no matter how hard we try. We may even give up trying to figure it out, because it doesn't seem worth the effort. In this section, we will see that (other things being equal) jokes and cartoons are most likely to be funny when they are at some moderate level of difficulty—when a moderate exertion of mental effort leads to full comprehension of the point of the intended humor.

Pleasure in Cognitive Mastery

Jean Piaget and various psychoanalytic writers emphasized decades ago that infants and young children derive pleasure in gaining a sense of intellectual mastery over an event.[1] A related source of pleasure is mastering a motor skill for the first time. It was suggested in Chapter 2 that this source of pleasure seems to be "built in" and does not need to be learned. From infancy on, we seem to derive pleasure from intellectual challenges. If a cartoon or joke offers such a challenge, it follows that the pleasure we experience from figuring out the point of the joke should add to other sources of pleasure contributing to the overall experience of funniness.

The potential significance of this source of pleasure for humor is heightened upon the realization that most jokes, cartoons, and other humorous circumstances pose a special form of problem to be solved.[2] Typically, some incongruous or otherwise

---

[1]KRIS, E. Ego development and the comic. *International Journal of Psychoanalysis,* 1938, 19, 77–90. PIAGET, J. *Play, dreams, and imitation in childhood.* New York: Norton, 1962.

[2]KOESTLER, A. *The act of creation.* New York: Dell, 1964. GOLDSTEIN, J. H., HARMAN, J., McGHEE, P. E., and KARASIK, R. Test of an information-processing model of humor: Physiological response changes during problem- and riddle-solving. *Jour-*

puzzling event is presented as a key component of the intended humor. We must figure out the puzzle or resolve the incongruity before we can appreciate the humor. As long as incongruity is the basis for the humor, problem-solving strategies must be set in motion—not unlike those required to figure out mathematical or other forms of nonhumorous puzzles and incongruities. (As noted in Chapter 1, the solution to the puzzle in jokes often makes sense only in a very restricted manner. It may make sense within the confines of the joke but not in the general world of experience.)

The notion of setting up a problem to be solved is most obvious in riddles, in which problems are clearly posed in the initial questions. Such a question may not seem like much of a problem to adults when the answer is heard, but even they find it difficult to come up with the correct joking answer on their own if they have not heard the joke before. The jokes presented in the last chapter, for example, were probably not very funny to readers of this book, because the answers seem immediately obvious and simplistic as soon as we read them. If an adult were to think up such riddles on his or her own, they would probably be a little funnier, because it takes more effort to create a joke than to simply understand it when told by someone else. If there were some way to make the riddle more difficult, even adults might find riddles funny. Accordingly, the following riddle should be funnier to the reader than were the riddles presented in the last chapter.

> QUESTION: What is purple and hums?
> ANSWER: An electric grape.
> QUESTION: Why does it hum?
> ANSWER: It doesn't know the words.[3]

The fact that this is a "double riddle" means that a little more effort is required on our part in order to understand it. Both answers are puzzling, but our experience with the objects or events of the riddle offer a means of resolution. The first puzzle is resolved upon the realization that grapes are purple and that

nal of General Psychology, 1975, 92, 59–68. SHULTZ, T. R. The role of incongruity and resolution in children's appreciation of cartoon humor. Journal of Experimental Child Psychology, 1972, 13, 456–477. SULS, J. M. A two-stage model for the appreciation of jokes and cartoons: An information-processing analysis. In J. H. Goldstein and P. E. McGhee (Eds.), The psychology of humor: Theoretical perspectives and empirical issues. New York: Academic Press, 1972.

[3]GOLDSTEIN et al., Information-processing model of humor.

electric gadgets typically produce a hum while operating. Because an electric grape would have both of these qualities, it seems to be a satisfactory answer to the question posed. We immediately recognize it as a joking answer because we know that there is no such thing as an electric grape. This is a basic quality of many of the jokes of both children and adults: that is, the answer both makes sense and does not make sense at the same time. The humor results from the fact that we recognize that it makes sense only in a manner that is nonsensical in the larger world of reality. The second question and answer merely serve to enrich the riddle (by making it more complex), because it provides yet another answer that makes sense only within the confines of the joke. We know that people often hum tunes when they do not know the words; so a grape might do the same. The importance of this added complexity may be seen by simply asking several adults the riddle questions. More often than not, the first answer will produce a groan or other form of negative reaction (translated to mean it's too simple to merit laughter), whereas the second is more likely to produce a smile or laugh. Only after hearing the second answer is an adult likely to view the riddle as being clever.

Ernst Kris, an early psychoanalytic writer, distinguished between the pleasure in humor and the general pleasure derived from cognitive mastery.

> Pleasure in mastery plays itself out in the present, and is experienced as such ... comic pleasure ... refers to a past achievement of the ego which has required long practice to bring it about.[4]

This clearly establishes the notion that, although the effortful exertion of our intellectual capacities may be pleasurable both in humorous and in nonhumorous situations, there remain important differences between the two. As indicated in Chapter 2, cognitive pleasure of the nonhumorous variety derives from the establishment of new knowledge. This pleasure is related to a permanent change in the concepts or ideas that have already been developed. The pleasure in cognitive exertion required for humor stems from the distortion (in fantasy) of previously established knowledge—not from its initial formation. Equal amounts of ef-

---

[4]KRIS, Ego development and the comic.

fort may be necessary in each case, but humor results only when the effort exerted leads to a resolution or understanding that is nonsensical in the world of reality at the same time that it is perfectly sensible in the world of fantasy. The pleasure experienced in each case is derived from the accommodation or change of existing concepts. Only in nonhumorous pleasure, though, is change in existing knowledge or concepts a permanent one. In humor, a child only temporarily changes relevant concepts to make the otherwise incongruous information fit. This occurs only at the fantasy level, with the child being aware the full time that this temporary change has no implications for the real world. Thus, in the electric grape riddle, a child would not walk away concluding that grapes can hum or that they can be electrified. The pleasure in contemplating such absurdities occurs only in connection with fantasy distortions of existing knowledge about grapes; the child never considers modifying what is already known about grapes.

As also noted in Chapters 1 and 2, the general level of cognitive mastery achieved by a child plays an important role in determining whether an attempt is made to interpret an incongruous event (such as an answer to a riddle question) at the level of reality or fantasy. As progressively higher levels of cognitive development are achieved with increasing age, children become increasingly confident of which interpretation is called for. Similarly, a high level of familiarity with the objects or events composing the incongruity is required in order for the child to be certain of which interpretation is correct. Even an adult will be confused about how to interpret an incongruous event if the circumstances are unfamiliar.

Supporting Research Findings

Evidence presented in Chapter 2 suggested that even one-year-old infants derive pleasure from successful efforts at understanding their world. The enjoyment of recognizing an initially unrecognizable event is manifested as smiling or laughter and in the appearance of delight on the infant's face. It has been noted that events that are moderately new (that is, having some familiar and some unfamiliar components) are most likely to be met with smiling. Presumably, this is because such events take just the right amount of effort to relate the new event to memories of old familiar ones. Even objects that are initially very interesting (and lead to smiling) tend to become boring if repeatedly presented to an infant. They become boring because the child recognizes them at a glance and has already explored any unusual qualities of the object. All it takes is a slight change in the now familiar object in order to make it interesting again. This change is likely to lead not only to renewed looking, but to a reappearance of smiling. With its changed appearance, the infant must exert a little more effort to recognize the object. Again, however, this pleasure does not seem to have anything to do with humor in infants, even though it might contribute to humorous forms of pleasure in the years after infancy.

Older children also give evidence of enjoying successful mental exertion if an optimal amount of effort is required. As noted in Chapter 2, after struggling to find the solution to an interesting but difficult problem, children are likely to smile or laugh when they finally get the answer. Again, this pleasure seems to be of the nonhumorous variety. Although no attempt has been made to demonstrate this relationship with adults, there is every reason to believe that adults function the same way. But each of us undoubtedly has our own individualized optimal level of challenge. One person may derive maximal pleasure from only extremely difficult problems, whereas another may get the most enjoyment from finally coming to grips with problems that are only mildly challenging. Also, each of us may prefer varying levels of challenge at different times of the day. In the morning when we are fresh and alert, we may thrive on struggling through complex problems to a final understanding; in the evening, after a hard day's work, we might find such struggles too taxing to be enjoyable. When mentally or physically fatigued, we might find it more enjoyable to deal with minimally challenging tasks.

The notion that the degree of intellectual challenge offered by a cartoon or joke might play an important role in determing a child's appreciation of it was first advanced by Edward Zigler and his associates in 1966.[5] They presented a series of cartoons to

---

[5]ZIGLER, E., LEVINE, J., and GOULD, L. Cognitive processes in the development of children's appreciation of humor. *Child Development*, 1966, 37, 507–518.

children in grades two, three, four, and five and found that the older the child, the greater the comprehension. This is to be expected because the older children have attained a higher level of intellectual development and have a broader range of experience. The most interesting part of this study, though, is the finding that smiling and laughter at the cartoons increased progressively between grades two and four, but decreased between grades four and five. The researchers advanced a "cognitive congruency" principle to account for these findings, arguing that "cartoons which make few cognitive demands elicit a lower mirth response than those that are in keeping with the complexity of the child's cognitive apparatus." Other investigators have obtained similar findings and have interpreted them in the same way.[6]

In a follow-up to this study, children in grades three, five, and seven were asked to explain why a series of cartoons was funny.[7] Their answers were scored for degree of comprehension of the cartoons, and these comprehension scores were then used to obtain groups of cartoons matched in difficulty level for each of the three grade levels. If a child received a high comprehension score for a given cartoon, the assumption was made that the cartoon must have been easily understood. A low comprehension score, on the other hand, was assumed to correspond to considerable difficulty in understanding the cartoon. Although the assumption that specific amounts of cognitive effort are reliably related to particular comprehension scores is clearly a weak one, the greatest amount of smiling and laughter (at all three grade levels) occurred in connection with comprehension scores in the middle ranges: that is, children who seemed to either fully understand the cartoons or not understand them at all were least likely to laugh and smile. So these findings also seem to support the view that cartoons that are moderately challenging are likely to be funniest.

Another investigator tested the cognitive congruency principle by developing jokes whose comprehension requires particular

[6]WHITT, J. K., and PRENTICE, N. M. Cognitive processes in the development of children's enjoyment and comprehension of joking riddles. *Developmental Psychology*, 1977, 13, 129–136.

[7]ZIGLER, E., LEVINE, J., and GOULD, L. Cognitive challenge as a factor in children's humor appreciation. *Journal of Personality and Social Psychology*, 1967, 6, 332–336.

intellectual capacities that children are known to acquire at about six or seven years of age.[8] Piagetian concepts provide an ideal means of testing the importance of cognitive challenge for humor appreciation, because we can determine in advance how well equipped a child is to understand a joke based on the violation of those concepts. For example, the following jokes have as their bases the violation of conservation and class inclusion concepts:

> Mr. Jones went into a restaurant and ordered a whole pizza for dinner. When the waiter asked if he wanted it cut into six or eight pieces, he said: "Oh, you'd better make it six! I could never eat eight!"

> Mr. Barley teaches first grade. One day his class was talking about religion; so he asked how many of the children were Catholic. When Bobby didn't raise his hand, the teacher said: "Why, Bobby, I thought you were Catholic too!" "Oh no," said Bobby, "I'm not Catholic; I'm American."

These jokes are admittedly not very funny to readers of this book, but then that was precisely the point of the study. Because the intellectual capacities required to understand these jokes are typically acquired in the first grade, they pose little challenge to adults. They strike us as obvious and simple-minded. However, for the child who has just learned that the total number of parts into which something is cut does not influence the total amount present, great enjoyment may be derived from the absurdity of pretending that six bigger pieces would be easier to eat than eight smaller pieces (as long as you're going to eat the whole pizza). Similarly, for the child who has only recently realized that concepts can be arranged in a hierarchy (e.g., objects may be arranged into edible and nonedible varieties; edible objects may be subdivided into fruit, vegetables, meat, etc.; fruit may be reclassified as apples, pears, bananas, etc.), it may require some thought to come to the conclusion that being a Catholic and an American are not mutually exclusive events. Elementary-school children experience great delight in younger children's errors along these lines (e.g., "I don't wany any meat! Just give me a

---

[8]McGhee, P. E. Children's appreciation of humor: A test of the cognitive congruency principle. *Child Development*, 1976, 47, 420–426.

"No, don't cut it into eight pieces. I'm on a diet."

hamburger!") Assuming that children who have just acquired conservation and class inclusion concepts must exert more mental effort to understand jokes based on these concepts than do children who acquired them several years before, the latter group should find the jokes less funny than the former group. Because the concepts are still relatively new for the younger group, violation should offer a greater challenge to them.

Because most children acquire conservation and class inclusion concepts in the first grade, jokes like those just presented were read to children in grades one, two, and five. Of the first-graders, half had already acquired both concepts, but the other half had not acquired either one. As expected, the jokes were viewed as funnier by first-graders who had already acquired conservation and class inclusion concepts than by both the first-graders who did not possess the concepts and the two older groups. The first-graders who had not acquired the concepts had no way of understanding the jokes, and the fifth-graders apparently considered them too simple to be funny.

This finding is similar to that obtained for infants (see Chapter 2), whose smiling was most likely to be produced by distortions of events only recently learned. It seems clear, then, that jokes and cartoons will generally be funniest if a moderate amount of effort is required to understand them. This influence upon humor appreciation is probably always operating to an extent, although it will be stronger in some cases than in others. It may be that the contribution of cognitive challenge to humor appreciation is greatest when other influences on funniness (such as the presence of sexual, aggressive, or superiority themes) are minimized. If a joke has strong sexual overtones, it does not have to be very clever or challenging to produce vigorous laughter. An equally complex joke that lacks a sexual or aggressive theme may not produce more than a smile; in fact, even if it is at an optimal level of difficulty, the pleasure derived from the challenge to the intellect is much less likely to produce hearty laughter than is a joke with an emotionally charged theme. It may be that, even in the context of a joke, the pleasure derived from cognitive challenge is an intellectual form of pleasure; although it may be accompanied by smiling or light laughter, it rarely is accompanied by vigorous laughter. Only if the context of the joke includes arousing material is it likely to lead to extended laughter.

A fascinating study along these lines was completed recently using older men and women (ranging from fifty to eighty years of age).[9] Conservation jokes of the type just described were presented to these subjects, and they were asked to rate them for funniness. The idea behind this study was the common finding that certain intellectual and physical skills tend to deteriorate with increasing age in later years. The capacity for logical thought (like that described by Piaget) is among those that regress in old age. Generally speaking, cognitive skills tend to be lost in the reverse order of that in which they were initially acquired in childhood. This suggests that, during the progressive deterioration of the capacity for logical thought, a point should be reached at

---

[9]SCHAIER, A. H., and CICIRELLI, V. C. Age changes in humor comprehension and appreciation. *Journal of Gerontology*, 1976, 31, 577–582.

which conservation (and other children's) jokes should become sufficiently challenging to be funny again. This is precisely what was found. Comprehension of conservation jokes became progressively worse with increasing age, whereas appreciation increased with age. These findings are exactly opposite the trend observed for children's humor earlier in this chapter, and they strengthen the conclusion that, throughout the life span, humor is maximized at a moderate level of difficulty.

Additional Cognitive Influences

It has been emphasized at several points in this book that children must be in the right frame of mind to find incongruous or puzzling events funny. The optimal frame of mind seems to be a playful one in which the incongruous event is interpreted as only occurring in a fantasy or pretend sense, although we have seen that some incongruous events are funny precisely because they really do happen. Only one study has examined the effect of the child's frame of mind on the perceived funniness of observed incongruities. The incongruous events in that study consisted of violations of conservation of weight, either in the context of a joke or demonstrated with a two-pan balance.[10] In the latter case, two piles of "potatoes" (actually, little pieces of Play-doh) were placed on the two pans and then altered until the two sides had the same weight. The material on one pan was then "mashed" into a single pile of potatoes and placed back on the balance. By discreetly removing a small portion during the mashing, the mashed potatoes were made to appear to be lighter than the unmashed potatoes. It seemed, then, that mashing the potatoes really did reduce their weight. This apparent violation of conservation of weight was also demonstrated by cutting two loaves of bread made out of Play-doh into either thick or thin slices (the thinly sliced loaf appeared to weigh less).

Some children witnessed these violations of conservation in the absence of any other comments by the examiner, but others

---

[10]McGHEE, P. E., and JOHNSON, S. F. The role of fantasy and reality cues in children's appreciation of incongruity humor. *Merrill-Palmer Quarterly*, 1975, 21, 19–30.

were read a story that paralleled the events with the balance. One of these stories follows:

> Mary is six years old and went to the bakery one day to get five one pound loaves of bread for her mother's party. When she saw that the bread was cut into very thick slices, she said, "Oh, you'd better slice it thin! I could never carry them home cut that thick."

A third group of children heard only the stories and did not see conservation being violated using the balance. Finally, a fourth group also heard the stories without seeing the balance demonstration, but were told in advance that the stories were jokes. So some of the children (all third- and fifth-graders) experienced a violation of conservation of weight only in a fantasy sense, whereas others experienced it under conditions that suggested that it really happened. The fourth group received the strongest "cues" suggesting a fantasy violation, and the first group received the strongest cues suggesting a real violation. The importance of fantasy elements in seeing puzzling or incongruous events as humorous may be seen in the fact that children in group four rated the violations as being most funny, followed by children in groups three, two, and one. Children who know that changing the shape of Play-doh or cutting it in different ways cannot influence its weight simply did not find much humor in seeing their beliefs disconfirmed. The stronger the evidence that it was only a pretend violation, the funnier it was.

It has been suggested that children automatically make an effort to resolve or make sense out of incongruous events, regardless of whether they occur in a reality or fantasy context. It has also been seen that the pleasure derived from this process can be interfered with if too much mental effort is required for understanding. One study has demonstrated that some children make a more active effort to explain incongruous events than do others.[11] Children who simply react to such events without laboring over how to interpret them tend to laugh more when absurd or strange happenings do occur. It may be, then, that the intellectual process of examining and interpreting an event disrupts the kind of spontaneity that is important for bringing forth hearty laughter. In

---

[11]KREITLER, H., and KREITLER, S. Dependence of laughter on cognitive strategies. *Merrill-Palmer Quarterly*, 1970, 16, 163–177.

Chapter 6, it will be shown that there are distinctive personality types along these lines. Although some children (and adults) are prone to laugh spontaneously at jokes or other humorous events and do not spend time trying to "figure it out," others tend to reflect more about what is actually going on in the joke. The latter may say that they think the joke is funny but are not likely to laugh as much as their more spontaneous peers.

One of the most problematic aspects of trying to study reactions to humor by experimentation is that simply being asked to explain the point of a cartoon or joke may interfere with how funny it is perceived to be. The extent to which this interferes with appreciation, however, depends on how difficult the joke or cartoon is.[12] Being asked to explain a simple joke does not interfere with laughter at it, although laughter is reduced in attempting to explain more challenging jokes. Even if adults explain to children what is going on in a joke or cartoon, they do not see as much humor as they do when no explanation is given.[13] This, again, suggests the importance of the child's frame of mind in seeing events as humorous. Regardless of whether one attempts to explain the point of a joke oneself or listens to someone else do the same, this seems to create a more serious frame of mind, which disrupts the spontaneous flowering of laughter.

Finally, the nature and intensity of children's reactions to incongruous events may depend on the context in which they occur. It was demonstrated more than fifty years ago that infants sometimes cry and sometimes laugh at the same event, depending on the circumstances.[14] For example, an infant may laugh at its mother wearing a mask if she was seen putting it on, but cry if she walks into the room already wearing it.[15] In Chapter 1, it was noted that an important factor in this regard may simply be whether the child interprets the situation to be a safe (often trans-

[12]McGHEE, P. E. Unpublished data, 1975.

[13]ROTHBART, M. K. Incongruity, problem-solving and laughter. In A. J. Chapman and H. C. Foot (Eds.), *Humour and laughter: Theory, research and applications.* London: Wiley, 1976.

[14]JONES, M. C. The development of early behavior patterns in young children. *Pedagogical Seminary*, 1926, 33, 537–585.

[15]SCARR, S., and SALAPATEK, P. Patterns of fear development during infancy. *Merrill-Palmer Quarterly*, 1970, 16, 53–87. SROUFE, L. A., WATERS, E., and MATAS, L. Contextual determinants of infant affective response. In M. Lewis and L. A. Rosenblum (Eds.), *The origins of fear.* New York: Wiley, 1974.

lated to mean familiar) or threatening one.[16] Any arousing event, such as a strange mask, in a threatening context is likely to lead to crying, whereas the same event in the absence of any threat should produce laughter.

Creativity and Humor

There has been an ongoing controversy during the past several decades regarding the nature and measurement of creativity. The most commonly accepted view at present is that creativity is best thought of as involving divergent (rather than convergent) thought processes.[17] Divergent thinkers tend to have more unique associations to ideas and events and a greater abundance of them than do convergent thinkers. Divergent thought is characterized by a rapid fluctuation between several different directions of thought, whereas convergent thought is characterized by consistent thought within a single direction. The eminent writer Arthur Koestler made a significant contribution to our understanding of the cognitive nature of creativity, with his view that all forms of creativity are based on a common mental process, which he calls "bisociation." The bisociative act is "the perceiving of a situation or idea . . . in two self-consistent but habitually incompatible frames of reference. . . ."[18] Through bisociation, two domains of thought that have never before been considered to have any meaningful relationship are suddenly seen to have a common thread of similarity. A bisociative insight is relatively more creative than others when this relationship is not initially easy to see but is obviously appropriate once realized. Within this view, the creative individual has more such insights than the uncreative one does.

According to Koestler, the type of thinking involved in creating humor is identical with that required for scientific, literary, artistic, or other forms of creative activities. In order to create a

---

[16]ROTHBART, M. K. Laughter in young children. *Psychological Bulletin*, 1973, 80, 247–256. SROUFE, L. A., and WUNSCH, J. P. The development of laughter in the first year of life. *Child Development*, 1972, 43, 1326–1344.

[17]GUILFORD, J. P. Three faces of intellect. *American Psychologist*, 1959, 71, 164–174.

[18]KOESTLER, *Act of creation.*

cartoon or joke, an object or event must be seen outside of its normal context; an unexpected or unusual relationship must turn out to be essential to get the point of the joke. The generally creative or bisociative thinker should have the advantage in this situation, because he or she automatically tends to bring a broad range of ideas and relationships to bear on any event. So creative thinkers should be better than less creative individuals both at creating humor spontaneously and at quickly understanding the humor initiated by others.

The nature of children's creativity is less well understood than is that of adults. The seemingly unorganized and disjointed conversations and reactions of very young children have often prompted the conclusion that they are generally more creative than adults. Because they do not feel the same need for being logical in their thinking that older children and adults feel, they are freer to extend ideas in unlimited directions. But what are the signs of creativity in preschoolers? Jerome Singer has recently suggested that, from the second year on, it may be possible to see the early precursors of creativity in children's make-believe play.[19] Children know as soon as they begin to engage in fantasy activities that one object or event may be brought together with another, and endless hours are spent mentally superimposing different events upon one another.

All children enjoy fantasy play, but Singer notes that some children become more preoccupied with it than others. In his view, the child who is often engaged in make-believe activity in the early years may become predisposed toward an "as if" way of thinking, thereby setting the stage for heightened creativity in subsequent years. Consistent with this view, artistically more creative college students have been found to have spent more time daydreaming in childhood.[20] High-school students who produce more-creative literary works are more likely to have had imaginary companions in childhood.[21]

---

[19]SINGER J. L. *The child's world of make-believe: Experimental studies of imaginative play.* New York: Academic Press, 1973.

[20]HELSON, R. Childhood interest clusters related to creativity in women. *Journal of Consulting Psychology*, 1965, 29, 353–361.

[21]SCHAEFER, C. E. The self-concept of creative adolescents. *Journal of Psychology*, 1969, 72, 233–242.

Studies relating creativity to humor in children have been rare, but the research that has been completed suggests that a close relationship does exist between them. Given the importance of play for humor, the finding that more-creative children tend to be more playful is especially interesting.[22] If humor and playfulness really are closely connected, the same relationship should hold for humor: that is, more-creative children should engage in clowning or joking more often and should also be funnier than their less-creative peers. During childhood, more-creative individuals are already viewed by their peers as having a better sense of humor.[23] By adolescence, they attach greater importance than their less-creative peers to having a good sense of humor.[24] Given this greater interest in humor, it is not surprising that more-creative individuals are generally more appreciative of humor,[25] understand it better,[26] initiate it more often,[27] and produce funnier material when they are trying to be funny.[28] In Chapter 2, it was suggested that most children use the production of fantasy incongruities and absurdities to maintain an optimally varied and interesting environment. If this pattern is characteristic of

[22]GETZELS, J. W., and JACKSON, P. W. *Creativity and intelligence.* New York: Wiley, 1962. LIEBERMAN, J. N. The relationship between playfulness and divergent thinking at the kindergarten level. *Journal of Genetic Psychology,* 1965, 107, 219–224. LIEBERMAN, J. N. *Playfulness: Its relationship to imagination and creativity.* New York: Academic Press, 1977. TORRANCE, E. P. Priming creative thinking in the primary grades. *Elementary School Journal,* 1961, 62, 139–145. WALLACH, M. A., and KOGAN, N. *Modes of thinking in young children.* New York: Holt, Rinehart, and Winston, 1965.

[23]HAUCK, W. E., and THOMAS, J. W. The relationship of humor to intelligence, creativity, and intentional and incidental learning. *Journal of Experimental Education,* 1972, 40, 52–55.

[24]GETZELS and JACKSON, *Creativity and intelligence.*

[25]GIDYNSKY, C. G. Associative shift, peer rejection and humor response in children: An exploratory study. Unpublished doctoral dissertation, Columbia University, 1972. WEISSBERG, P. S., and SPRINGER, K. J. Environmental factors in creative function. *Archives of General Psychiatry,* 1961, 5, 64–74.

[26]GIDYNSKY, Associative shift, peer rejection and humor response in children. ROUFF, L. L. Creativity and sense of humor. *Psychological Reports,* 1975, 37, 1022.

[27]BABAD, E. Y. A multi-method approach to the assessment of humor: A critical look at humor tests. *Journal of Personality,* 1974, 42, 618–631. GETZELS and JACKSON, *Creativity and intelligence.*

[28]BRODZINSKY, D. M., and RUBIEN, J. Humor production as a function of sex of subject, creativity, and cartoon content. *Journal of Consulting and Clinical Psychology,* 1976, 44, 597–600. TREADWELL, Y. Humor and creativity. *Psychological Reports,* 1970, 26, 55–58.

children generally, it may be that creative children are simply more concerned with maintaining such a stimulating environment than are other children. Humorous fantasy creations afford an ideal way of producing new exciting events, because the child always has immediate access to them. Also, because the child has complete control over imaginative activity, it is easy to switch to other fantasy ideas as soon as the present one becomes boring. Finally, the production of humorous incongruities in fantasy probably fosters the development of creative thinking, because the child must continually look for new ways to alter or distort familiar ideas.

6 Social and Personality Influences

So far, humor has been discussed as if all children showed the same general developmental trends. This is an appropriate way to begin, because the basic pattern of change in humor at different ages depends on underlying changes in intellectual development. But most opportunities for humor arise in the presence of others, and their reactions may play an important role in establishing a more individualized pattern of humor development. Such reactions may also be more important to some children than to others, thereby providing for a greater social influence on their humor development. In this chapter, then, consideration will be given to the ways in which social factors lead to individual differences in children's sense of humor and to the kinds of social influences on humor that hold for children generally.

Children show basic differences in many aspects of behavior as early as infancy. If these differences were to influence either how they react to humor (both their own and others') or how much they engage in clowning or joking activity, this would enhance individualization within the general developmental pattern resulting from cognitive developmental changes. In the latter half of this chapter consideration will be given to personality and other "individual difference" factors that have a bearing on humor development. Sex differences constitute the single largest source of individual differences in humor; so that topic will be treated in a chapter by itself.

Social Influences

The social aspects of children's humor have only recently begun to be studied in a systematic fashion. It seems clear, though, that children learn very early that laughter and humor can be very effective in achieving certain social goals. The extent to which a child adopts laughter or humor initiation as part of a habitual way of relating to others may depend on the reactions of parents, peers, and other persons having considerable contact with the child. Social models of humor and laughter may be equally important. Although it is safe to assume that these social influences help to mold the child's sense of humor, it is not clear just when their influence begins.

The Beginning of Socially Shared Humor

Many adults and children of school age cannot resist telling an especially funny or clever joke to others. This strong urge to communicate humor to others, however, is not present when children first begin to experience humor. In Chapter 2, the origin of humor in the second year of life was linked to the achievement of a specific milestone of cognitive development; namely, the ability to represent the world by simple image-symbols. This capacity enables the child to engage in pretend play with objects and to create incongruous relationships between objects and the actions directed toward them. When the child is in a playful frame of mind, such "nonfitting" actions are funny precisely because they are known to be inappropriate for those particular objects. Pleasure is derived from examining and figuring out such incongruities, but it does not take the form of humor unless the child is in a playful mood. The important point for our present concerns is that this early humor may or may not occur in the presence of others. When it does occur in a social context, social factors have no bearing at all on the enjoyment derived from the activity. In its original and simplest form, humor is a private experience. There is no realization initially that others might also enjoy the incongruities produced.

Between the ages of two and three, children begin to want to share their humor with others. The example of Chukovsky's three-year-old daughter described earlier (see Chapter 2) clearly demonstrates the enjoyment derived from passing on one's humorous insights to others.[1] Once she thought up the idea of a

---

[1]CHUKOVSKY, K. *From two to five.* Berkeley: University of California Press, 1966.

dog making the sound of a cat, she rushed to her father with a grin on her face and said: "Daddy, 'oggie miaow." How did this behavior get established, given that it had not been present a year or so earlier? Also, how are we to explain the fact that some children are more intent than others on communicating their humor to others?

The most plausible answer to each of these questions lies in the reactions that adults or older children have when they first begin to see the child producing incongruous fantasy activities. Some parents take great delight in the fantasy play of their children, whereas others show no interest at all, dismissing it as nonsense or child's play. In the latter case, the child is not likely to receive any form of attention or social reinforcement in connection with fantasy constructions. This should not make the child's humor less enjoyable than it was to begin with, but it should restrict the pleasure derived to that intrinsically resulting from enjoyment of the incongruity produced. In this sense, this child's humor should be enjoyed in a very "pure" way. In the former case, on the other hand, if the child repeatedly encounters smiling, laughter, and other positive forms of adult attention in connection with fantasy constructions during play, he or she should quickly learn to connect the two together. As this relationship is strengthened, the child can be expected to repeat these fantasy creations for other people. This child, then, has two sources of pleasure associated with humor, instead of one. As social forms of reinforcement become increasingly intertwined with the intrinsic pleasure derived from humor, joking and clowning behavior might increasingly be initiated primarily for the social rewards it leads to.

The habit of clowning or joking for social reasons may also be established in some children because of adult reactions to actions or statements not completely understood. Children are continually extending their understanding of their world, but they sometimes come to seemingly reasonable conclusions that are funny to adults. For example, one investigator observed one three-year-old reprimanding another by saying: "Don't say Goddam! That means bullshit!"[2] In this case, the child is making a genuine attempt to meaningfully link together two words known

---

[2]SINGER, J. L. *The child's world of make-believe.* New York: Academic Press, 1973.

to be forbidden. There is no attempt to be funny, and the predictable outcome is likely to be confusion at the laughter of onlooking adults. In spite of this lack of insight into the humor involved, the child may attempt to reproduce this and similar statements later. Because the child has already learned the social value of joking, this kind of experience might encourage him or her to initiate humor that he or she does not even understand. This effect is especially apparent in many five- and six-year-olds who repeatedly tell riddles before they understand the double meanings that are usually involved.

Social Laughter

Just as joking, clowning, and the production of simple incongruities with one's action can be initiated either because of the sheer enjoyment of the funny outcome or in order to produce laughter in others, so a child's laughter may be either a genuine reaction to humor or a primarily social response. Researchers studying humor have noted that there are many different kinds of laughter, but only one of them is related to humor.[3] Social laughter is probably the most common of the nonhumorous forms of laughter and may even be more common than humorous laughter. Social laughter tends to occur as a part of normal conversation, and its function is to cover up nervousness, make others feel at ease, fill in gaps, and generally make conversation more relaxed and enjoyable. Polite laughter at unfunny jokes or stories is another form of social laughter designed to seem like humorous laughter.

Preschool children often laugh at jokes and other forms of humor that they do not yet understand, but they do not generally use polite laughter to hide the fact that they do not understand or appreciate the point of a joke. Their laughter is more likely to be a spontaneous and genuine response to the humorous incident. The conversational forms of laughter observed among preschoolers differ from those of adults in that they are more likely to reflect the joy and excitement of activities accompanying the conversation. It may be that a child first uses polite laughter in

---

[3] GILES, H., and OXFORD, G. S. Toward a multidimensional theory of laughter causation and its social implications. *Bulletin of the British Psychological Society*, 1970, 23, 97–105.

response to incomprehensible or unfunny jokes at about age six or seven, when new cognitive skills enable the child to begin empathizing with others and seeing things from their perspective.

Laughter as a Means of Gaining Approval   The greatest motivation behind social laughter may be a desire for social acceptance or approval. A person who laughs readily in the course of normal social interchange and who laughs predictably at others' efforts at being funny is usually considered to be warm and friendly. This invites others to be warm and accepting in return and increases the chances that the person will be liked. When someone else tells a joke or makes some other effort at humor, laughter is the obvious way to gain approval, even if the effort is a poor one. As will be seen in Chapter 7, children with an early tendency to seek attention, affection, and approval are more likely than their peers to develop a heightened sense of humor.

Laughter and In-group Acceptance   As children progress through the grade-school years, they tend to form cliques and other informal groups. Social laughter seems to be a useful tool for helping establish a child's membership in an "in-group."[4] Assuming that

---

[4]Foot, H. C., and Chapman, A. J. The social responsiveness of young children in humorous situations. In A. J. Chapman and H. C. Foot (Eds.), *Humour and laughter: Theory, research and applications.* London: Wiley, 1976.

the members of the group share certain attitudes or likes and dislikes, the child can demonstrate the possession of similar attitudes by laughing with the other members at the ideas or actions of out-group members. Thus, laughter facilitates acceptance by other members of an in-group by demonstrating that a common bond exists between them and the child.[5]

Social Facilitation of Humor and Laughter

It will come as no surprise to the reader that children (and adults) show greater appreciation of humor in groups than when they are alone.[6] They do laugh at jokes or cartoons when alone, but the laughter is less boisterous and more restricted. Only during play with other children does intense and extended laughter occur. This pattern seems to get stronger as children get older.[7] As long as the other person present is another child, that person does not even have to laugh in order to produce increased laughter. The mere presence of another child seems to be enough to stimulate laughter if the child is in the right frame of mind for it.[8] An unresponsive adult, on the other hand, has the opposite effect. Children do not laugh much in the presence of an adult unless the adult joins in. This may simply indicate young children's general sensitivity to adult reactions. They may assume that the adult's failure to laugh or show some kind of playfulness indicates disapproval or a generally bad mood.

But is this increased laughter in the presence of others humorous or social laughter? That is, do children actually find things funnier in social situations? The answer to this question is not clear at this point, but it seems likely that both possibilities

[5]HERTZLER, J. O. *Laughter: A socio-scientific analysis.* New York: Exposition Press, 1970.

[6]BRACKETT, C. W. Laughing and crying of pre-school children. *Journal of Experimental Education,* 1933, 2, 119–126. KENDERDINE, M. Laughter in the preschool child. *Child Development,* 1931, 2, 228–230. FOOT and CHAPMAN, Social responsiveness of young children.

[7]DING, G. F., and JERSILD, A. T. A study of laughing and crying in preschool children. *Journal of Genetic Psychology,* 1932, 40, 452–472. CHAPMAN, A. J., SMITH, J., and FOOT, H. C. Humour, laughter, and social interaction. In P. E. McGhee and A. J. Chapman (Eds.), *Children's humour.* London: Wiley, forthcoming.

[8]CHAPMAN, A. J. Social aspects of humorous laughter. In A. J. Chapman and H. C. Foot (Eds.), *Humour and laughter: Theory, research, and applications.* London: Wiley, 1976.

hold to an extent: that is, a child is likely to show social laughter in the presence of others for the reasons just outlined. The fact that the social facilitation of laughter is greater among friends than strangers supports this view.[9] It is the child's friends whose acceptance and approval are most important; so social laughter should be especially likely in their presence. But laughter seems to be part of a generalized increase in intimacy among friends. They also talk to, look at, and touch each other more than when among strangers.[10] On the other hand, being in the presence of friends should also put a child sufficiently at ease to produce the playful frame of mind essential to humor. This should lead the child to find things genuinely funnier, so that the increased laughter is a true indication of greater appreciation.

Tony Chapman and his associates in Cardiff, Wales, have created special social circumstances in the laboratory in order to study the social aspects of humor and laughter. In one study, for example, they trained "confederate" children to exhibit varying amounts of looking, smiling, and laughter while attending to humorous materials. When the confederates laughed and smiled more, the other children did the same.[11] In a situation in which children listened to humorous tapes through head phones, the mere presence of another child was enough to increase laughter at the tape, even if the second child could not hear the tape.[12] Other experiments completed by Chapman have led him to conclude that the desire to share the social situation leads children to laugh more in the presence of others. It is not so much the sharing of the humor that facilitates laughter, but the shared participation in a social situation that just happens to include humor. If two confederates are planted in the situation in which the child experiences the humor, the amount of laughter depends on how much time the confederates spend looking at each other. The more the confederates look at each other, the less the third child laughs at the jokes presented. As they begin to look at the third

---

[9]DING and JERSILD, Laughing and crying in preschool children.

[10]FOOT, H. C., SMITH, J. R., and CHAPMAN, A. J. Sex differences in children's responses to humour. In A. J. Chapman and H. C. Foot (Eds.), It's a funny thing, humour. Oxford, England: Pergamon Press, 1977.

[11]CHAPMAN, Social aspects of humorous laughter.

[12]CHAPMAN, A. J. Social facilitation of laughter in children. Journal of Experimental Social Psychology, 1973, 9, 528–541.

child more, that child begins to laugh more.[13] This increased eye contact presumably increases the feeling that the child is sharing the social situation with the other two children and leads to increased laughter accordingly. Given that the humor is shared (i.e., experienced) regardless of how much the children look at each other, the sharing of the humor must not be as important as the sharing of the social situation generally. Increasing the closeness of children's seats while witnessing humor also tends to increase the amount of laughter.[14] This phsyically produced increase in social intimacy also serves to increase the feeling that children are sharing the social situation.

The Contagion of Laughter   The fact that laughter is very contagious may account for part of a child's tendency to laugh more when in groups than when alone ("Laugh and the world laughs with you"). Both children and adults find it difficult to resist laughter in the midst of hilarious belly laughter by others. This infectious quality of laughter can even make us laugh when we have no idea what is behind the laughter. It is not known when this develops in children, but it is certainly present by the preschool years. It is not uncommon to find a whole class of nursery- or elementary-school children breaking up into tear-producing laughter simply because a few children got "tickled" over some event. This contagion of children's laughter is especially likely during ongoing play activities and may indicate a generally increased excitement or arousal making the children especially prone toward laughter. It is not uncommon for the laughter to quickly accelerate and combine with screaming, yelling, and generally increased physical activity. One investigator has referred to this phenomenon as "group glee."[15]

The contagion of laughter is the main motivation behind the inclusion of laugh tracks or "canned laughter" in both children's and adults' comedy programs. Presumably, this added laughter increases appreciation of the program by making the viewer

---

[13]CHAPMAN, A. J. Humorous laughter in children. *Journal of Personality and Social Psychology*, 1975, 31, 42–49.

[14]CHAPMAN, Social aspects of humorous laughter.

[15]SHERMAN, L. W. An ecological study of glee in small groups of preschool children. *Child Development*, 1975, 46, 53–61.

laugh more. Among high school students and adults, canned laughter does increase viewer laughter, but there is only a corresponding increase in viewers' intellectual judgment of the funniness of the program among females.[16] Males, then, do not seem to be as influenced by their own increased laughter when they decide how funny the program is. Whether younger children are similarly able to form judgments about funniness independent of their own laughter remains to be seen.

"Laughing With" versus "Laughing At"

Young children have a reputation for being especially cruel in their laughter, because they generally make no effort to hide their laughter at mental and physical deformities or other odd characteristics of other persons. This laughter at others should not, however, be equated with similar forms of laughter in adults. Although an adult who laughs at another person in his or her presence is likely to be fully aware of the effect that this has on the "victim," a child less than the age of about seven does not have this awareness. Piaget noted long ago that children less than this age are very egocentric in their thinking and that they have great difficulty in taking the perspective of another person.[17] Because they are not aware of the other person's feelings, their laughter is not really (necessarily) hostile in intent. As underlying cognitive development enables them to put themselves in their victim's position, they begin to inhibit this kind of laughter—at least as long as the victim is present—and consider mitigating circumstances in deciding what is and is not funny.[18]

The prevalence of hostile forms of humor in our society suggests that adults are prone to enjoyment of cruel forms of humor. Thus, we continue to laugh at incompetence, deformities, and oddities of behavior in others, just as children do. The only differences are that we require a little more distance between

---

[16]CHAPMAN, A. J. Funniness of jokes, canned laughter and recall of performance. *Sociometry*, 1973, 36, 569–578. LEVENTHAL, H., and MACE, W. The effect of laughter on evaluation of a slapstick movie. *Journal of Personality*, 1970, 38, 16–30.

[17]PIAGET, J. *The origins of intelligence in children.* New York: International Universities Press, 1952.

[18]McGHEE, P. E. Moral development and children's appreciation of humor. *Developmental Psychology*, 1974, 10, 514–525.

ourselves and the victims of our laughter than do children and require a little more sophistication or abstraction in the depiction of the object of our laughter. Some children older than age seven (as well as some adults) continue their direct laughter at others, in spite of their awareness of how devastating this can be. It is these children who are truly cruel in their laughter.

Social factors may again enter in to sustain laughter at others beyond the first or second grade. As in-groups and out-groups become formed in a child's school or neighborhood, laughter at members of the out-group may become very common among members of the in-group. This laughter serves to draw members of the in-group closer together and to sustain a hostile disposition toward members of the out-group.[19] A child may even feel pressure from other members of the in-group to laugh at or otherwise derogate members of the out-group as evidence of allegiance to the in-group. In this situation, then, laughing at and laughing with may occur simultaneously: that is, the child is enjoying a joyous and shared form of laughter with in-group members at the same time that laughter is being directed at a particular person or group. As children approach adolescence, some appear to have internalized this habit of laughing at others in order to favorably impress people by whom they want to be liked or accepted. In these individuals, such hostility in laughter and humor may become sufficiently general that it becomes the prominant feature of their sense of humor. Other children are able to restrict this kind of laughter to situations in which it occurs simply as an outcome of group comraderie. For these individuals, laughter at others remains a purely social form of laughter and does not develop into a stable aspect of their sense of humor.

Personality Influences

An investigator studying the effects of personality on humor development recently described children's reactions to the following joke told by a fourth-grade boy who was asked to relate a favorite joke to the rest of the class:

---

[19]Martineau, W. H. A model of the social function of humor. In J. H. Goldstein and P. E. McGhee (Eds.), *The psychology of humor: Theoretical perspectives and empirical issues.* New York: Academic Press, 1972.

Did you hear about the woman who got married four times? Her first husband was a millionaire; her second was a famous actor; her third was a well-known minister; and her fourth was an undertaker. Oh, I see. One for the money; two for the show; three to get ready; and four to go.[20]

The reaction of the class to this joke was typical of the reactions obtained whenever a joke or cartoon is presented to a large number of children or adults. Although some children laughed uproariously, others showed very little reaction at all. Still others laughed only mildly, chuckled, or simply smiled broadly. What are we to make of this broad range of reactions to the joke? Some of the responses may have resulted from a failure to understand the joke or a lack of familiarity with the phrase "one for the money. . . ." Yet, when the teacher asked the children to indicate how funny they thought the joke was, almost 80 percent of the class indicated that they thought it was very funny. This suggests that most of the children did understand the joke. Because the number of children who said that they thought the joke was funny was greater than the number who laughed, it seems that some children are more prone toward laughter at humorous incidents than are others.

One basic personality characteristic that has been studied helps account for this pattern in children's laughter. David Brodzinsky has completed a number of studies relating "conceptual tempo" to children's comprehension and appreciation of humor.[21] In this line of research, two types of children are distinguished: reflectives and impulsives.

Impulsive children scan stimuli in a more global fashion, and ignore a greater percentage of relevant task information than reflective children. Furthermore, the impulsive child is more likely to adopt a less successful problem-solving strategy than his reflective counterpart. On the other hand, as a result of his cautious, system-

[20]Brodzinsky, D. M. Conceptual tempo as an individual difference variable in children's humour development. In A. J. Chapman and H. C. Foot (Eds.), *It's a funny thing, humour.* Oxford, England: Pergamon Press, 1977.

[21]Brodzinsky, D. M. The role of conceptual tempo and stimulus characteristics in children's humor development. *Developmental Psychology,* 1975, 11, 843–849. Brodzinsky, Conceptual tempo as an individual difference variable in children's humour development. Brodzinsky, D. M., and Rightmeyer, J. Pleasure associated with cognitive mastery as related to children's conceptual tempo. *Child Development,* 1976, 47, 881–884.

atic, and detailed approach to problems, the reflective child is more likely to pick out the nuances of stimuli that often escape the impulsive child, which in turn, presumably leads to more accurate performance.[22]

When presented with cartoons or jokes, impulsive children laugh and smile more than reflective children do, in spite of the fact that reflective children show better comprehension when asked to explain why they are funny.[23] Even more revealing of the expressiveness of impulsive children was the finding that they also laughed more at the stimuli presented when the humor was removed. Thus, impulsive children seem to react more emotionally generally. It seems likely that much of this increased laughter is of the social variety just discussed, given that impulsive children continue to laugh a lot even when the funny aspects of the cartoon or joke have been removed. Reflective children's laughter tended to subside either when the humor was removed or when they did not really understand the point of the joke. Thus, although reflectives generally smile and laugh less, their affective reactions may be a better index of how funny they really think a joke is.

The poorer comprehension of humor by impulsive children seems to be simply a result of their cognitive style—not a result of poorer intellectual ability. This has been demonstrated by simply asking both types of children to reconsider the meaning of a joke. When prompted to think more carefully about what is going on in a joke, comprehension of the point of the joke by impulsive children proved to be just as good as that of reflective children, although the former still laughed more than the latter.[24] Reflective children's laughter depended on the complexity of the joke, whereas impulsive children laughed the same amount regardless of how difficult the jokes were to understand.

Given that impulsive children are more emotional in their reactions to humor, they might also be more influenced than

---

[22]BRODZINSKY, Conceptual tempo as an individual difference variable in children's humour development, p. 352.

[23]BRODZINSKY, Conceptual tempo and stimulus characteristics in children's humour development. BRODZINSKY, Conceptual tempo as an individual difference variable in children's humour development.

[24]BRODZINSKY, D. M. Children's comprehension and appreciation of verbal jokes in relation to conceptual tempo. *Child Development*, 1977, 48, 960–967.

reflectives by the kinds of social factors described earlier in this chapter. One study has shown this to be the case by presenting jokes to children using a videotape that either included or did not include audience laughter after each joke.[25] Although all children laughed more when jokes were followed by audience laughter, the increase in laughter was greater for impulsive children than for reflective children. So the impulsive child's increased laughter in response to humor is partly due to a general pattern of increased emotional expressiveness and partly due to a heightened susceptibility to influence by the social reactions of others.

It is tempting to conclude that impulsive children enjoy humor more than reflective children do, becasue they are easily drawn into intense laughter. Reflective children seem not to be as appreciative simply because they are not as emotionally labile. It is really impossible to make this kind of comparison, though, because we have no way of comparing what goes into different children's laughter or their statements that a joke is very funny. Some impulsive children may genuinely think a joke is as funny as their laughter suggests, whereas others may say a joke is only a little bit funny while they are breaking up in laughter. The more reflective child may experience a more intellectualized form of appreciation of humor and may accordingly be drawn to more abstract, sophisticated, or subtle forms of humor. Brodzinsky concluded that

> children from various conceptual tempo groups differ not so much in their appreciation of humor ... but in the way their appreciation is expressed affectively in "social" situations. The affective level expressed by impulsive ... children seems to depend more on cues emanating from the social environment than on internal cognitive evaluations of funniness. For reflective ... children, however, the affective and evaluative domains are more interdependent. In other words, for these children there is less of a tendency to smile and laugh at a joke (regardless of social cues) unless one has evaluated the joke as at least somewhat funny.[26]

The possession of a positive self-concept seems to facilitate humor development. Children with a better self-concept are

---

[25]BRODZINSKY, D. M., CUNDARI, L., and AIELLO, J. R. Sex of subject and group composition as factors in humor appreciation. Unpublished manuscript, 1978.

[26]BRODZINSKY, D. M., TEW, J. D., and PALKOVITZ, R. Control of humorous affect in relation to children's conceptual tempo. Unpublished manuscript, 1978.

able to tell more jokes or humorous stories on request, suggesting that they must spend a greater amount of time listening to and telling jokes generally. Children with poor self-concepts not only relate fewer jokes or funny incidents when asked to do so, but also include more hostility in the few jokes that they do tell.[27] Their humor, then, may reveal an underlying hostility that they feel about themselves and their interaction with others.

Much attention has been given in recent decades to the differences in the physical and psychological environment in which first-born and later-born children are raised. Of special importance with respect to humor development is the fact that attention and affection toward first- or early-borns must be reduced when later children are born. The longitudinal study of humor development described in Chapter 7 has demonstrated that children with an early concern about gaining adult attention and affection are most likely to laugh, joke, and clown more in later childhood. Thus, first-borns might be expected to initiate more humor and laugh more than do later-borns. The only study to examine the importance of birth order for humor appreciation indicated that first-borns do laugh more than later-borns, especially in situations in which they are likely to feel uneasy or under stress.[28] This makes sense, because first-borns tend to become especially affiliative under stressful conditions, and laughter is highly effective at strengthening affiliative bonds.[29]

Sex-role development has a major effect on children's personality development during the preschool years. As boys and girls learn that they are one sex or the other, and that this cannot be changed, they develop a progressively stronger identification with important members of that sex. Some children develop stronger and more exclusive identifications with their own sex than do others. Although all preschoolers take great delight in playfully pretending to be the opposite sex or in calling children

[27] LaChance, A. A study of the correlation between humor and self-concept in fifth-grade boys and girls. Unpublished doctoral dissertation, University of Maryland, 1972.

[28] Chapman, A. J., and Speck, L. J. M. Birth order and humour responsiveness in young children. In A. J. Chapman and H. C. Foot (Eds.), *It's a funny thing, humour.* Oxford, England: Pergamon Press, 1977.

[29] Schachter, S. *The psychology of affiliation: Experimental studies of the sources of gregariousness.* Stanford, California: Stanford University Press, 1959.

by names of the opposite sex (see Chapter 2, p. 74), the humor produced by such changes is greatest among those children who have the strongest identification with their own sex. Because three- and four-year-olds are still experiencing anxiety about what it means to be a boy or girl, and are not sure that they cannot be made into the opposite sex, they may not see the silliness of distorting the behavior or characteristics of the opposite sex. The child who is very confident about his or her own sex and about the behavior and characteristics related to each sex, however, does see sex-inappropriate behavior as silly or humorous.[30] Mastery of sex-role expectations, then, contributes to a child's humor in the same way that all other forms of learning do. Once you know how things actually occur in the real world, it is funny to imagine them occurring in an incompatible or incongruous manner.

These and other still unexplored personality characteristics, then, play an important role in producing the diversity of humor preferences, joking, and clowning among children of the same age or cognitive level. In the next chapter, we will see that the quantity as well as the quality of a child's sense of humor is closely related to patterns of behavior and personality characteristics of earlier childhood.

---

[30]McGhee, P. E., and Grodzitsky, P. Sex-role identification and humor among preschool children. *Journal of Psychology*, 1973, 84, 189–193.

Photographs by Edie Pistolesi

7 The Making of a Humorist: Early Childhood Influences

The concern in this chapter is not with the general trends in humor development which hold for all children, but rather with those children who become especially interested in humor during childhood and develop greater humor skills than their peers do. What causes some children to become intensely preoccupied with humor and laughter, whereas others simply give the same attention to humor that they give to other interesting events? Do humorous children tend to have humorous parents? Do parents influence their children's humor development in ways not directly linked to their own clowning or joking? Does increased development of the sense of humor result from a happy childhhood, or an unhappy one full of conflict and distress? How early can the budding humorist be detected? Has the older child or adult humorist always been funny? What are the early behavioral characteristics of children who subsequently show special skills at humor? Are humorists born or made? Professional comedians typically claim that comics or comedians are born, not made. Some of us presumably have a gift or an "intuitive feel" for humor from the beginning, whereas others of us not only don't have it, but could not possibly develop it if we devoted all of our energy to it. This is undoubtedly overstating the case, because no behavior or capacity as complex as the initiation or experiencing of humor has ever been shown to be linked exclusively to genetic inheritance. A safer interpretation of this claim would be that particular behavioral characteristics in early childhood more strongly predispose some children to become clowns or jokesters than others. In this case, our task is reduced to studying the same children for many years and noting those early characteristics or behaviors that are predictive of increased initiation of (or responsiveness to) humor in later childhood or adulthood. I recently completed such a longitudinal study of the early-childhood antecedents of humor development, and the findings of that study are the primary source of information presented in this chapter.[1]

It was noted in the last chapter that widespread individual differences in responsiveness to and initiation of humor can be seen early in the preschool years. On the reactive side, some children are very impulsive and overt in their laughter, whereas others are more reflective about what they find funny. The latter children seem to have a more "serious" ("intellectual" might be more accurate) appreciation of humor than do their impulsive peers and tend to be more restricted in their display of smiling and laughter. There may be constitutional differences along these lines as early as birth, given that it has been demonstrated that infants vary considerably in the extent to which they smile, laugh, or cry at interesting or unusual events during the first year of life.[2] It may be that the impulsive child who is quick to show emotional reactions becomes the overt performer who loves to clown around or tell jokes, whereas the more reflective and analytical child tends to develop a "drier" sense of humor. Professional comedy writers have noted that this basic dichotomy exists among adults;[3] so it is plausible to argue that children are predisposed to developing particular forms or styles of humor.

The Meaning of "Sense of Humor"

The expression "sense of humor" has generally been avoided throughout this book. This may seem surprising in a book concerned with humor development in children, but it is because there is little agreement among those investigating humor about just how sense of humor should be defined. For example, does a "good" sense of humor depend on initiating jokes, funny anecdotes, puns, or other forms of verbal humor more often than do

[1]McGhee, P. E. Sex differences in children's humor. *Journal of Communication*, 1976, 26:3, 420–426. McGhee, P. E. Development of the sense of humour in childhood: A longitudinal study. In P. E. McGhee and A. J. Chapman (Eds.), *Children's humour*. London: Wiley, forthcoming.

[2]McCall, R. B., and Kagan, J. Individual differences in the infant's distribution of attention to stimulus discrepancy. *Developmental Psychology*, 1970, 2, 90–98. McCall, R. B., and McGhee, P. E. The discrepancy hypothesis of attention and affect in infants. In I. C. Uzgiris and F. Weizman (Eds.), *The structuring of experience*. New York: Plenum, 1977. Sroufe, L. A., and Wunsch, J. P. The development of laughter in the first year of life. *Child Development*, 1972, 43, 1326–1344.

[3]Fry, W. F., and Allen M. *Make 'em laugh*. Palo Alto: Science and Behavior Books, 1975.

others? Do clowning, acting silly, and other behaviors count as much toward a good sense of humor as do verbal efforts at humor? Does possession of a sense of humor depend on being able to "see the light side" of things, or laugh in the midst of adversity? Does the chronic laugher who rarely initiates humor possess as good a sense of humor as the persistent clown or joker who rarely laughs? Through the decades, psychologists, philosophers, and other writers have stressed one or another of these qualities as being central to the possession of a good sense of humor. It is precisely for this reason that psychologists studying humor avoid the term. It seems that different individuals have widely varying senses of humor. Thus, it is not a question of having or not having a sense of humor, depending on whether one tells a lot of jokes, laughs "at the drop of a hat," and so forth. Our own personalities and developmental histories may determine whether we tend to be mainly responders or initiators of humor, but we all have a sense of humor as long as we are in some way especially tuned into the enjoyment of humor.

Because initiating and responding to humor are equally important to the possession of a sense of humor, sense of humor will be defined here with respect to both characteristics. Similarly, because both behavioral and verbal forms of humor are enjoyed by most people, they will be given equal weight. Thus, the person with a more developed sense of humor (the term "better" should probably be avoided, because of its questionable value connotations) generally initiates more behavioral or verbal forms of humor and smiles and laughs more at the humor of others. Thematic content of the humor that a person enjoys or initiates may influence our perception of the quality that person's sense of humor, but it has no bearing on the extent to which the sense of humor has been developed—that is, on the quantitative aspects of the sense of humor. Finally, humor development may be equal in two people even though one of them initiates humor frequently and the other mainly reacts to the humor of others.

A Longitudinal Study of Humor Development

This chapter is primarily concerned with the identification of early childhood behaviors and influences that are especially conducive to the development of the three basic qualities that have been identified as central to the sense of humor: laughter and the behavioral and verbal initiation of humor. The only longitudinal study of humor development was recently completed by the author at the Fels Research Institute.[4] As part of the ongoing data gathering procedures for the Fels longitudinal program, measures of maternal behavior toward children were obtained every six months during the first six years of each child's life by a regular Fels Home Visitor. Numerous aspects of the child's own behavior were also rated during the semiannual Fels Nursery School (for three- to five-year-olds) and the annual Fels Day Camp (for six- to eleven-year-olds). Because these antecedent child and maternal behavior data were available in the permanent data files, it was possible to relate prior maternal and child behavior to the child's laughter, clowning, and joking at later points in childhood.

The two separate age groupings used in the study were a preschool sample (from the nursery-school children) and an elementary-school sample (from the day-camp children). Separate ratings were obtained of the three basic components of sense of humor during the unstructured free-play activities. Amount of laughter was determined by the frequency of laughter during the period in which a child was being observed. Thus, the intensity of laughter was not considered in this rating. Also, no attempt was made to determine whether the event (in the case of another child's behavior) was intended to be funny. Children who laughed more often received a higher laughter rating, regardless of the nature of the laughter-producing event. Behavioral attempts to initiate humor included silly or clowning activity, arranging objects in incongruous positions or using them in incongruous ways, teasing through gestures, and so forth. Verbal humor included the distortion of familiar word sounds, puns, riddles, "bathroom" jokes and words, other "canned" jokes, incongruous or meaningless word combinations, and playful verbal teasing. The mean frequency of these three behaviors was used to define the extent to which the children had developed a sense of humor.

Continuity of Humor and Laughter

Before the findings of this longitudinal study are discussed, it should be noted that the oldest children studied were only

---

[4]McGHEE, Sex differences in children's humor. McGHEE, Development of the sense of humour in childhood.

eleven years of age. At this point, we have no way of knowing whether the young humorist maintains this strong humor orientation into adulthood. Studies of comedy writers and comedians, however, suggest that there may be considerable continuity of joking and clowning between childhood and adulthood.[5] Interviews with adults have shown that most professional humorists tended to be funny from childhood on.[6] There are notable exceptions, however (e.g., Carol Burnett), who did not develop special skills at humor until late adolescence.[7] When humor skills were late in developing though, there were usually strong humor models present in the home throughout childhood, so that there was still extensive exposure to humor.

The amount of laughter exhibited by young children is highly stable over a one-year period,[8] but it is not known whether attempts to initiate humor are similarly stable. It would be surprising, however, if joking and clowning were not stable behaviors during childhood, because initiating humor successfully requires considerable skill. Like most skills, continued practice should improve the capacity to evoke laughter in others. Unless the child begins to extend joking and clowning into inappropriate circumstances (e.g., in a classroom or in church), early humor skills should extend into a greater capacity for new forms of humor as they evolve with changes in cognitive development. Because humor is generally received favorably by others, ongoing social reinforcement should help the preschool comic develop into an adult with special humor skills.

Parental Influences

Given that all children show the same general developmental trends in the kinds of humor appreciated and produced, how are we to explain the fact that some children possess

[5]FRY and ALLEN, Make 'em laugh. JANUS, S. S. The great comedians: Personality and other factors. American Journal of Psychoanalysis, 1975, 35, 169–174. WILDE, L. The great comedians. Secaucus, New Jersey: Citadel Press, 1968.

[6]FRY and ALLEN, Make 'em laugh. SCHWARTZ, T. Comedy's new face. Newsweek, April 3, 1978, 60–71.

[7]MERYMAN, R. Carol Burnett's own story. McCall's, February, 1978.

[8]BRACKETT, C. W. Laughing and crying of preschool children. Journal of Experimental Education, 1933, 2, 119–126.

greater skill than others in producing and using humor? Temperamental differences may account for some of the variability, as noted earlier, but such differences cannot account for the full range of humor-related behavior engaged in by children. Of the various environmental influences on humor development, those of parents might be expected to be the strongest. Because parents (at least mothers) usually spend the greatest amount of time with a child, they are in an ideal position both to be humor models and to reinforce the child's attempts at humor. Other aspects of parental behavior might also indirectly produce conditions optimal for heightened humor development.

Modeling and Reinforcement of Humor

Interviews with comedy writers[9] and comedians[10] have shown that professional humorists typically had strong and consistent models of joking and clowning in one or both parents (and, in many cases, grandmothers) throughout childhood. In some cases, radio or television provided additional models that children imitated.[11] Psychologists have known for some time that children can learn from models without necessarily incorporating what they have learned into their own behavior. They are most likely to adopt the modeled behavior for themselves if the model is positively reinforced in some way. In the development of humor, such positively reinforcing events as smiling, laughter, attention, and affection usually result from the successful joke or clowning routine (barring the expression of overt hostility in the process). Under these conditions, we would expect a child to adopt these behaviors regardless of whether parents made a specific effort to praise or otherwise reward the child for attempts at jokes and comical antics.

It was argued in Chapters 2 and 3 that humor and other forms of fantasy play are intrinsically rewarding. Young children usually have a strong drive to become competent in executing newly evolved skills and are automatically drawn to using and

[9]FRY and ALLEN, Make 'em laugh.
[10]MERYMAN, Carol Burnett's own story. WILDE, The great comedians.
[11]SCHWARTZ, Comedy's new face.

improving them.[12] They also derive pleasure from distorting the world as they know it, once they begin to develop a firm understanding of familiar objects and events. Parents do not have to show children how to engage in pretend play with objects or words. They do it on their own and have great fun in the process. This accounts for the fact that nearly all preschoolers love fantasy games—both humorous and nonhumorous. When humor is modeled and reinforced (through laughter, attention, affection, etc.), the child learns that humor is not only enjoyable in its own right, but also very effective in eliciting favorable reactions from the people most important to the child. It may be, then, that it is those children who, for whatever reasons, have an especially great need for attention, affection, or recognition who are especially likely to adopt humor as a predominant component of their interaction with others. Support for this view will be presented later in this chapter.

The Role of Early Maternal Behavior

Data from the longitudinal study of humor development have shown that certain aspects of maternal behavior toward the child other than modeling or reinforcement of humor may also have an important bearing on whether unusually high amounts of laughter and humor initiation become established.[13] Surprisingly, though, the relationship between mothers' behavior and children's laughter and humor depends on the age at which their sense of humor was observed. Among preschoolers, boys and girls with a heightened sense of humor had a history of very positive relationships with their mothers. Their mothers were generally warm and approving, and tended to baby and overprotect them. These children were raised in an environment free of conflict, danger, and difficult-to-solve problems. In very young children, then, a heightened interest in humor is more likely to be related to a positive, conflict-free frame of mind than a distressed or otherwise negative one. There are signs, however, that this state

---

[12]WHITE, R. W. Motivation reconsidered: The concept of competence. *Psychological Review*, 1959, 66, 297–333.

[13]McGHEE, Sex differences in children's humor. McGHEE, Development of the sense of humour in childhood.

of affairs may be changing as early as age three. Preschoolers with a more developed sense of humor tended to have mothers who showed little affection toward them after age three, even though they continued to be protective, babying, and generally approving (uncritical).

Further evidence of a reversal of maternal influences on humor development may be seen in the elementary-school sample of children. In these older children, it was a lack of prior maternal babying and protectiveness that predicted increased laughter and humor. Thus, humor development was fostered by exposure to tough and potentially hazardous situations and the withholding of help in solving problems. It seems, then, that a transition occurs between the preschool and elementary-school years in the kinds of maternal behavior that foster humor development. By the time children enter grade school, those who have been allowed to cope with problems and conflict show greater degrees of humor development than those who have been protected from such circumstances by their mothers. In this sense, it appears to be the "tougher" child who shows the greatest humor development. This supports the psychoanalytic view that humor develops, to a great extent, as a means of coping with difficult or anxiety-arousing circumstances.[14]

The Role of Early Conflict and Distress

The antecedents of humor in elementary-school girls (but not boys) further support the view that humor is used by children to ease the distress they may experience. Girls whose homes were characterized by conflict, unpleasantness, repression, and insecurity during their first three years of life not only initiated more joking, but were more hostile in the process. Additional support for the "coping" theory of humor development has come from interviews with professional comedians and comedy writers about their early childhood experiences. The following examples seem to be quite typical. First, Norman Lear described early family dissension and noted that the only way to deal with this was to

[14]BERGLER, E. A clinical contribution to the psychogenesis of humor. *Psychoanalytic Review*, 1937, 24, 34–53. FREUD, S. *Wit and its relation to the unconscious.* New York: Moffat Ward, 1916. WOLFENSTEIN, M. *Children's humor.* Glencoe, Illinois: Free Press, 1954.

"I wish I could make them happy."

find something funny about it (such as scoring points during fights between parents, depending on who seemed to be winning). Second, Ruth Flippen's parents fought often, and she described experiencing much conflict and disappointment as a child. Her approach was to turn dreadful things into funny stories and to use joking as a means of keeping from crying. Third, Bob Henry described ongoing family conflicts and distress, with a persistent source of difficulty stemming from a driving and energetic mother with high expectations. His family, however, seemed to be continually full of laughter and joking in the midst of such havoc. Fourth, several other writers specifically mentioned using humor as a means of coping with parental or other sources of distress in childhood.[15]

Among comedians, Carol Burnett's background seems to be typical of the early experiences of professional humorists.[16] Her parents were both alcoholics and had frequent fights. She has described her childhood as a difficult one, noting that one responds either by getting stronger (and humor seems to be an especially effective means of gaining such strength) or "buckling under." The generality of this pattern of poor home adjustment and early stress is apparent in a study in which fifty-five professional comedians were interviewed (only four were female).[17] Most of these comedians had a good relationship with their mother, but a poor one with their father. Many described feeling belittled or picked on while growing up. Their early lives were "marked by suffering, isolation, and feelings of deprivation. Humor offered a relief from their sufferings and a defense against inescapable panic and anxiety."[18] There is considerable support, then, for the view that a problematic childhood is especially conducive to humor development. Children who are not old enough to deal with sources of distress in a rational way ease their plight by making the source of concern a cause for joking and laughter and by generally getting themselves into a more playful frame of mind. This frame of mind makes it easier to tune out the painful aspects of their lives and to focus on more positive events. Once an interest

---

[15]FRY and ALLEN, Make 'em laugh.
[16]MERYMAN, Carol Burnett's own story.
[17]JANUS, The great comedians.
[18]Ibid., p. 174.

in humor has been established on this basis, the extra attention to and practice at producing humor should strengthen the child's capacity for both appreciating and initiating humor in social interaction. In the words of one psychoanalyst, "The child who has found in joking a particularly valuable device for solving emotional difficulties, or for expressing unacceptable impulses, is apt to gain a quicker mastery of joke technique."[19] This increased mastery should lead to sufficient positive social reinforcement that the path toward the development of joking or clowning as a general life-style could become firmly established.

Early Characteristics of the Humorous Child

The longitudinal study referred to throughout this chapter showed that early precursors of a heightened sense of humor are much more evident in the child's own prior behavior than in the behavior of mothers toward their children. It is also interesting to note that the number of prior behaviors predictive of subsequent humor was greater for elementary-school children than for preschoolers. This again suggests that the period just before entering grade school may be especially important for humor development.

The single most striking aspect of the early childhood of children who showed more joking, clowning, and laughter than did their peers was their physical and verbal aggressiveness. In both the preschool and elementary-school samples, both boys and girls with more pronounced humor development had a long history of aggressiveness in their interactions with peers. This is an especially important finding, in light of the view long held by psychoanalysts that humor provides a socially acceptable means of expressing unacceptable aggressive feelings or impulses.[20] Because these children developed their aggressive behavior patterns very early, they undoubtedly encountered frequent criticism and other forms of negative reactions from both parents and other children. Although there are many potential rewards for the suc-

[19]WOLFENSTEIN, M. Children's understanding of jokes. *Psychoanalytic Study of the Child*, 1953, 9, 162–173.

[20]FREUD, *Wit and the unconscious*.

cessful wielder of aggression, there are also invariably pressures to conform to a more sociable style of interaction. Given these pressures, humor may have been adopted as a means of expressing hostility, while claiming that it was only meant as a joke.

Sense of humor was also strongly predicted by other forms of dominance in interaction with peers. Children who subsequently became clowns or jokers were highly assertive as early as the third year of life. They were used to having social power in their dealings with other children, and humor seems to have enabled them to continue this pattern. The child or adult who is constantly joking or clowning maintains control of most ongoing social interaction by creating circumstances to which others are obliged to react. Through the use of humor, then, domination of others can continue in a manner that is not only socially acceptable, but usually lavishly rewarded.

Verbal forms of dominance were especially characteristic of children who subsequently showed greater amounts of humor development. They were not only more talkative than their peers, but also generally more precocious in their language development. Because they did not have higher IQs, this language facility cannot simply be attributed to a higher overall intelligence. Although it is difficult to account for the origins of such a heightened language capacity in these children, it is not surprising that it was channeled into developing a sense of humor. As noted in Chapter 2, humor is essentially a symbolic or representational capacity. Thus, children with a special language facility might be expected to become especially interested in humor because of the great enjoyment that comes from symbolic manipulations and distortions of events.

Humor development was also found to be strongly associated with a history of attempts to seek attention, affection, and emotional support, along with frequent requests for help on tasks and recognition-seeking for achievement-related performances. So the budding clown or joker had a history of being especially sensitive to adult reactions and geared much of his or her behavior to obtaining some form of positive reaction from adults. It is difficult to account for the origin of these concerns, but it may be that the physically and verbally overbearing style of interacting with peers produced sufficiently negative reactions from them that these children became especially concerned about gaining the favor of adults. Humor should have provided a very effective means of accomplishing this. Early family conflicts or a lack of affection may also have made these children uncertain about their parents' love for them. In any case, these findings suggest that a desire to please others, and gain positive reactions from them, may be especially important in producing motivational circumstances conducive to heightened humor development.

Children's early achievement-related behavior showed an especially interesting pattern of prediction of subsequent development of the sense of humor. Although certain forms of achievement facilitated humor development, others interfered with it. Those children who were unusually persistent in their efforts to master gross motor skills (jumping, climbing, baseball, etc.) showed increased humor development, whereas those who were equally persistent in their efforts to master fine motor skills (craft work, puzzles, tinker toys, etc.) showed reduced levels of humor development. In the preschool sample, children who were highly persistent at intellectual achievement tasks (e.g., anagrams, twenty questions, geography names, etc.) also clowned, joked, and laughed less frequently during nursery school free-play sessions. The important distinction between these kinds of achievement may lie in the nature of the child's frame of mind while performing the tasks required for each kind. For intellectual and fine motor tasks, a child is likely to be serious. Because a serious frame of mind tends to be incompatible with humor, it is not surprising that children who spend large amounts of time engaged in such activities and who are greatly concerned about performing well show reduced levels of laughter and humor. Gross motor activities, on the other hand, which are generally physically vigorous and undertaken in the midst of social play, are likely to be accompanied by a more playful frame of mind. Both the social nature of the situation and the child's mental state during such activities are more conducive to laughter, humor, and generally having "fun." Children who spend more time engaged in these activities during their early years, then, may gradually develop clowning, joking, and other means of having fun as a stable part of their developing personalities and behavior.

A popular belief is that fat people have a better sense of

humor than skinny people. The findings of the longitudinal study of the preschool sample supported this view. Overweight children initiated humor more often than their peers, but they did not laugh more (which is really at the heart of the belief, given that fat people are assumed to be "more jolly"). Generally speaking, though, it was the taller and heavier children who showed the greatest humor development. It may have been increased physical stature that led to the development of aggressive patterns of behavior, as described earlier. Because measures of height and weight were not predictive of any of the humor measures at the elementary-school level, though, it would seem that this influence affects only very young children.

Are Humorists Born or Made?

We are now in a better position to answer the question raised at the beginning of this chapter. It seems that humorists are neither born nor made, but develop as a result of a combination of environmental influences and behavioral characteristics present very early in life. Broad constitutional and temperamental differences in infancy may account for heightened humor development in some children more than others. For example, a high activity level or increased physical stature may increase the odds of a child developing aggressive and dominating forms of behavior, which may subsequently be channeled into humor in the manner we have described. The constitutional tendency to exhibit affect in response to interesting or incongruous events may predispose some children toward heightened development of the laughter component of sense of humor. It is difficult to speculate, however, whether such increased laughter might also lead children to develop superior joking and clowning skills. Finally, the precocious language development noted as a consistent antecedent of heightened humor development may be partly due to maturational or genetic factors. It has already been noted that an increased interest in humor is a predictable outcome of precocious language development.

In most cases of complex human behavior, it is impossible to sort out how much of a given behavioral characteristic is attributable to genetic or constitutional factors and how much to

specific environmental influences. It can be concluded, ho'
that several distinctive types of behavior during the pre
and early elementary-school years are closely related to subsequent humor development. The following behavioral profile
during early childhood maximizes the probability of a child's
showing increased joking, clowning, and/or laughter in middle
childhood: (1) a highly assertive style of interaction with peers,
characterized by dominance and both physical and verbal aggression; (2) talkativeness and precocious language development;
(3) sensitivity to adult attention, affection, and recognition for
achievement efforts; and (4) high amounts of persistence and
effort in gross motor activities, but low amounts in intellectual
and fine motor tasks. A poorly adjusted home, characterized by
conflict and distress, and exposure by mothers to difficult and potentially hazardous situations also maximizes the probability of
heightened development of a sense of humor. In some unknown
fashion, these child and maternal behavioral characteristics combine to nurture the development of the young humorist.

8 Sex Differences: A Sense of Humor Distinctly Male or Female?

As noted earlier, the greatest single source of individual differences in humor may be whether the child is male or female. To the extent that such differences are reliable, we might consider the existence of a distinctive sense of humor associated with each sex. In considering this possibility, attention will be given to (1) the initiation of joking and clowning, (2) preferences for different types of cartoons and jokes, (3) early developmental influences and precursors in the child's own behavior, and (4) social influences. The extent to which a distinctive sense of humor exists for males and females in adulthood will be discussed first and then its development will be traced through childhood.

Sex Differences in Adults

Joking

The most obvious difference between male and female humor is that a male is more often than not the joke-teller, whereas a female is typically in the position of reacting to humor.[1] The fact that this difference does not begin to appear until the end of the preschool years, as described later in this chapter, suggests that humor might be related to certain sex-role expectations in our society. As noted in Chapter 6, the person who frequently uses

---

[1]Coser, R. L. Some social functions of laughter. *Human Relations*, 1959, 12, 171–182. Middleton, R., and Moland, J. Humor in negro and white subcultures: A study of jokes among university students. *American Sociological Review*, 1959, 24, 61–69. Pollio, H., and Edgerly, J. Comedians and comic style. In A. J. Chapman and H. C. Foot (Eds.), *Humour and laughter: Theory, research and applications*. London: Wiley, 1976. Smith, E. E., and Goodchilds, J. D. Characteristics of the witty group member: The wit as leader. *American Psychologist*, 1959, 14, 375–376.

humor is typically very good at controlling the pattern of social interaction. In Chapter 7, it was noted that children who do more clowning and joking have a history of social assertiveness, including both physical and verbal aggression. The close association of humor with aggressive and dominating forms of behavior indicates that our society may consider the initiating of humor to be more appropriate for males than females. For a female to develop into a clown, joke-teller, or story-teller, she must violate the cultural expectation that females should not aggressively dominate mixed-sex social interaction.

The Importance of Status   In occupational settings in which clear status differences exist between employees, individuals in positions of higher status initiate more jokes and other witty remarks than do people in low-status positions.[2] This supports the view that the humorist tends to have more social power than others. Employees in positions of lower status seem to feel that they are stepping beyond the bounds of their positions by taking the assertive role of jokester. Not only do employees in more authoritative positions initiate more jokes, but their humor is also more likely to be at the expense of others. In short, high-status employees are free to put down lower-status employees in their humor, but the latter group does not enjoy the same privilege. Rather, these employees are more likely to tell jokes that are self-depreciating in some way. Thus, everyone puts down someone in their humor, but only low-status persons put down themselves.

These findings have clear implications for sex differences in humor, because it is commonly assumed that women occupy a lower status in society than men. If status in connection with sex-role expectations operates in the same manner as status in connection with occupational-role expectations, women might be expected not only to initiate joking less frequently than men, but to be more self-disparaging in their humor as well. It is not clear what factors associated with lower-status occupational roles are responsible for these findings, but, if the status effect is a valid one, we should see both an increase in joking and more other-disparaging jokes as an individual's status increases. If we can

[2]Coser, R. L. Laughter among colleagues. *Psychiatry*, 1960, 23, 81–95.

assume that the feminist movement of recent years has been effective in improving the general status enjoyed by women, then we should expect to see a pattern of self-disparaging humor developing into other-disparaging humor as women become increasingly liberated from the traditional female sex role. Evidence in support of this transition is discussed below.

Humor Appreciation

Unfortunately, researchers studying humor have not yet begun to look for differences in the type of humor initiated by men and women. Ideally, these studies would be completed both for same-sex and mixed-sex groups. We do know, however, how men and women react when they are presented with cartoons or jokes. If we assume that people are likely to tell jokes and initiate witty remarks in a way consistent with the kind of humor they enjoy most, these studies are a source of insight into how men and women might be expected to differ in their joking patterns.

Sexual and Aggressive Humor   It is commonly assumed (perhaps only by men) that humor that is sexual or aggressive is more popular among men than women. Several studies have produced findings in support of this view,[3] but they may be misleading because of the research methods used. In the study of aggressive humor, no attempt was made to control which sex was the initiator and which the recipient of the hostile act. As will be seen in the next section, the funniness of a joke depends on who is aggressing toward whom, and whether one has a positive or negative attitude toward the protagonists. Because females are usually sexual objects in sexual jokes and cartoons, and more likely than males to be the butt of the joke, it would not be surprising if women find sexual humor less funny than men do. The only fair comparison would require either developing nonsexist forms of

[3]MALPASS, L. F., and FITZPATRICK, E. D. Social facilitation as a factor in relation to humor. *Journal of Social Psychology*, 1959, 50, 295–303. SPIEGEL, D., BRODKIN, S. G., and KEITH-SPIEGEL, P. Unacceptable impulses, anxiety, and the appreciation of cartoons. *Journal of Projective Techniques and Personality Assessment*, 1969, 33, 154–159. TERRY, R. L., and ERTEL, S. L. Exploration of individual differences in preferences for humor. *Psychological Reports*, 1974, 34, 1031–1037. THOMAS, D. R., SHEA, J. D., and RIGBY, R. G. Conservatism and response to sexual humor. *British Journal of Social and Clinical Psychology*, 1971, 10, 185–186.

sexual humor, or balancing the number of male-sexist and female-sexist jokes. When this is done, men and women show comparable levels of appreciation of sexual humor.[4] There are no grounds, then, for the assumption that men respond more to sexual humor than do women.

Self-disparaging versus Other-disparaging Humor   Most hostile cartoons or jokes have a clearly identifiable aggressor and a victim or butt. It should come as no surprise to the reader that our reaction to hostile humor generally depends on our attitude or disposition toward the protagonists depicted.[5] We derive the greatest enjoyment from jokes when we have a favorable attitude toward the aggressor and a negative attitude toward the victim. Similarly, appreciation is more likely to be interfered with when a liked person is victimized by a disliked person. This pattern also seems to hold with respect to issues about which we might have strong feelings, such as racial and political issues. Blacks find antiwhite jokes funnier than do whites (and vice versa), and Democrats find anti-Republican jokes funnier than do Republicans (and vice versa).[6] It should come as no surprise, then, that the same pattern holds for the sexes: that is, males find jokes funnier when females are the butt, whereas females find them funnier when males are the butt.[7] There seems to be no doubt about this

---

[4]CHAPMAN, A. J., and GADFIELD, N. J. Is sexual humor sexist? *Journal of Communication*, 1976, 26, 141–153.

[5]LaFAVE, L. Humor judgments as a function of reference group and identification classes. In J. H. Goldstein and P. E. McGhee (Eds.), *The psychology of humor: Theoretical perspectives and empirical issues.* New York: Academic Press, 1972. LaFAVE, L., HADDAD, J., and MAESEN, W. A. Superiority, enhanced self-esteem, and perceived incongruity humour theory. In A. J. Chapman and H. C. Foot (Eds.), *Humour and laughter: Theory, research, and applications.* London: Wiley, 1976. ZILLMAN, D., and CANTOR, J. R. A disposition theory of humour and mirth. In A. J. Chapman and H. C. Foot (Eds.), *Humour and laughter: Theory, research, and applications.* London: Wiley, 1976.

[6]LaFAVE, HADDAD, and MAESEN, Superiority, enhanced self-esteem, and perceived incongruity humour theory. ZILLMAN and CANTOR, Disposition theory of humour and mirth.

[7]LaFAVE, Humor judgments and reference group and identification classes. PRIEST, R. F., and WILHELM, P. G. Sex, marital status, and self-actualization as factors in the appreciation of sexist jokes. *Journal of Social Psychology*, 1974, 92, 245–249. WOLFF, H. A., SMITH, C. E., and MURRAY, H. A. The psychology of humor. I. A study of responses to race-disparagement jokes. *Journal of Abnormal and Social Psychology*, 1934, 28, 341–365.

pattern for males, but the picture for females has become more complicated in recent years. Although some women do respond like men in that they prefer jokes victimizing the opposite sex, many women actually derive greater enjoyment from jokes in which men victimize women![8]

The finding that women prefer jokes disparaging women to those disparaging men is a puzzling one, because it is counter to the general trend in this kind of study. There is agreement among theorists that women should not derive pleasure from seeing others like themselves put down.[9] In one study, an attempt was made to determine whether it made a difference to women whether it was a male or a female who victimized another woman in the joke.[10] By presenting jokes with all possible combinations of aggressor's sex and victim's sex, it was determined that women rate jokes as being the funniest when a woman is the butt of the joke, regardless of the sex of the aggressor! The important determinant of appreciation for women, then, seems to be the sex of the victim, not the person who humiliates the victim. Not only do women find great humor in seeing other women victimized in jokes, but they even rate such jokes as funnier than males rate them: that is, men show the greatest enjoyment of jokes in which women are put down, but women seem to enjoy them even more. This strengthens the view that self-disparagement may play a unique role in the establishment of a female sense of humor.

Although the disparagement of females appears to be the optimal condition for humor among women generally, there is reason to believe that the enjoyment of self-disparagement may be much broader than this. Females give higher funniness ratings than males to self-disparaging jokes, regardless of the sex of the person being disparaged.[11] The researchers who completed this

---

[8]CANTOR, J. R. What is funny to whom? *Journal of Communication*, 1976, 26, 164–172. Losco, J., and EPSTEIN, S. Humor preference as a subtle measure of attitudes toward the same and the opposite sex. *Journal of Personality*, 1975, 43, 321–334.

[9]LaFAVE, Humor judgments and reference group and identification classes. LaFAVE, HADDAD, and MAESEN, Superiority, enhanced self-esteem, and perceived incongruity humor theory. ZILLMAN and CANTOR, Disposition theory of humour and mirth.

[10]CANTOR, What is funny to whom?

[11]ZILLMAN, D., and STOCKING, S. H. Putdown humor. *Journal of Communication*, 1976, 26, 154–163.

study suggested that this may reflect the fact that females are typically less concerned than males with the issue of dominance and infallibility. Self-disparaging acts may be threatening to men, even though they are in a humorous context. If this kind of threat is present, it is not surprising that men do not find humor in the putting down of other men—especially by a woman.

One popular definition of sense of humor emphasizes the individual's ability to laugh at shortcomings, see the "light side" of things, and laugh at one's own expense. In this respect, women appear to have a better sense of humor than men. Undoubtedly, the early socialization history of males and females plays the key role in producing this difference. Women may be more used to accepting subordinate roles in society, and so may be freer to laugh at their own expense. Women are traditionally trained to "put others first" before considering their own needs, desires, and aspirations (at least to a greater extent than men), and the extent to which this is internalized may be indicated by their humor preferences. If this line of reasoning is correct, then, women's humor preferences should change as they begin to reject or become dissatisfied with such subordinate roles. Positive evidence of such a change is presented in the following section.

The role of self-disparagement in humor among women can even be seen in the routines of professional comediennes. One analysis of the recordings of male and female comics indicated that 63 percent of comediennes' cuts included self-disparagement, whereas only 12 percent of comedians' cuts did so.[12] When male comics did make disparaging remarks about their own sex, it was usually done in an impersonal way, rather than being directly at their own expense. Females were more prone toward self-victimizing. Professional comics give careful attention to the development and presentation of joking routines to audiences. Female comics must have discovered during the development of their comedy skills that audiences responded more favorably when they put themselves down than when they made others the butts of their jokes. This is consistent with the findings just discussed, because both men and women in the audience should find humor in the victimizing of women.

---

[12]LEVINE, J. B. The feminine routine. *Journal of Communication*, 1976, 26, 173–175.

The Effect of the Feminist Movement

The fact that a few studies show that women enjoy antimale jokes may reflect the changing attitudes, values, and beliefs of women about themselves. The findings obtained in any particular study may depend on the extent to which females in the sample are satisfied or dissatisfied with the traditional female role in society. The importance of this dimension may be seen in a study that found that women who expressed strong support for the movement for sexual equality were more likely to enjoy male-disparaging than female-disparaging jokes.[13] Thus, more-liberated women respond to jokes just as males do. Feminists not only failed to see much humor in jokes disparaging women, but also indicated that their support for the movement was actually strengthened by such jokes.[14] It is also interesting to note that males who indicated strong beliefs in male supremacy were especially likely to show the usual pattern of enjoyment of antifemale jokes.

Clearly, then, a preference for self-disparaging forms of humor is not characteristic of a generalized female sense of humor. It may, however, be characteristic of individuals who occupy (or feel they they occupy) lower-status positions in society. As noted earlier, job status has a definite bearing on whether one puts oneself or others down in joking. Women may develop a generally lower sense of self-regard during the development of traditional female sex-role values (at least lower than that of males), such that finding themselves put down in humor is not that different from the image they already have of themselves. Once the initial stages of dissatisfaction with the traditional female role begin, and a sense of personal pride and self-esteem is increasingly fostered, the depreciation of women in jokes or any other context may become increasingly unacceptable.

In the 1960s and early 1970s, the accusation was frequently heard that women were losing their sense of humor (see the cover of *Ms* magazine, November, 1973). In retrospect, we can now see that, although it was changing, it was not disappearing. Women

---

[13]CHAPMAN and GADFIELD, Is sexual humor sexist? GROTE, B., and CVETKOVITCH, G. Humor appreciation and issue involvement. *Psychonomic Science*, 1972, 27, 199–200. LaFAVE, Humor judgments and reference group and identification classes.

[14]GROTE and CVETKOVITCH, Humor appreciation and issue involvement.

were simply coming to be more like men in their sense of humor. This change seems to be a healthy one, because it parallels a desire to eliminate perceived inequities. But if the enjoyment of humor at one's own expense is considered crucial to a healthy sense of humor, this interpretation becomes questionable. Women do seem to lose their capacity to laugh at themselves as they become more deeply involved in the feminist movement. And yet their sense of humor is approaching that of males in this respect. Does this mean that males do not have a healthy sense of humor?

The weakness of this line of reasoning may be seen in the fact that the humor of any hostile joke depends on who tells the joke and under what circumstances. Thus, a female-disparaging joke will be funnier to women if it is told by another woman than if a man tells it. Similarly, the joke should be funnier to women if it is told by either a man or woman known to support the feminist movement than if it is told by a woman known to be against the movement. In each case, the latter would be more likely to meet with a hostile response, because the joke would be interpreted as a genuine reflection of attitudes toward women. In short, the joke would be interpreted as a hostile attack on women.

Throughout this book frame of mind has been emphasized as an important influence on whether any joke is found to be funny. In order to fully appreciate humor, we must be in a playful frame of mind that is receptive to the consideration of incongruities or inequities in life. In many cases, comical incongruities can be imposed on otherwise serious or unhappy conditions. It is the ability to step beyond the broader set of unfortunate conditions of the real world into a momentary playful contemplation of humorous incongruities that is really at the heart of the conception of sense of humor referred to earlier. A person with a good sense of humor presumably does not let the desperateness of his or her situation prevent the enjoyment of potentially comical events when they occur. In order to maintain this kind of frame of mind, and appreciate the humor of a joke even if one's own sex is put down, a woman must feel confident that the joke is, in fact, only meant in a playful or joking sense. If the joke is perceived to be merely a vehicle for expressing the joker's real sentiments about women, it would be surprising if the woman hearing the joke disregarded this and responded *as if* it were meant playfully. Yet it may be that this is exactly what women have traditionally done.

As noted in Chapter 6, women seem to be generally more sensitive to the reactions of others than are men. Laughter at others' jokes (even when they aren't very funny) is one means of assuring continued liking and acceptance by others, and women may have acquired the tendency to be responders to the humor of others (especially that initiated by men) partly for this reason. We all feel pleased when others laugh at our jokes, and we are likely to come to like those who share their laughter with us. In short, women may use laughter as a "social lubricant" more than men do. Along these lines, it has been suggested that women may laugh at events or jokes they really don't find very funny simply in order to present a "charming" personality in public.[15] More liberated women are likely to find this practice distasteful and to laugh only if they find the joke funny. If this were the case, it would help account for the belief that women lose their sense of humor as they progressively reject traditional female attitudes and values. This trend actually suggests that we will now be able to get a better glimpse of the female sense of humor. Stripped of the sense of necessity to engage in artificial laughter, women may now be free at last to discover and develop their own sense of humor.

Sex Differences in Children

Joking and Clowning

The limited evidence on sex differences in humor at different ages suggests that boys and girls do not differ in their attempts at verbal humor during the preschool years.[16] By age six, though, the typical pattern for adults begins to appear: that is, by the beginning of the elementary-school years, boys show more silly rhyming, naughty words, (playful) untrue or incongruous statements, and so forth. It is interesting to note that this is precisely the age at which children first begin to become fascinated by word-play jokes. As noted in Chapter 4, it is only at age six or

---

[15]WEISSTEIN, N. Why we aren't laughing . . . anymore. *Ms* magazine, November, 1973.

[16]McGHEE, P. E. Sex differences in children's humor. *Journal of Communication*, 1976, 26, 176–189.

seven that children become intellectually capable of keeping both meanings of a double entendre in mind at the same time—a necessary prerequisite for understanding any word-play joke. Once they acquire this new level of understanding, boys seem to become more preoccupied with endless joke-telling and joke-hearing sessions than do girls. Both sexes show an increased enjoyment of jokes and riddles during the years between six and ten or so, but they have already begun to show the pattern of sex differences in joke-telling that characterizes adults.

The humor of the preschooler was described in Chapter 4 as being based mainly on the physical or perceptual properties of objects and events. Early humor also commonly consists of the child doing (rather than saying) something that is funny. Boys make more frequent behavioral attempts at humor than do girls as early as the preschool period. During nursery-school play, boys are more likely than girls to clown around, act silly, make faces, and so forth. Whatever the factors are that lead to sex typing in humor, then, they must be operating as early as age three. It is not known at this time whether the increased joking and clowning eventually shown by boys is due to more frequent attempts at humor by boys as they get older, less frequent attempts by girls, or a combination of the two. Because boys are generally positively reinforced for most forms of assertive behavior, whereas girls tend to be negatively reinforced for such behavior, it is likely that girls reduce their joking activities at the same time that boys begin to increase theirs. It may also be, however, that as girls get older they simply restrict their clowning and joking activities to situations in which only girls are present. Boys, on the other hand, may feel free to initiate humor in the presence of either sex.

The fact that boys tell jokes and riddles and clown around more than girls does not necessarily mean that boys' humor is more creative than that of girls. During the joke-telling or riddle-telling phase of the early grade-school years, most children simply repeat verbatim the jokes that they have heard from other children. Many jokes and riddles are handed down generation after generation in this fashion. The level of creativity shown when children make up their own humor probably depends on general differences in creativity, rather than differences in experience at repeating memorized jokes. The greater backlog of experience with humor does, however, enable boys to tell a greater number of jokes than girls when asked to tell their favorite jokes.[17] When asked to create their own funny answers to "elephant joke" riddles (based on exaggeration or absurdity), boys were also more successful than girls at coming up with a joking answer.[18] They were also better at making a general statement about what is required to make an answer to such riddles funny. This means that boys are not simply parroting answers to memorized riddles without extracting some generalized understanding of them. It was undoubtedly this increased awareness of the requirements for a joking answer that enabled them to make up more new joking answers of their own.

Humor Appreciation

It is difficult to be certain that preschoolers' laughter during play means that something is funny. Like adults, children may laugh for reasons that have nothing to do with humor. For example, children commonly laugh during ongoing play simply because of the excitement of the moment, and because they are having a good time. Because most studies of preschoolers' humor take place in the context of spontaneous play in naturalistic situations (usually a nursery school), humorous and nonhumorous forms of laughter tend to get lumped together in one category. So studies of this age group should probably be considered studies of laughter—not humor.

The same pattern found for initiated humor is found for laughter. Boys and girls show equal amounts of laughter during nursery-school free play,[19] but boys begin to show more laughter than girls during social play after age six.[20] The picture for reactions to humor is more complicated than that for humor initiation, however, in that girls begin to smile more than boys at about the same age that boys begin to laugh more.[21] One study,

---

[17]YORUKOGLU, A. Children's favorite jokes and their relation to emotional conflicts. *Journal of Child Psychiatry*, 1974, 45, 677–690.

[18]McGHEE, P. E. Development of children's ability to create the joking relationship. *Child Development*, 1974, 45, 552–556.

[19]BRACKETT, C. W. Laughing and crying of preschool children. *Journal of Experimental Education*, 1933, 2, 119–126. McGHEE, Sex differences in children's humor.

[20]Ibid.

[21]CHAPMAN, A. J. Some aspects of the social facilitation of "humorous laughter" in children. Unpublished doctoral dissertation, University of Leichester, 1972.

completed nearly fifty years ago, found more smiling in girls than boys as early as the preschool years.[22] The researchers who completed this study argued that exaggerated laughter was not considered "ladylike" and that girls began to react to social pressures to inhibit laughter as early as four years of age. It is difficult to extend this interpretation to the more liberated society of today, but a later section in this chapter will demonstrate that this same pattern of sex differences continues to exist.

By the time children reach school age, it is possible to present preselected cartoons, jokes, and stories to them and determine their level of comprehension and appreciation by asking them to rate their funniness or explain why they are funny. Using this approach, numerous studies have documented the fact that boys and girls show similar levels of both comprehension[23] and appreciation[24] of most forms of humor. If girls do have less experience with humor, then, it does not seem to have any effect on either their comprehension or their appreciation of the humor in most cartoons or jokes designed for children. In the only exception to this pattern, boys are generally more appreciative of hostile forms of humor than are girls (see following section). Barring

---

[22]JUSTIN, F. A genetic study of laughter provoking stimuli. *Child Development*, 1932, 3, 114–136.

[23]BRODZINSKY, D. M. Conceptual tempo as an individual difference variable in children's humour development. In A. J. Chapman and H. C. Foot (Eds.), *It's a funny thing, humour.* Oxford, England: Pergamon, 1977. MAW, W. H., and MAW, E. W. Differences between high- and low-curiosity fifth-grade children in their recognition of verbal absurdities. *Journal of Educational Psychology*, 1972, 63, 558–562. PRENTICE, N. M. and FATHMAN, R. E. Joking riddles: A developmental index of children's humor. *Developmental Psychology*, 1975, 11, 210–216. ZIGLER, E., LEVINE, J., and GOULD, L. Cognitive processes in the development of children's appreciation of humor. *Child Development*, 1966, 37, 507–518. ZIGLER, E., LEVINE, J., and GOULD, L. Cognitive challenge as a factor in children's humor appreciation. *Journal of Personality and Social Psychology*, 1967, 6, 332–336.

[24]BRODZINSKY, Conceptual tempo as an individual difference variable in children's humour development. PRENTICE and FATHMAN, Joking riddles. ROTHBART, M. K. Incongruity, problem-solving and laughter. In A. J. Chapman and H. C. Foot (Eds.), *Humour and laughter: Theory, research and applications.* London: Wiley, 1976. SHULTZ, T. R. The role of incongruity and resolution in children's appreciation of cartoon humor. *Journal of Experimental Child Psychology*, 1972, 13, 456–477. SHULTZ, T. R. Development of the appreciation of riddles. *Child Development*, 1974, 45, 100–105. SHULTZ, T. R., and HORIBE, F. Development of the appreciation of verbal jokes. *Developmental Psychology*, 1974, 10, 13–20. ZIGLER, LEVINE, and GOULD, Cognitive processes and children's appreciation of humor. ZIGLER, LEVINE, and GOULD, Cognitive challenge and children's humor appreciation.

the presence of aggressive themes in the joke or cartoon, then, when boys and girls are rated differently for laughter, smiling, or funniness, this difference must be due to factors not specifically related to the humor stimulus itself. We shall see shortly that the social circumstances of the humorous event may be especially important in this respect.

Sexual and Aggressive Humor   We continue to know little about the development of sexual humor in children. Bathroom jokes begin to be replaced by sexual jokes by the early elementary-school years, but this aspect of development has simply not been studied. This is no doubt due to the hesitance of researchers to present sexual jokes or cartoons to children. However, there is generally no objection raised to presenting aggressive materials to children in our society; so our understanding of developmental trends in hostile forms of humor has progressed more rapidly. Consistent with the findings for adults, boys' humor initiated during spontaneous play tends to be more hostile than that of girls, although it is not clear whether this pattern first appears at the preschool level[25] or about the first grade.[26] Moreover, if children are asked to make a direct choice between aggressive cartoons and cartoons based on a nonsensical incongruity, boys are more likely to choose the aggressive cartoon as the funnier one as early as age four or five.[27] The pervasiveness of hostility in boys' humor can be seen, then, in the kind of humor they are most responsive to, as well as in the humor they initiate.

Social Influences   Girls and women have been found to have a generally higher need for social approval than boys and men.[28] From the early elementary-school years on, then, females' behavior should be more likely than that of males to be directed toward either the gaining of approval or the avoidance of disapproval. Because laughing at someone's joke is a socially appropriate response and should generate a positive reaction from the person telling the joke, reactions to humor should relate positively to the tendency to give socially desirable responses (often used as an index of strength of the need for social approval). The only investigation that considered this relationship found a stronger correlation among girls than among boys between amount of laughter at cartoons and the tendency to behave in socially desirable ways.[29] These findings suggest that girls are more likely than boys to show exaggerated laughter because it is the kind of behavior called for in the current social situation. Boys with higher concerns about behaving in socially appropriate ways may show exaggerations of other forms of behavior (perhaps including the initiation of joking), but they do not exaggerate their laughter more than other boys.

Tony Chapman and his associates at the University of Wales have completed a series of studies both in naturalistic situations and in the laboratory in an effort to determine the effect of differ-

---

[25]GROCH, A. Joking and appreciation of humor in nursery school children. *Child Development*, 1974, 45, 1098–1102.

[26]McGHEE, Sex differences in children's humor.

[27]KING, P. V., and KING, J. E. A children's humor test. *Psychological Reports*, 1973, 33, 632.

[28]CRANDALL, V. C., CRANDALL, V. J., and KATKOVSKY, W. A children's social desirability questionnaire. *Journal of Consulting Psychology*, 1965, 29, 27–36.

[29]McGHEE, P. E. Unpublished data.

ent social conditions on children's smiling and laughter at humorous events (see Chapter 6). In their laboratory studies, seven- and eight-year-olds typically listened to humorous tapes or watched film cartoons alone, in pairs, or in triads, of either the same or the opposite sex. In these situations, girls generally smiled and looked at their companions more than boys did.[30] When placed in a cartoon-viewing room with a friend, girls increased their smiling, whereas boys increased their laughter.[31] Boys and girls also responded differently when in mixed-sex groups. In this situation, girls reciprocated boys' laughter more often than boys reciprocated girls' laughter. Boys also tended to laugh the same amount regardless of whether they were with a boy or a girl. Girls, on the other hand, both smiled and laughed more with boys than with girls.[32]

It seems, then, that girls are generally more prone to smiling whereas boys laugh more. When the social situation calls for laughter, though, girls do show increased laughter with their smiling, especially if boys are present. Chapman and his associates felt that the fact that girls looked more at their companions in addition to smiling more than boys suggested that girls (at least seven- and eight-year-olds) are more concerned than boys with "sharing the prevailing social situation." In their view, boys tend to respond more to the cartoons or jokes themselves, whereas girls are more prone to being influenced by the social circumstances. This is consistent with the finding that girls have a stronger need for approval than do boys, and this may lead them to be more likely to give the reaction that seems appropriate at the time.

Canned Laughter   An interesting pattern of sex differences in social influences upon humor has also been obtained in connec-

[30]SMITH, J. R., FOOT, H. C., and CHAPMAN, A. J. Nonverbal communication among friends and strangers sharing humour. In A. J. Chapman and H. C. Foot (Eds.), *It's a funny thing, humour.* Oxford, England: Pergamon, 1977.

[31]FOOT, H. C., SMITH, J. R., and CHAPMAN, A. J. Sex differences in children's responses to humour. In A. J. Chapman and H. C. Foot (Eds.), *It's a funny thing, humour.* Oxford, England: Pergamon, 1977.

[32]FOOT, H. C., and CHAPMAN, A. J. The social responsiveness of young children in humorous situations. In A. J. Chapman and H. C. Foot (Eds.), *Humour and laughter: Theory, research and application.* London: Wiley, 1976.

tion with the addition of canned laughter to film comedies. Both male and female tenth-graders showed increased laughter at a slapstick film when a laugh track was added.[33] When asked to rate the film for its funniness afterward, however, only females judged the film to be funnier with than without a laugh track. The film was also shown to children between grades one and five; they were asked to either laugh a lot at the film or not laugh at all, and also subsequently rated it for funniness. Again, both sexes laughed and smiled more in the laughter-facilitation condition, but only girls also rated the film funnier when they laughed at it more. In both situations, then, the intellectual evaluation of the film and overt expressions of mirth (artificially elevated) were more independent among boys than among girls. Boys were more likely to discount the canned laughter or their own laughter in making judgments about the funniness of the film, whereas girls' judgments seemed to be more heavily influenced by how much they themselves laughed. Moreover, this effect was strongest for girls who were initially less expressive. These findings are surprising, because the boys and girls were equally aware that their own laughter was artificially boosted. Why, then, was it only the boys who seemed to take this into consideration when judging the film's funniness? The experimenters who completed these studies suggested that the findings result from the fact that females generally take their own expressive reactions into account in making judgments about events, whereas males are more likely to keep their expressive reactions independent of intellectual judgments.

The generality of these findings was demonstrated in a series of studies by Howard Leventhal and his associates using college students instead of children. They, too, found that both men and women laughed more at cartoons accompanied by audience laughter, but only women also rated them funnier when audience laughter was included than when it was not.[34] Women also both laughed more and rated cartoons funnier at an end-of-the semester beer party than in a laboratory, whereas men laughed more at

---

[33]LEVENTHAL, H., and MACE, W. The effect of laughter on evaluation of a slapstick movie. *Journal of Personality*, 1970, 38, 16–30.

[34]CUPCHIK, G. C., and LEVENTHAL, H. Consistency between expressive behavior and the evaluation of humorous stimuli: The role of sex and self-observation. *Journal of Personality and Social Psychology*, 1974, 30, 429–442.

the cartoons at the party without rating them funnier.[35] Again, males seemed to be responding more to the objective qualities of the humor, whereas females seemed to be basing their judgments on their own elevated mirth. This interpretation is strengthened by the fact that women can base their judgments more exclusively on objective criteria if instructed to do so.[36] When both sexes were asked to pay careful attention to both the quality of the cartoon and the nature of the audience reaction when forming their own judgments about funniness, the two sexes gave comparable funniness ratings. Without these instructions, women again gave higher funniness ratings when the audience reaction was strong and enhanced their own expressiveness.

It was concluded earlier that females are generally more sensitive than males to the social opinions and reactions of others. It might be argued that this sensitivity is sufficient to lead females to genuinely change their views of the funniness of a film when they see others laughing at it. However, Leventhal and his co-workers favor the view that the important factor is whether a person's expressive reaction is heightened by watching the film—not whether she witnesses laughter or other social reactions by others. Their underlying explanation for the importance of this factor is a most intriguing one.

Several investigators have emphasized that the two cerebral hemispheres process information in different ways. The right hemisphere, characterized as holistic, processes information emotionally, whereas the left hemisphere processes information objectively.[37] In Leventhal's view, the greater reliance of females on emotional or holistic cues in forming judgments indicates that

---

[35]LEVENTHAL, H., and CUPCHIK, G. C. The informational and facilitative effects of an audience upon expression and evaluation of humorous stimuli. *Journal of Experimental Social Psychology*, 1975, 11, 363–380.

[36]PANAGIS, D. H., LEVENTHAL, H., and CAPUTO, G. C. Sex differences in integrating focal and contextual cues. Unpublished manuscript, University of Wisconsin, 1975. (Cited by Leventhal, H., and Cupchik, G. C. A process model of humor judgment. *Journal of Communication*, 1976, 26, 190–204.)

[37]BROADBENT, D. C. *Decision and stress.* London: Academic Press, 1971. CARMON, A., and NACHSON, I. Ear asymmetry in perception of emotional nonverbal stimuli. *Acta Psychologica*, 1973, 37, 351–357. HAGGARD, M. P., and PARKINSON, A. M. Stimulus and task factors as determinants of ear advantages. *Quarterly Journal of Experimental Psychology*, 1971, 23, 168–177. KIMURA, D. The asymmetry of the human brain. *Scientific American*, 1973, 228, 70–80.

their decisions must be more strongly influenced by the right hemisphere. Support for this view was obtained by feeding the sound track (including audience laughter) or cartoons into either the left ear (right hemisphere) or right ear (left hemisphere).[38] Amazingly, females rated the cartoons funnier when heard through the left ear, whereas males rated them funnier when heard through the right ear. Even more astounding was the fact that this effect was the greatest among women with a stronger identification with the traditional female sex role. If subsequent research confirms the existence of general differences in hemisphere dominance among females and males, we will have arrived at a satisfactory explanation for many of the sex differences in the social aspects of humor that have been studied. We will still have the task, however, of sorting out the extent to which biological and early learning factors contribute to the development of such hemispheric dominances. A biological basis for sex differences in sense of humor will have to be acknowledged if sex differences in hemispheric domination prove to have a biological origin.

Early Developmental Precursors and Influences

The relationship between different aspects of early child and maternal behavior and subsequent joking, clowning, and laughter in the child was discussed earlier. Although these developmental antecedents were, on the whole, very similar for males and females, evidence of several important sex differences was also obtained. The following discussion deals with only those antecedents that differ significantly for the two sexes.

Precursors in the Child's Own Behavior The reader will recall from Chapter 7 that, in the longitudinal study of humor development completed by the author, four observational ratings were made of the amount of humor-related behavior engaged in by a group of six- to eleven-year-olds during spontaneous play activities at a two-week summer day camp.[39] These humor mea-

---

[38]Caputo, G. C., and Leventhal, H. Sex differences in lateralization effects for holistic-subjective processing. Unpublished manuscript, University of Wisconsin, 1975. (Cited by Leventhal and Cupchik, A process model of humor judgment.)

[39]McGhee, Sex differences in children's humor.

sures included: (1) frequency of behavioral attempts to initiate humor, (2) frequency of verbal attempts to initiate humor, (3) amount of laughter, and (4) degree of hostility evident in the child's laughter or humor. Ratings of nineteen antecedent child behaviors (obtained regularly between age three and the current day-camp session) were correlated with these four humor measures.

Sex differences in antecedents in children's own prior behavior were not manifested until after age six. There were numerous precursors in a child's behavior during the preschool years (see Chapter 7), but they were of a broad developmental nature, holding equally for both boys and girls. The most striking cluster of sex differences in humor predicted from the child's prior behavior after age six centered on the relationship between humor and measures of social assertiveness and power. It was suggested in Chapter 6 that the initiation of humor in most social situations serves as a means of gaining and holding control over the nature of the ongoing social interaction: that is, the joker, wit, or clown is typically a dominating social force who holds considerable social power. Consistent with this view, as noted in Chapter 7, children who generally initiated more humor or who responded more to it had early histories of dominance over their peers and were physically and verbally aggressive. Although this pattern of antecedents was obtained for both sexes, the correlations were generally significantly higher for girls than for boys. So it is the dominating and aggressive girl who seems to be especially drawn to clowning and other forms of humor. Such girls were also more likely to eventually develop high levels of hostility in laughter and humor.

It was also noted in the last chapter that this general pattern of antecedents is not surprising, because humor provides a socially acceptable (even rewarded) means of rechanneling hostile feelings or impulses.[40] The child who directly vents hostile feelings while interacting with peers is likely to learn that, although aggression is rewarding in some respects, it also creates problems in the cultivation and maintenance of friendships. Although some children retain their initial aggressiveness into adulthood, others learn to channel it into assertive behavior in sports, school work,

---

[40]FREUD, S. *Jokes and their relation to the unconscious.* New York: Norton, 1960.

or other areas of skill development. Humor, though, may provide the best means of expressing aggressive tendencies, because it is almost universally responded to favorably in social situations. Also, and perhaps most important, if the hostile nature of a child's clowning or joking becomes apparent at some point, that child can always claim to be only joking or playing around. With this means of expression of aggression, then, there is always an "out" that enables the child to deny any hostile intent.

The use of humor as an outlet for aggressive tendencies and a desire to dominate others may be especially important for girls, given that dominance and aggression are incompatible with the traditional female sex role. As girls become increasingly aware during the elementary-school years that dominance and aggression are more acceptable for males than females, they must learn to either inhibit these qualities or express them in a more socially appropriate fashion. Humor provides an ideal means of maintaining these qualities in a disguised way. Even though initiating humor seems to be more strongly linked to the male than the female sex role, this certainly constitutes less of an intrusion of traditional masculinity than most direct expressions of dominance and aggression. This may account for the fact that, although this pattern of antecedents held for both sexes, it was stronger for girls' than for boys' subsequent behavioral attempts at humor. It also helps explain why these early behaviors predicted amount of hostility in a child's humor more strongly for girls than for boys.

As noted earlier, girls have a generally stronger concern than boys about gaining approval and behaving in socially appropriate ways. If a concern about others' reactions to their behavior plays an important role in girls' rechanneling of physical and social assertiveness into humor, there should be evidence of early sensitivity to the reactions of other people. This evidence was obtained for three different measures of early behavior, each of which indicates a concern about gaining attention or positive reactions from adults: (1) seeking instrumental help (on tasks) from adults, (2) seeking affection and emotional support from adults, and (3) seeking recognition for achievement from adults. These measures were generally positively related to the different humor measures for both sexes but were more strongly related for girls with respect to both behavioral attempts to initiate humor and amount of hostility shown in humor. So girls who subsequently did more clowning and acting silly, and who were more hostile in all aspects of their humor, were more likely than boys to have had an early history of concern about obtaining adult attention and affection. These developmental findings add further support to the view that the humor-related behavior of females is more susceptible to social influence than that of males.

It was noted in the last chapter that the exertion of large amounts of effort in an attempt to master fine motor skills (such as crafts, puzzles, sewing, block building, woodworking, painting, etc.) is incompatible with the development of a sense of humor: that is, children who are very persistent and work hard at perfecting skills and producing a high-quality product subsequently make fewer attempts to initiate humor and laugh less than their less achievement-oriented peers. It was suggested that the significance of this finding may lie in the more serious frame of mind that usually accompanies persistence in achievement tasks. Because the initiation or appreciation of humor requires a playful frame of mind, a strong achievement orientation (at least in the areas of intellectual and fine motor skills) may be incompatible with the full development of a child's sense of humor. Evidence has been obtained that suggests that this incompatibility is greater for girls than for boys. Girls who were more persistent and exerted more effort in fine motor and intellectual tasks were more likely than boys exhibiting the same behavior to show restricted amounts of both laughter and verbal joking. It is difficult to explain this sex difference, because a more serious task-oriented frame of mind should be equally disruptive of humor and laughter for both sexes. It is worth noting, however, that the same types of achievement effort in gross motor activities (such as climbing, jumping, baseball, running, etc.) are positively related to humor development for both sexes. Further research will be required to clarify the significance of these findings.

A puzzling pattern of sex differences was also obtained for predictions from the amount of restless activity shown by children in earlier years. Restlessness among girls was not related to any of the measures of humor some years later. Among boys, it was positively related to the amount of laughter shown and frequency of verbal attempts to initiate humor but negatively related to the hostility of the child's humor. Inactive boys, then, subsequently showed the most hostility in their humor, whereas more active boys showed little hostility—even though they exhibited large amounts of laughter and joking. This suggests that the high levels of activity of the restless boys gave them an outlet for aggression that the inactive boys lacked. Without such a physical outlet, their aggression may have been channeled into humor. The fact that boys showing high levels of hostility in their humor also tended to have poor body coordination may have led them to avoid active engagement in social activities requiring physical skill. We have no explanation for why these factors seem to be important for boys' humor development, but not that of girls.

Parental Influences   Does the budding humorist come from a family in which humor is prominant in some way? Do parents have any influence at all on a child's humor, or are children simply "born with it?" As noted in the last chapter, virtually nothing is known about the influence of parents on the humor development of their children. The longitudinal study that has been discussed in detail demonstrated that mothers' early joking is not related to the humor development of either boys or girls.[41] Mothers who did more joking in various ways with their children did not have more humor-oriented sons or daughters. These findings cannot be safely extended to fathers, though, because, as already noted, joking forms of behavior are more typical of males than females. If only one parent is the strong humor model for a child, it is likely to be the father. But we know only that men initiate more joking behavior than women among other adults. We will have to determine in future research whether men who are humor initiators when with adults also joke and clown with their children. If parents provide humor models for their children consistent with their behavior in other situations, girls should acquire from mothers the habit of reacting to humor without initiating it too frequently, whereas boys should acquire from fathers the pattern of joking and clowning around. If a girl identifies strongly with a regularly clowning or joking father, however, she might also pick up the masculine pattern of initiating humor.

One aspect of parental behavior that does seem to have a

---

[41]McGhee, Sex differences in children's humor.

differential effect on the humor development of boys and girls concerns the amount of emotional conflict in the home. Poor home adjustment in the first three years was related to increased attempts to initiate humor both verbally and behaviorally to a greater extent among girls than among boys.[42] Thus, it is girls who grow up in homes filled with dissention and conflict during their earliest years who are especially likely to try to be funny during later childhood. This supports the psychoanalytic view of humor as a means of coping with stress and conflict (see Chapters 1, 7, and 9). Such girls may have been drawn to humor because it took their minds off their problems, led to positive reactions from parents, or was simply enjoyable in its own right. Once again, though, it is not clear why girls coming from such homes should be more likely than boys coming from comparable homes to adopt humor as a means of adjusting to their difficult circumstances.

Mass Media Influences   Television comedy may make an important contribution to the establishment of sex-typed behavior in the area of humor. It has become apparent in the past two decades that the observation of live or film models is an effective means of learning by children.[43] Because most children spend several hours each day watching television, the patterns of behavior viewed should have some effect on their own behavior and development. Our specific concern here is whether the patterns of humor depicted on television influence children's own humor development.

It is now well documented that both children's and adults' television programs are highly stereotyped in their depiction of sex-role behavior.[44] Also children who are heavy television viewers are more aware of these stereotypes than are those who sel-

[42]Ibid.

[43]BANDURA, A. Social-learning theory of identificatory processes. In D. A. Goslin (Ed.), *Handbook of socialization theory and research*. Chicago: Rand McNally, 1969. MISCHEL, W. Sex-typing and socialization. In P. H. Mussen (Ed.), *Carmichael's manual of child psychology*. Vol. 2. New York: Wiley, 1970.

[44]COURTNEY, A. D., and WHIPPLE, T. E. Women in TV commercials. *Journal of Communication*, 1974, 24, 110–118. STERNGLANZ, S. H., and SERBIN, L. A. Sex role stereotyping in children's television programs. *Developmental Psychology*, 1974, 10, 710–715. TEDESCO, N. S. Patterns in prime time. *Journal of Communication*, 24, 55–64.

dom watch.[45] If initiating humor is more strongly identified with
the male sex role and reacting to humor is more consistent with
the female sex role, as has been suggested, then television comedy
programs undoubtedly reflect these patterns in their humor. Unfortunately, the extent of stereotyping along these lines has not
been investigated by those studying the pervasiveness of sex-role
stereotypes in television broadcasting. In the only study having
some bearing on this issue, males on prime-time television initiated disparaging forms of humor more often than females did.[46]
An informal observation of a broad range of television humor
suggests that investigations of sex-typed behavior in the area of
humor will show that the amount of humor of all kinds initiated
by males far surpasses that initiated by females. Assuming that
this finding is borne out, there is every reason to believe that
children watching hour after hour of males initiating and females
responding to humor will acquire the attitude that this differ-
entiation is an appropriate one for males and females generally:
that is, because it has been demonstrated that children learn sex-
role stereotypes in connection with other areas of behavior by
watching television, it would be most surprising if they did not
learn them with respect to humor.

Although male performers on television do seem to initiate
humor more frequently than female performers, there are some
notable exceptions. The tradition of a few female comics on television was started by Lucille Ball ("I Love Lucy") and has been
continued more recently by Mary Tyler Moore, Carol Burnett,
"Maude", "Laverne and Shirley", and others. A recent analysis
of television situation comedies indicated that the proliferation
of sitcoms (actually "kidcoms"), which started in the late 1970s,
will be close to the saturation point by the beginning of the
1980s.[47] Many of the new comedy shows include a female performer as either the primary or the secondary comic in the pro-

---

[45]FRUEH, T., and McGHEE, P. E. Traditional sex role development and amount of
time spent watching television. *Developmental Psychology*, 1975, 11, 109. McGHEE,
P. E., and FRUEH, T. Television viewing and the learning of sex role stereotypes.
Sex Roles, in press.

[46]STOCKING, S. H., SAPOLSKY, B., and ZILLMAN, D. Is there sex discrimination in
humor on prime time television? *Journal of Broadcasting*, 1977, 21:4, 447–457.

[47]WATERS, H. F., KASINDORF, M., HUCK, J., COPELAND, J. B., and WILSON, C. H. TV
comedy: What it's teaching the kids. *Newsweek*, May 7, 1979, pp. 64–72.

gram. Males probably still outnumber females as possible models of humor for children, but there may now be enough funny female performers on television that girls are learning that joking or clowning is not incompatible with the female sex role. If this is the case, the new popularity of comedy programs (nine out of Nielson's Top Ten shows are situation comedies at the time of this writing) may serve to foster humor development in females, rather than interfere with it.

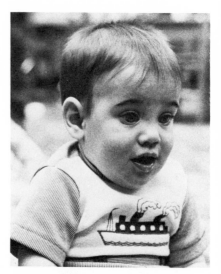
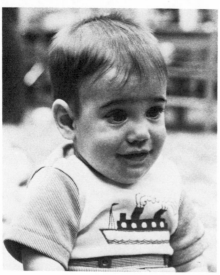

9 Laughter, Humor, and Mental Health

The possession of a good sense of humor is commonly assumed to be necessary for good mental health. We tend to regard people who show little laughter or humor as being poorly adjusted, but we also question the adjustment of those who laugh indiscriminately or in inappropriate situations. This belief in humor's importance for good mental health seems to have resulted from the common experience of most people that humor is often capable of elevating us from the grips of depression or other negative mental states. Both as a nation and as individuals, we often seek out comedy or some other form of "escape" when forced to endure hard times. Millions of dollars are spent each year in support of humor through the mass media, and it is often argued that the real value of situation comedies during prime-time television lies in their therapeutic potential. For the person who must work all day at a hated job, or who must continually cope with stress and conflict on the job, the simplistic humor of situation comedies and comedy variety programs may play an important role in dismissing the problems of the day. In this chapter, the evidence in support of this function of humor will be discussed, and particular attention will be given to humor's capacity to promote healthy adjustment in children.

Humor as a Coping Mechanism ?

It is generally assumed that if humor does promote good mental health, it does so by enabling us to cope with sources of conflict and distress. Although some children have more difficult childhoods than others, the process of growing up entails a certain amount of stress for all children. Thus, we all have a poten-

227

tial need for the therapeutic properties of humor. It is difficult to determine the origins of the notion that humor can ease psychological pain, but the strongest influence on contemporary thinking along these lines clearly stems from the writings of Freud.[1]

Sex and Aggression

According to Freud, sexual and aggressive impulses are sources of conflict for all children, because society only permits their direct expression under certain limited circumstances. Generally speaking, children must learn to curb these impulses as part of the socialization process. Because it would be very unhealthy for children to simply inhibit or repress these impulses, they must learn how to express them in a socially acceptable manner. As noted earlier, Freud considered humor (actually, wit) to serve precisely this function; it is a basic psychological mechanism for reducing pent-up sexual and aggressive impulses. Humor is ideal for this purpose because it is not only socially acceptable, but actually welcomed and rewarded by both children and adults. If a joke goes too far and becomes overtly sexual or aggressive, a child can always reduce its offensiveness by claiming that he or she was only joking. We have seen that as children approach the elementary-school years, they begin to recognize the need to disguise the sexual, aggressive, or otherwise offensive nature of their jokes; that is, they see the need for a joke facade.[2]

The importance of this outlet for sexual and aggressive "energy" may be seen in the increased intensity of laughter at sexual and aggressive jokes, relative to jokes based solely on incongruous relationships lacking such emotionally sensitive themes. According to Freud, laughter provides a release of the psychic energy previously used to block expression of socially or personally unacceptable impulses. The important question is what would happen to this energy or tension if it were not released through humor? Although some people would probably be successful in keeping their sexual and aggressive impulses repressed or otherwise under control without humor, others might express these impulses directly in their behavior. It seems safe to

[1]FREUD, S. *Jokes and their relation to the unconscious.* New York: Norton, 1960.
[2]WOLFENSTEIN, M. *Children's humor.* Glencoe, Illinois: Free Press, 1954.

argue that either of these extremes would not be conducive to healthy adjustment (although the latter should promote good mental health as long as appropriate circumstances for such direct expression are sought out). If laughter does have this cathartic function, then, children who develop laughter and humor as a means of expressing unacceptable impulses should be better adjusted than children who have equally strong impulses, but do not use humor and laughter regularly as a release mechanism.

Anxiety

Psychoanalytic writers have long stressed that humor also facilitates healthy adjustment by helping children cope with anxiety.[3] All children confront sources of anxiety and distress during childhood, and many of their jokes and riddles deal with tasks or conflicts that they are trying to master or have recently mastered. Martha Wolfenstein has argued that, for many children, laughter and humor play a central role in the ultimate success of attempts to cope with anxiety and distress.[4] In fact, she feels that the transformation of painful or difficult situations into enjoyable ones is actually the main motivating force behind joking and other forms of humor. This is an extreme position, though, and a difficult one to defend. We have seen that the capacity for humor evolves as a natural outcome of progressive changes in cognitive development. There is an intrinsic source of pleasure in humor, which results simply from the enjoyment of a playful challenge to one's intellect. It has also been noted that there are social sources of pleasure in humor that have nothing to do with either this intrinsic pleasure of intellectual exertion or the kind of pleasure Wolfenstein is talking about. A more plausible interpretation of Wolfenstein's position, then, would be that certain children learn to use humor as a means of reducing anxiety and distress and that this constitutes yet another source of pleasure for them. We cannot deny the reasonableness of the position that substituting laughter and humor for tension and anxiety should be enjoyable and self-reinforcing. There are no grounds, however, for arguing that this

---

[3]Kris, E. Ego development and the comic. *International Journal of Psychoanalysis.* 1938, 19, 77–90. Wolfenstein, *Children's humor.*

[4]Ibid.

is the prime motivating force behind laughter and humor for all—or even most—children. All of these sources of pleasure undoubtedly contribute to the enjoyment of humor in children, although to varying degrees. An extreme reliance on the coping functions of humor is likely only for (some of) those children suffering unusually great amounts of stress during childhood.

Jokes told by children during therapy sessions offer support for the view that humor is often used to help cope with conflict.[5] For example, many of the anxieties felt by children concern parent-child relationships in some way. When children are asked to tell their favorite jokes during therapy, the jokes often center on parent conflicts or other sources of family dissention. One twelve-year-old girl whose father frequently belittled the mother, and became angry and critical over trivial matters, told the following joke:

> A girl asked her father what the word "war" meant. The father began to explain, "Suppose one of our neighboring countries tried to occupy our land. . . ." Right at this moment the mother entered the room and told her father to explain it in as few words as possible. So they got into an argument over how to explain it best. The girl said: "That's enough, now I know what war means!"[6]

It is probably no coincidence that this joke was described as the child's favorite joke, because it captures the kind of conflict commonly witnessed between her parents. The fact that children experiencing such distress are able to joke about it is generally considered by clinicians to be a sign that they have not been totally overcome by the conflict but are making an effort to come to grips with it in some way. The child who responds to such problems by either withdrawing or becoming hostile appears to be less well adjusted than the child who can "laugh it off" through the medium of humor: that is, by "seeing the light side" of the situation.

---

[5]Ibid. YORUKOGLU, A. Children's favorite jokes and their relation to emotional conflicts. *Journal of Child Psychiatry*, 1974, 13, 677–690. ZWERLING, I. The favorite joke in diagnostic and therapeutic interviewing. *Psychoanalytic Quarterly*, 1955, 24, 104–114.

[6]YORUKOGLU, A. Favourite jokes of children and their dynamic relation to intrafamilial conflicts. In A. J. Chapman and H. C. Foot (Eds.), *It's a funny thing, humour*. Oxford, England: Pergamon Press, 1977, p. 408.

Importance of a Playful Frame of Mind   How is humor able to accomplish such a magical conversion of pain into pleasure? One important factor seems to be the substitution of a frame of mind incompatible with anxiety or distress. Getting oneself into a playful frame of mind seems to be especially effective in this regard. It is difficult to be angry, frightened, or depressed if one is genuinely in a playful mood. It is no easy task, however, to establish such a mood in the midst of strong anxiety or conflict. Many of us have had the experience of trying to change a bad mood; although we can go through the motions of laughing or smiling, we have difficulty actually changing our frame of mind. Young children must first realize that laughter and humor can help produce a mood that enables them to forget their troubles, or at least put them sufficiently in the background that they can minimize the feeling of anxiety. Once this is understood, they must have some success in overcoming difficulties with humor. The development of good joking or clowning skills may be especially important in achieving such success. For the child to develop a habit of using humor to help cope with sources of anxiety, humor would probably have to be initiated during the early stages of development of the conflict. If the anxiety or conflict is already well developed or chronic, it may be impossible to establish a genuinely playful frame of mind.

The Role of Mastery   Jacob Levine (among other psychoanalytic writers) has argued that the coping functions of humor may be closely linked to the general pleasure derived from cognitive mastery (see Chapter 2).[7] Following the earlier lead of Robert White and Jean Piaget,[8] he suggested that infants and young children experience a feeling of "effectance" upon gaining a sense of mastery of both the cognitive and interpersonal aspects of their environment. It has already been seen that smiling and laughter are natural, unlearned (although they may be modified by later learn-

---

[7]LEVINE, J. Humour as a form of therapy: Introduction to symposium. In A. J. Chapman and H. C. Foot (Eds.), *It's a funny thing, humour.* Oxford, England: Pergamon Press, 1977.

[8]PIAGET, J. *The origins of intelligence in children.* New York: International Universities Press, 1952. WHITE, R. W. Motivation reconsidered: The concept of competence. *Psychological Review*, 1959, 66, 297–333.

ing) reactions to the enjoyment derived from this mastery. Thus, humor is a form of pleasure closely related to the original pleasure in mastery, and yet different from it. The feeling of effectance results from both the original understanding of some aspect of the environment and from the appreciation of humor based on a violation of that understanding. The incongruity of a humorous situation may produce the pleasure of effectance by both reminding the child of the initial gaining of an understanding of the event and by producing a sense of being very knowledgeable.

Regardless of the nature of the pleasure in incongruity humor, Levine has argued that the relationship between humor and mastery over objects and events in the environment may be duplicated for sources of anxiety and distress.[9] Regardless of how one has gone about overcoming a past source of conflict, a joke that centers on that conflict allows the child to re-experience the pleasure of no longer being troubled by it. In dealing with anxiety, a "gratifying state of effectance" (provided by humor) is substituted for a "painful state of helpelessness." The child who is successful in making such substitutions will presumably be better adjusted than the child who is unable to do so. The ability to establish a playful frame of mind may play a central role in this process.

The most extreme examples of using humor to cope with distress can be found in what is commonly referred to as "gallows humor," as evidenced by the following joke about a man who is about to be shot by a firing squad. When asked if he would like a last cigarette, he refused, saying "No thanks, I'm trying to give up smoking." Laughter has also been noted among individuals about to be shot or burned, apparently in a desperate attempt to master the fear of death. In ritual burnings in India in the past, individuals were expected to laugh as they approached their fiery deaths.[10] In these situations, the individual may not actually be in a playful frame of mind but may be trying to go through the motions of humor in order to prevent being overtaken by the fearfulness of the situation.

---

[9]LEVINE, Humour as therapy.

[10]VICTOROFF, D. New approaches to the psychology of humor. *Impact of Science on Society*, 1969, 19, 291–298.

Laughter and Liberation

Harvey Mindess has recently expanded psychoanalytic views on the coping functions of humor, emphasizing the importance of the liberating qualities of humor generally. In his view, "the most fundamental, most important function of humor is its power to release us from the many inhibitions and restrictions under which we live our daily lives."[11] All of us feel certain pressures to conform our behavior to the expectations held for us by certain subgroups of society. Such conformity robs us of spontaneous and flexible behavior, but humor weakens the bonds of conformity. It is during the preschool years that children first begin to feel pressure from parents, teachers, and others to conform their behavior to particular rules and standards. Although a three-year-old's play tends to be free-flowing and uninhibited, a six-year-old has already begun to have a built-in sense of restricting play along certain rule-bound lines. In virtually every aspect of our lives, we become increasingly automatic or mechanical in our behavior as we get older. This is very stifling, in Mindess's view, and so we need occasional releases from the demands for conformity. Humor is liberating because of its ability to release us from such demands.

Humor functions in the same fashion to give us freedom from morality and feelings of inferiority. From adolescence on, society places strong demands on us for moral behavior, providing both legal and social forms of retaliation for failure to meet such demands. The restraints on sexual and aggressive behavior are especially strong in this respect. In the playful context of the joke, every taboo against hostility and sexuality can be violated, again producing a feeling of liberation. In inferiority,

> the very act of making fun of our inferior position raises us above it. This is true not only of subordinated social status but of all inferiorities of any kind. The laughter with which we mock our weakness asserts that while we suffer them we also transcend them, look down on them from a height, make light of them, and thus live on enjoyably despite them.[12]

---

[11]MINDESS, H. *Laughter and liberation.* Los Angeles: Nash, 1971.
[12]Ibid., p. 48.

Freud,[13] Levine,[14] and other psychoanalysts argued that we also need periodic releases from the obligation to be rational and logical all of the time. Young children easily and frequently move from sense to nonsense, from reality to fantasy. As new achievements in cognitive development permit children to think more logically at about seven years of age, however, they are expected to be more rational. Especially after age ten or eleven, children who have failed to become more rational are thought of as immature and childish. It has been argued throughout this book that children (and adults, presumably) find it intrinsically pleasurable to distort the world as they know it. In the realm of fantasy, they can twist logic and engage in endless strings of nonsense and absurdity. We have seen that the kinds of incongruities or nonsense that are most appreciated become more sophisticated as children's own intellects become more sophisticated, but the enjoyment of the basic nonsensical aspects of humor remains throughout life. In the psychoanalytic view, those adults who show very little initiation of and responsiveness to humor may be the very ones who need it the most. It is these individuals who have become most chained to the social expectations for reasonable behavior and thinking. Because humor is generally responded to favorably by other people, it would seem that individuals who show little humor in their lives have simply gone too far to meet society's demands for rational behavior. Humor for these individuals would free them from their excessive rationality, presumably yielding a better state of mental health in the process.

Do Laughter and Humor Indicate Healthy Adjustment?

If humor does help children release sexual and aggressive impulses in a socially acceptable way, and facilitates attempts to master sources of anxiety or distress, it must be considered to promote good mental health. Similarly, it must make adjustment to the demands for rational, moral, and generally conventional behavior easier by providing periodic freedom from the stifling

---

[13]FREUD, Jokes and the unconscious. LEVINE, Humour as therapy.
[14]Ibid.

restrictiveness of those demands. But does it follow that children or adults who laugh, joke, or clown more are better adjusted than those who demonstrate humor less often? This conclusion is questionable for several reasons. We have seen that the coping functions of humor constitute only one basis for the establishment of frequent laughter and humor in a child's behavior. In many children, the same heightened laughter and clowning or joking occurs simply as a by-product of joyful experiences during play.

Theoretically, we might be able to locate two distinct groups of children, both of whom display high amounts of humor and laughter. One group would come from well-adjusted homes, characterized by minimal conflict or family dissention. The other would come from poorly adjusted homes, characterized by continuous family disturbances. Children in the former group would generally be happy and show relatively few signs of tension or anxiety, whereas children in the latter group would tend to be more unhappy and anxious. Thus, in one case, humor and laughter result from a very positive set of childhood experiences; in the other, they stem from an environment that obliges the child to cope with conflict. The children from the first group would usually be considered to be mentally healthier, and yet children from the second group would appear to have successfully coped with a most difficult set of circumstances. Asking which group of children is better adjusted in a general sense is tantamount to asking whether having successfully overcome adversity would make one better adjusted than would not having had to face such adversity to begin with. It is impossible to answer this question satisfactorily; so such comparisons are probably best not attempted. The most pertinent question, then, is whether a child who has early distress and conflict to cope with is better adjusted as a result of using humor to deal with it than he or she might otherwise have been.

The greatest risk in relying on humor as a means of reducing anxiety or overcoming conflict is that a child might never get around to confronting the source of difficulty: that is, the problem may be avoided at the same time that it is being transcended. For example, assume that a girl develops hostility toward her mother because of a belief that she is not loved by her. The child might learn to use humor as a means of getting attention and approval from people other than her mother. She might also enjoy jokes or cartoons in which mothers are berated. This preoccupation with humor might last into adulthood and serve to prevent the child from dealing with her own feelings about her mother. In this sense, laughter and humor as a coping mechanism would interfere with the achievement of good mental health. It seems, then, that humor can interfere with healthy adjustment at the same time that it is helping the child overcome sources of distress.

Studies focusing on the relationship between sense of humor and mental health have been rare, but the research that has been done supports the view that humor is positively related to healthy adjustment. Degree of humor appreciation among adults has been found to be positively correlated with other psychological measures of maturity and seems to be a fairly stable personality characteristic.[15] More restricted forms of reaction to humor tend to correlate with a generally more repressive life style.[16] On the other hand, no significant relationship has been found between reduced sense of humor and pathology scores on psychological tests.[17] So far, measures of adjustment or mental health among children have not been related to the amount of laughter and humor shown. There is evidence, however, that poorly adjusted children (as indicated by teachers' ratings) more greatly appreciate aggressive and nonsocial forms of humor than do well-adjusted children.[18]

The strongest evidence of the importance of laughter and humor in children comes from studies of extreme cases of their presence or absence. Many institutionalized infants and young children, along with others who have received only limited amounts of mothering, rarely smile or laugh.[19] This is usually in-

[15]O'CONNELL, W. E. The adaptive functions of wit and humor. *Journal of Abnormal and Social Psychology*, 1960, 61, 263–270.

[16]O'CONNELL, W. E., and COWGILL, S. Wit, humor, and defensiveness. *Newsletter for Research in Psychology*, 1970, 12, 32–33. O'CONNELL, W. E., and PETERSON, P. Humor and repression. *Journal of Existential Psychology*, 1964, 4, 309–316.

[17]O'CONNELL, W. E. Maturity, sex, and wit-humor appreciation. *Newsletter for Research in Psychology*, 1969, 11, 14–15.

[18]NICHOLSON, W. S. Relation between measures of mental health and a cartoon measure of humor in fifth grade children. Unpublished doctoral dissertation, University of Maryland, 1973.

[19]BOWLBY, J. Grief and mourning in infancy and early childhood. In G. E. Daniels (Ed.), *New perspectives in psychoanalysis*. New York: Gruen and Stratton, 1965. MAHLER, M. S. On sadness and grief in infancy and childhood: Loss and restora-

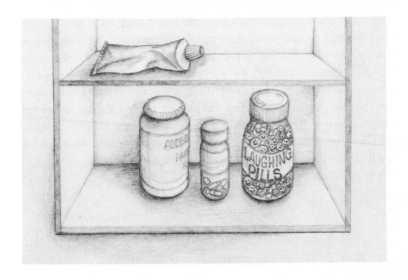

terpreted as a sign of severe emotional disturbance. Infants who have had little sensory and social stimulation tend to show little excitement and only a limited range of expression of emotion. There is no doubt in these cases that the lack of any form of laughter or humor is related to poor mental health. At the other extreme, some children show incessant laughter.[20] They may use it as a means of warding off unbearable anxiety or as a means of attacking others. Extreme laughter tends to be viewed suspiciously because it seems to be out of the laugher's control. If there is no apparent explanation for a person's laughter, it gives the appearance of hysterical or psychotic laughter.[21]

It seems safe to conclude, then, that either incessant laughter, playfulness, joking, and other humor-related behaviors or the lack of them is a sign of maladjustment in children. It is more difficult to draw conclusions when these are exhibited in more moderate degrees. There seem to be many different ways in which

tion of the symbiotic love object. *Psychoanalytic Study of the Child*, 1961 (Vol. 16). PROVENCE, S., and RITVO, S. Effects of deprivation on institutionalized infants: Disturbance of development of relationship to inanimate objects. *Psychoanalytic Study of the Child*, 1961 (Vol. 16).

[20]WOLFENSTEIN, M. Mad laughter in a six-year-old boy. *Psychoanalytic Study of the Child*, 1955, 19, 381–394.

[21]LEVINE, J. Humor and mental health. In A. Deutsch and H. Fishman (Eds.), *Encyclopedia of mental health*, (Vol. 3), 1963.

a sense of humor within this moderate range can be manifest in children and adults, and it is not known currently whether some types of sense of humor are more healthy than others. The possession of a good sense of humor increases the odds of a person's being well adjusted, but emotional difficulties may also develop that cannot be mastered by means of humor: that is, although humor may be effective in dealing with certain sources of anxiety and distress, there is no evidence that it is a cure-all for all emotional difficulties that children encounter.

Humor as a Diagnostic Tool

Several attempts have been made in the past three decades to develop some kind of humor test to be used as a tool for diagnosing mental disorders in clinical settings. The tests attempted have generally been restricted to adults and have failed to point to a clear diagnostic use for humor. Some studies have shown no difference in humor appreciation between traditional diagnostic groups, such as neurotics, schizophrenics, and normals.[22] Other studies, however, have demonstrated that schizophrenic and neurotic patients are more likely than normal people to be disturbed by cartoons or jokes.[23] The most typical finding of studies using clinical populations is that cartoons or jokes closely related to the area of conflict are rated very low in funniness.[24] This is not surprising, because we have all had the experience of failing to see the humor of jokes that touch on areas that we are sensitive about. In the 1960s, most people had difficulty laughing at jokes about the Vietnam war, presumably because the war was a

---

[22]DERKS, P. L., LEICHTMAN, H. M., and CARROL, P. J. Production and judgment of "humor" by schizophrenics and college students. *Bulletin of the Psychonomic Society*, 1975, 6, 300–302. VERINIS, J. S. Inhibition of humor: Differential effects with traditional diagnostic categories. *Journal of General Psychology*, 1970, 82, 157–163.

[23]LEVINE, J., and ABELSON, R. Humor as a disturbing stimulus. *Journal of General Psychology*, 1959, 60, 191–200.

[24]ECKER, J., LEVINE, J., and ZIGLER, E. Impaired sex-role identification in schizophrenia expressed in the comprehension of humor stimuli. *Journal of Psychology*, 1973, 83, 67–77. FRANKEL, E. B. An experimental study of psychoanalytic theories of humor. Unpublished doctoral dissertation, University of Michigan, 1953. REDLICH, F. C., LEVINE, J., and SOHLER, T. P. A mirth response test: Preliminary report on a psychodiagnostic technique utilizing dynamics of humor. *American Journal of Orthopsychiatry*, 1951, 21, 717–734.

source of emotional distress. We simply had a difficult time reacting to the war in a playful fashion—a necessary prerequisite for seeing the depiction of incongruous aspects of the war as humorous. Similarly, feminist women have often been accused of lacking a sense of humor—especially with respect to jokes victimizing women. The generality of this pattern suggests that, although responsiveness to selected jokes or cartoons might be helpful in understanding the source of difficulty in an individual already categorized as emotionally disturbed, humor reactions cannot be used as a basis for determining whether or not an individual is neurotic, schizophrenic, or otherwise disturbed. One study specifically demonstrated that both psychiatric patients and highly intelligent normal individuals showed a puzzling inability to understand normally easily understood cartoons when the cartoons touched off strong emotional conflicts.[25]

One of the most promising uses of laughter and humor as a diagnostic tool may be for cases of extreme depression. The amount of laughter and joking shown is a good index of the depth of depression and of the progress being made in dealing with it.[26] Because depression and playfulness are incompatible frames of mind, and playfulness is a prerequisite for humor, humor and laughter provide a good day-by-day record of progress. They have also been found to be a good indicator of health-related progress through time[27] and of the level of adjustment achieved outside the hospital setting[28] for patients with other psychiatric classifications.

No attempt has been made to develop diagnostic humor tests for children. The most popular use of humor in clinical settings with children is that of the favorite-joke technique. Because children use humor as a means of working out at least some anxiety or conflict, the child's favorite joke may help the therapist or counselor discover the nature of the child's problem.

[25]LEVINE, J., and REDLICH, F. C. Failure to understand humor. *Psychoanalytic Quarterly*, 1955, 24, 560–572.

[26]NUSSBAUM, K., and MICHAUX, W. W. Response to humor in depression: A predictor and evaluator of patient change? *Psychiatric Quarterly*, 1955, 24, 560–572.

[27]HARRELSON, R. W., and STROUD, P. S. Observations of humor in chronic schizophrenics. *Mental Hygiene*, 1967, 51, 458–461.

[28]STARER, E. Reactions of psychiatric patients to cartoons and verbal jokes. *Journal of General Psychology*, 1961, 65, 301–304.

When exposed to jokes, a particular child picks out one uncon-
sciously which corresponds to his/her inner needs, and he/she begins to use it repeatedly to express a certain conflict. . . . As a con-
densed form of the emotional conflict, the favourite joke serves as a
means to escape the censorship. Thus, the internal conflict breaks
through into the consciousness in a disguised form. In other words,
the favourite joke is an attempt . . . to resolve the conflict. As a
healthy defense mechanism, the joking affords a pleasurable dis-
charge for the painful affect which is related to the repressed
conflict.[29]

The skilled therapist will be able to relate emotion-laden qualities
of the joke to information already obtained about the child,
thereby clarifying the nature of the child's conflict.

Humor in Therapy

The material presented in this chapter makes it difficult to
question the therapeutic properties of humor. Humor has the capacity to relax tensions, provide outlets for otherwise unacceptable behavior or impulses, and put a child in a frame of mind
more conducive to effective interchanges with others. It would
seem, then, that humor might be a very effective technique in
psychotherapy for either children or adults. Again, little attention
has been given to this possibility with children, although discussion of its usefulness in therapy for adults has been going on
among therapists for many years. Most therapists are agreed on
humor's potential usefulness in therapy,[30] although some have
warned that humor initiated by a therapist can be very destructive to progress by the client, especially in the early stages of
therapy.[31] For example, a patient may assume that the therapist
is laughing *at* rather than *with* him or her. The general concensus,
however, is that humor is like any other tool at the therapist's

---

[29]YORUKOGLU, Favourite jokes of children and intra-familial conflicts, p. 410.

[30]GREENWALD, H. Humor in psychotherapy. *Journal of Contemporary Psychotherapy*, 1975, 7, 113–116. GROTJAHN, M. *Beyond Laughter.* New York: McGraw-Hill, 1957. MINDESS, *Laughter and liberation.* O'CONNELL, W. E. Freudian humour: The eu-psychia of everyday life. In A. J. Chapman and H. C. Foot (Eds.), *Humour and laughter: Theory, research and application.* London: Wiley, 1976.

[31]KUBIE, L. S. The destructive potential of humor in psychotherapy. *American Journal of Psychiatry*, 1971, 127, 861–866.

disposal, in that it's effectiveness depends on how skillfully it is used. When used skillfully, humor in therapy can (1) create a more relaxed atmosphere, (2) encourage communication on sensitive matters, (3) be a source of insight into conflict, (4) help overcome a stiff and formal social style, or (5) facilitate the acting out of feelings or impulses in a safe, nonthreatening way.[32] If humor is able to put the individual into a frame of mind in which he or she can more readily deal with sources of conflict in everyday life, it's effectiveness along these lines should even be increased when in the hands of an experienced therapist.

It has already been seen that asking a child his or her favorite joke is a technique used with much success in therapy. When children initiate joking on their own in the course of therapy, the focus of their humor is most often themselves, again suggesting that the joking may be an attempt to deal with personal conflicts.[33] In addition to fears and anxieties, common themes of children's jokes during therapy are knowing and not knowing, aggression, and being triumphant or superior. Each of these themes represents an area of special concern to many children during the school years. By joking, the child may experience the feeling not only of being assertive, but of being knowledgable and superior to others. In many therapists' view, taking the first step toward such feelings in the context of humor is important because the experience is unobtainable in any other way. In therapy, as in everyday living, then, humor can serve the very important function of opening the doors to an open, spontaneous, flexible, and generally healthy interaction with others.

---

[32]HERSHKOWITZ, A. The essential ambiguity of, and in, humour. In A. J. Chapman and H. C. Foot (Eds.), *It's a funny thing, humour.* Oxford, England: Pergamon Press, 1977.

[33]ORFANDIS, M. M. Children's use of humor in psychotherapy. *Social Casework,* 1972, 53, 147–155.

10 Concluding Remarks

This book may have gone further than the reader would like in examining the nature of humor and its development throughout childhood. Many of us have a vaguely defined fear that too much investigation of laughter and humor may destroy our capacity to fully appreciate it. When symposia are devoted to discussions of research on humor at meetings of the American Psychological Association or other professional organizations, it is not uncommon for newspaper journalists reviewing the symposia to express concern that maybe this is one area of human behavior that should remain safely out of the hands of scientists. The rationale for this view is usually something along the following line: "In today's complex technological society, life is hard and full of distress, but at least we have our sense of humor to pull us through. But now they're going to take that away from us!" It should be comforting to know, however, that psychologists, sociologists, and others studying humor have shown no signs of losing their sense of humor as they continue their research on humor. They only appear to have done so, because they tend to write seriously about a subject that is supposed to be entertaining and enjoyed "for the fun of it." If anything, their personal sense of humor has been enhanced by learning more about humor. If humor really is intrinsically pleasurable, as suggested in this book, the gaining of new knowledge about the nature of that pleasure should not interfere with the enjoyment derived unless it produces an analytical frame of mind in which the individual does not respond playfully to the humorous event.

Mankind has always had mixed feelings about the establishment of new knowledge. Although the gaining of knowledge for its own sake is now looked at much more favorably than it has been in past centuries, we continue to worry about the use that might be made of certain kinds of knowledge. For example, can we really afford to perfect the cloning of human beings? Also, many believe that we may yet meet our doom because of our accumulated knowledge of the atom. From this perspective, the study of humor seems to be a safe venture. In spite of Monty Python's claim in recent years to have discovered a "killer joke," which was so funny that people who heard it died laughing, humor seems to serve many more positive than negative functions— at both the personal and the societal level. Civilized society has always placed a premium on humor. Those with special skills to make us laugh have become as famous and respected as heads of state. If humor does provide a means of rechanneling sexual and aggressive impulses, this alone makes it essential to the smooth functioning of society. If such impulses were to receive direct expression on a massive scale, chaos and anarchy would be the certain result. Given the importance of humor, a better understanding of its nature could make a major contribution to maintenance of social harmony.

It is unlikely that we will ever understand humor well enough to predict in advance who will and who will not like a particular joke, or how funny it will be. This requires more information on the personal history of individuals than most of us would care to have. The individual difference element in humor may always elude us, but we have already made considerable progress in understanding the patterns of humor development that hold for children generally. We have seen that these patterns depend on the child's level of cognitive development, beginning with the simple pretend play with objects (which results from the beginning of the symbolic capacity), and terminating with the highly abstract forms of humor of the adolescent. Just as new cognitive skills transform the general thought qualities of children, so do they alter the kinds of humor they are capable of experiencing. For the most part, children prefer humor that is consistent with their intellectual capacities, but both adults and children of all ages continue to derive enjoyment from the humor of earlier developmental levels. Because the intellectual challenge is no longer enough to make such jokes and cartoons funny, something else must be added to sustain their humor. In most cases, sex or aggression elevates the funniness of simple forms of humor, although funniness may be increased by linking the content of the joke to any area that is emotionally salient to the individual. At some point in development, preferences are established for relatively more complex or simple jokes. We know virtually nothing about how this preference is established, when it is established, or how stable such preferences are throughout development. It is quite apparent, though, that there are widespread differences among adults in their preference for challenging or unchallenging forms of humor.

An attempt has been made in this book to draw attention to the complexity of the humor experience. Primary attention has been given to the role of the intellectual aspects of the overall humor phenomenon, because humor seems to be most essentially a cognitive event. Its original appearance depends on cognitive factors, and the process of understanding the point of a joke is an intellectual one. Amount of intellectual challenge even contributes to funniness once we have understood the point. Fantasy events and a playful frame of mind are cognitive in nature. The attainment of new cognitive levels (especially with the assistance of a language system) also seems to result in the transformation of apes from humorless creatures into animals who initiate purely intellectual forms of play. It would be a serious mistake, however, to conclude that we have understood humor and its development once we understand how all of these cognitive factors interact to produce the perception of funniness. In spite of the cognitive similarities of all kinds of humor, each person's sense of humor is as unique as his or her thumbprint. Certain early experiences and early behavioral characteristics are very important for subsequent humor development, but the influences on the individualized aspects of a sense of humor remain largely unknown. The few basic personality characteristics noted that serve to individualize a person's sense of humor hardly tap the range of diversity of humor appreciation that is believed to exist among people.

Although humor is basically a mental phenomenon, social and emotional factors may prove to be most important in determining the intensity of the overall experience. The addition of an emotional investment in the content of the humorous event and a social context give humor the zest of which it is capable. We have just begun to understand the social functions of humor, but it is already apparent that humor is commonly used as a "lubricant" for social interaction. It is difficult to imagine a substitute device that would be equally successful at promoting smooth and comfortable social interaction. The initiation of joking or clowning is a complex skill, and even casual observation of people is enough to make it readily apparent that some have become very proficient in this skill, whereas others are surprisingly incompetent at initiating any form of humor. The origins of this skill are little known at this point. We know that most children initiate various forms of humor as they develop, but we do not know how certain children come to be especially adept at producing humor. We also know that highly verbal children who are socially dominant and verbally and physically aggressive tend to become most skilled at initiating humor (at least they do it more often; no attempt was made to determine the funniness of humor initiated). Humor might provide the optimal means of rechanneling these characteristics in a manner that is socially acceptable. But not all children with these characteristics proceed to become clowns or jokers. There must be an added factor, then, that leads some children to become preoccupied with humor. Parental modeling of humor, or support for the child's efforts at humor, may play a crucial role in solidifying humor as a direction in which to channel aggressive and other forms of assertive behavior. This aspect of humor development has simply not been studied, except for occasional anecdotal studies of professional comics based on recall of early childhood.

At this point, there is much more to be learned than we already know about the nature and development of humor. This remains the case, in spite of the speculations that have been offered through many centuries. As long as analyses of humor remain at the level of speculation, this is likely to continue to be the case. This book summarizes the findings of experimental studies of humor development, and offers additional speculations based on what has been learned. It is hoped that it will serve as a milestone along the route to a fuller understanding of humor, and point the way to progress in its achievement.

Index